Collins

CAPE® REVISION GUIDE
ECONOMICS

Dave Ramsingh

Collins

HarperCollins Publishers Ltd
The News Building
1 London Bridge Street
London SE1 9GF

HarperCollins*Publishers*
Macken House
39/40 Mayor Street Upper
Dublin 1, D01 C9W8, Ireland

First edition 2015

10 9 8 7 6 5 4 3 2

© HarperCollins *Publishers* Limited 2015

ISBN 978-0-00-811604-0

Collins® is a registered trademark of HarperCollins Publishers Limited

CAPE® Revision Guide Economics is an independent publication and has not been authorised, sponsored or otherwise approved by **CXC**®.

CAPE® is a registered trade mark of the **Caribbean Examinations Council (CXC)**.

www.collins.co.uk/caribbeanschools

A catalogue record for this book is available from the British Library.

Typeset by QBS
Printed and bound by CPI Group (UK) Ltd, Croydon, CR0 4YY

All rights reserved. No part of this book may be reproduced, stored in a retrieval system, or transmitted in any form or by any means, electronic, mechanical, photocopying, recording or otherwise, without the prior permission in writing of the Publisher. This book is sold subject to the conditions that it shall not, by way of trade or otherwise, be lent, re-sold, hired out or otherwise circulated without the Publisher's prior consent in any form of binding or cover other than that in which it is published and without a similar condition including this condition being imposed on the subsequent purchaser.

Without limiting the exclusive rights of any author, contributor or the publisher of this publication, any unauthorised use of this publication to train generative artificial intelligence (AI) technologies is expressly prohibited. HarperCollins also exercise their rights under Article 4(3) of the Digital Single Market Directive 2019/790 and expressly reserve this publication from the text and data mining exception.

If any copyright holders have been omitted, please contact the Publisher who will make the necessary arrangements at the firstopportunity .

Author: Dave Ramsingh
Publisher: Elaine Higgleton
Commissioning Editor: Tom Hardy
Managing Editor: Sarah Thomas
Copy Editor: Keith Povey
Editor: Atalanta Willcox
Proofreader: Sylvia Worth

This book contains FSC™ certified paper and other controlled sources to ensure responsible forest management.

For more information visit: www.harpercollins.co.uk/green

Acknowledgements
p1: Peter Leask/Alamy, p7: Art Directors & TRIP/Alamy, p12: Bill Bachmann/Alamy, p29: Nigel Hicks/Getty Images, p35: Ariel Skelley/Getty Images, p42: Marcell Mizik/Shutterstock, p49: Eye Ubiquitous/Getty Images, p57: Light Bulb Studio/Shutterstock, p67: Rob Crandall/Alamy, p77: PhotosIndia.com LLC/Alamy, p84: TinnaPong/Shutterstock, p91: Wesley VanDinter/Gettyimages, p96: Kritchanut/Shutterstock, p106: AfricaImages/Istockphoto, p114: Hoberman Collection/Gettyimages, p122: LatitudeStock/Alamy, p128: Edhar/Shutterstock, p136: Michaeljung/Shutterstock, p147: CaraMaria/Istockphoto, p153: Thomas Cockrem/Alamy Stock , p163: Jack Sullivan/Alamy, p172: Robert Harding Picture Library Ltd/Alamy, p179: Amanaimages/Corbis, p183: Robert Harding World Imagery/Alamy, p189: Aleksey Stemmer/Shutterstock, p197: Ewais/Shutterstock, p207: Monkey Business Images/Shutterstock, p213: Karen Bleier/Getty Images

Contents

Guidelines for Revision iv

1. The Economic Problem 1
2. Economic Systems 7
3. Theory of Demand 12
4. Theory of Supply I 29
5. Theory of Supply II 35
6. Market Equilibrium 42
7. The Cost of Production 49
8. Price, Revenue and Profit Concepts 57
9. Imperfect Competition: Monopoly and Monopolistic Competition 67
10. Oligopoly and Contestable Markets 77
11. Market Failure 84
12. Role of Government and Market Failures 91
13. Theory of Income Distribution 96
14. Wage Differentials 106
15. Income Inequality, Poverty and Poverty Alleviation 114
16. National Income Accounting 122
17. Classical Models of the Macro-Economy 128
18. The Keynesian Model of the Macro-Economy 136
19. Investment 147
20. Unemployment and Inflation 153
21. Monetary Theory and Policy 163
22. Fiscal Policy 172
23. The Public Debt 179
24. Economic Growth and Sustainable Development 183
25. International Trade 189
26. Balance of Payments and Exchange Rates 197
27. Economic Integration 207
28. International Economic Relations 213

    Answers to multiple choice questions 223

    Index 225

Guidelines for Revision

In the classroom

A high percentage of your learning for examinations takes place in the classroom. You should be versed in the best ways to learn.

- **State of attention** Learning is best achieved if the human mind and body is at a state of attention, so remember to sit upright to achieve this.
- The **visile** learner is one who learns best by seeing. Keep a keen eye on your teacher and the board or screen, and try to focus until the point is made.
- The **audile** learner learns best from hearing. Listen intently and ask your teacher to kindly speak up if you cannot hear, or simply sit at the front. If you are unsure about a point made, be brave and ask a question.
- The **tactile** learner learns by doing – hence the reason for laboratories. In economics, as in similar subjects, it is achieved by writing, drawing and calculating.
- **Sharing**. Since all three types roughly make up over 70% of learning, it is not until you share your learning that you will know the gaps in your knowledge. Suggest this cooperative strategy to your teacher.
- All three types of learning involve the senses, so try not to write until you look at and listen to the point being made. Ask your teacher for a few minutes to make a brief note if one is not given to you.

Taking notes

- **Diagrams, formulae and bullet points** are condensed ways to record information. Remember: a picture is worth a thousand words. An entire lesson could be condensed on a single page if you get this technique right.
- Use **Abbreviations** for long words or use texting language to save time but be careful to avoid the use of text language in an exam.
- **Mnemonics** When you have to make a list of factors related to a concept, try making up a word to assist your memory – e.g. 'The rewards to the factors of production are WIRP (wages, interest, rent, profit)'.
- **Coloured pens and highlighters** For important points, use coloured pens or highlight markers. In all of the above, remember EASY STORE – EASY TO RETRIEVE.

At home

- Homework revision is of critical importance because your learning is independent of everyone, self-directed and self-empowering. The learning of other subject matter interferes with learning in economics (retroactive interference) and it is ONLY by revision that you can retain your learning. Also, you will not be overwhelmed at exam time if you continuously revise. Not following these practices may be the reason you are not making the high marks you deserve.
- **Avoid** lying down to study because you are sending a signal to your brain that you are ready to sleep. Select a chair that is comfortable and use proper lighting.
- **Music** It is also not advisable to have loud music playing when you study because it could distract you. However, based on brain research, music assists learning if you listen to your favourite music one hour BEFORE studying or writing a test.

Study timetable

- If you are attempting four subjects, make a timetable to revise all four – revising the day's notes of the most challenging subject first. The next day, rotate the order of revision.
- **Time allocation** Do not spend too much time on one subject. You should spend 40 minutes summarizing your condensed notes as a means of revising, mixing Papers 1 and 2 on consecutive days.
- **Diagrams, formulae, definitions, assumptions and examples** are part of your strategy for supporting your answers – reserve one night for revision of these.

GUIDELINES FOR REVISION

- **Redraw** your diagrams and **label** them as a form of practice.
- **Multiple choice questions** Remember: the fastest way to revise your entire subject is the use of multiple choice questions.
- Take a **10-minute music break** and start afresh with your next subject.
- **Writing** The only time you write extensively is three times a year for term exams and some practice tests in-between that time. Select a past paper question, do it in the time given and ask your teacher for his or her approval to email to them. It will enhance your writing skills and exam preparation.

In the examination room

- Before the paper is given to you, take a minute to **focus your thoughts** by meditating.
- When the paper is given to you **focus** on Section 1.
- **DO NOT** read the entire paper and waste precious time.
- **Selecting a question** Select one question from Section 1. Make sure you can answer all the parts of the structured question, ESPECIALLY the parts carrying high marks.

- **Time management**
  - Put a clock on your desk if you are allowed to do so. You have 150 minutes for Paper 2, which is 50 minutes per question for the three sections.
  - For Paper 1, you have 90 minutes to answer 45 questions, which is 2 minutes per question.
  - For Paper 2, check the marks allotted to each part of the question and spend more time on the part carrying higher marks first.

- **Planning your answers**
  - READ your selected question carefully and UNDERLINE the command words – e.g. define, list, identify, and so on.
  - Take 5 to 6 minutes to plan the content of the answer by quickly writing down every point you can remember related to the answer in no special order.
  - Then, place each point in order from the first to last.
  - Properly labelled diagrams remove doubt in the examiner's mind. Even if you make an error when explaining, a correct diagram would give you the benefit of doubt.
  - Write legibly. Illegible handwriting may cause the examiner to misinterpret your answer.
  - Reread your answer to ensure good grammar, spelling and punctuation.

- **Repeat the entire procedure for Sections 2 and 3**
  Paper 1 (Multiple choice)
  - Choose the easy questions first and use a red pen to circle the answer to allow more time on other items that require more thought. There are about 10 to 15 fairly easy ones to answer. When you are certain, THEN shade your answers.
  - Use 1 minute to eliminate the two wrong answers.
  - Then take a further minute to decide between the two that may be correct.
  - If even you guess, you have a 50% chance of being correct when choosing between options.
  - Do not spend more than 2½ minutes on any one question as this could cause you to rush the answers to others that were not difficult to answer.
  - Only shade your answer when you are satisfied it is your best response.

- **Common question commands**
  - **Account for:** Provide reasons to support a concept.
  - **Analyse:** Examine in detail the main characteristics and how they contribute to a concept.
  - **Assess:** Determine the positive or negative factors, strengths and weaknesses.
  - **Comment:** State your opinions on an issue in question, providing evidence in support of your views.
  - **Compare:** Identify characteristics that are similar, and also show an awareness of differences.
  - **Contrast:** Emphasize the differences between the items in question, but show some awareness of similarities.

- **Criticize:** Judge and scrutinize both the strengths and weaknesses of the statements in the question.
- **Define:** Give a concise and clear statement of a fact or concept.
- **Describe:** Provide details to make a concept better understood.
- **Discuss:** Examine and analyse the many positive and negative perspectives of an issue and reach a balanced conclusion.
- **Differentiate:** Observe and explain the difference between two or more variables.
- **Enumerate:** Concisely state points one by one.
- **Evaluate:** Carefully assess an issue, citing both strengths and limitations.
- **Explain:** To make clear the points being raised, giving detailed reasoning for important features.
- **To what extent:** Explain the degree to which, partly or wholly, a variable is applicable to an issue.
- **Illustrate:** The use of specific models, figures or diagrams to clarify or explain a concept.
- **Identify:** To point out or name.
- **Justify:** Provide proof or support for decisions or conclusions.
- **List:** To itemize points related to an issue.
- **Outline:** Provide the main and supporting points of an issue emphasizing a general framework.
- **Prove:** Providing evidence or facts to support a concept.
- **Relate:** Explain how variables are linked to each other in one or more ways.
- **Review:** Critically analysing, concluding and commenting on key issues and stages of development.
- **State:** Express the main points briefly and clearly.
- **Summarize:** To provide the main points or facts in condensed form without details and illustrations.

Chapter 1: The Economic Problem

REVISION GUIDE TO ECONOMICS

Learning Objectives

By the end of this chapter you should be able to:
- Define scarcity
- Explain opportunity cost
- Explain the production possibility frontier and decreasing, increasing and constant costs
- Identify three main choices – what, how and for whom to produce
- Describe economic systems – subsistence, free market, planned and mixed economy
- Explain Pareto optimality

Exam tip

All examination questions focus on learning objectives.

Exam tip

Always support your definitions with examples, formulae or diagrams.

Introduction

Scarcity exists when unlimited human wants cannot be satisfied because resources are limited – e.g. housing.

Resources generally consist of land, labour, capital and human enterprise, for example:

- LAND – anything above or below the ground that is provided by nature – e.g. air, sunshine, fish and minerals;
- LABOUR – human mental or physical effort of any kind – e.g. surgeon;
- CAPITAL – producer goods which enable future production – e.g. machines;
- ENTERPRISE – human resource which organizes and coordinates the other factor inputs to produce goods and services.

The three most basic choices all societies must make are:

- **What to produce** – this refers to the type of goods and services to be produced;
- **How to produce** – this relates to the combination of factors of production that should be used;
- **For whom to produce** – this relates to the distribution of goods and services.

The distribution of goods and services may take the following forms:

- Lotteries;
- Rationing;
- Food stamps;
- A system of merit or need;
- A price system;
- Queues.

Opportunity cost

Opportunity cost is defined as the sacrifice of the next-best choice whenever economic decisions are made. The opportunity cost of building a school is therefore giving up the next-best option of constructing a hospital.

Opportunity cost is illustrated by a diagram called a 'production possibilities frontier' (PPF) or a 'production possibilities curve' (PPC).

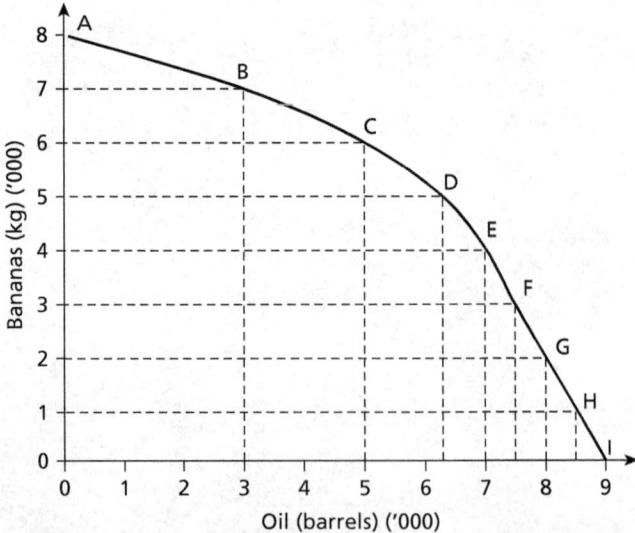

Figure 1.1 Combinations of a production possibilities curve showing increasing opportunity cost

THE ECONOMIC PROBLEM

A PPC shows the maximum of different combinations of two types of goods that a country's resources can produce. The assumptions that are made when drawing the PPF are:

- There are only two goods;
- Technology is fixed;
- No foreign trade exists;
- Output is measured on a yearly basis;
- The level of resources is fixed;
- Output is measured in units;
- Resources are perfectly mobile.

Note:

- A maximum of 8000 kg of bananas can be produced and 0 barrels of oil.
- A maximum of 9000 barrels per day (bpd) can be produced and 0 kg of bananas.
- Since society needs both goods, moving from combination A to B requires the allocation of resources from banana production to oil.
- 1000 kg of bananas are sacrificed to produce 3000 barrels of oil at a ratio of 1 kg of bananas to 3 barrels of oil.
- This exchange results in a loss of 1 kg of bananas to gain 3 barrels of oil.
- The opportunity cost of choosing combination B over A is 1000 kg of bananas given up.

The reason for the concave shape of the PPF

- The shape of the PPF is concave due to the law of increasing costs.
- Referring to Figure 1.1 shows that moving from combination A to combination B sacrifices the resources producing 1000 kg of bananas to achieve 3000 bpd of oil.
- Moving down the PPF to combination C, D, E and F, the same 1000 kg of bananas given up yield 2000 barrels of oil for combination C, but not for combination D, E and F.
- From B to C yields 2000 bpd, C to D 1300 bpd and only 500 barrels of oil for combinations E to F.
- This is so because resources are more suited to banana production than oil production.
- Also, adding extra resources to oil production eventually causes the rate of production to decrease.
- This is called the **law of diminishing returns** or the **law of increasing costs**.

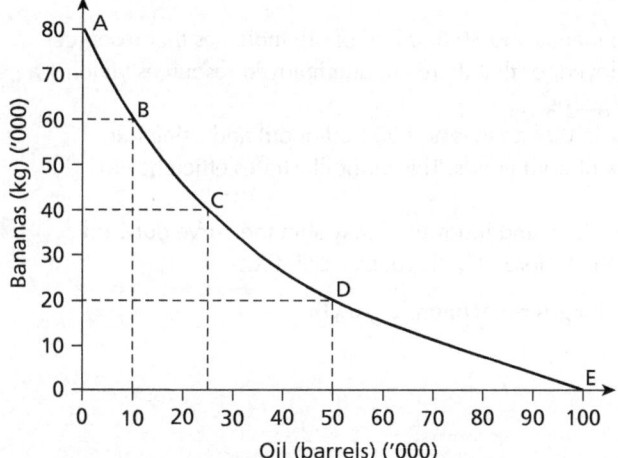

Figure 1.2 The convex shape of the production possibilities frontier showing decreasing opportunity cost

Note:

Also observe that in Figure 1.2.

- Moving down the curve between points A to D results in sacrificing resources producing 20 kg of bananas to produce an increased number of barrels of oil. For example, from combination A to B, 20 kg of bananas are given up to gain 10 barrels of oil.
- From combination C to D, the gain in oil is 25 barrels, and D to E the gain is 50 barrels. This is the **law of decreasing opportunity cost** or the **law of increasing returns** in production.

> **Exam tip**
>
> Differently shaped PPCs and points in and out of the curve appear as questions for both Papers 1 and 2.

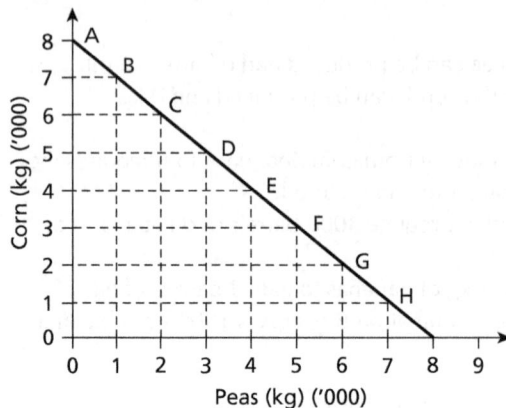

Figure 1.3 Combinations of the linear production possibilities frontier showing constant opportunity cost

The linear PPF

Observations on Figure 1.3:

- The linear PPF curve in Figure 1.3 shows that moving from combinations A through F indicates a 1:1 ratio – 1000 kg of corn given up would yield 1000 kg of peas.
- Resources are equally productive when they are allocated to either good.
- This phenomenon is the **law of constant opportunity costs**.
- This curve is typical of production of similar goods – e.g. production of corn and peas.

Points within and outside of the PPF

Note the following in Figure 1.4:

- Point X (i.e. 40,000 bananas and 50,000 bpd of oil) indicates that resources are inefficiently employed, or that there are unemployed resources yielding a lower output of both goods.
- Moving to point X_1 (75,000 bananas and 90 bpd of oil) and using idle resources yields more of both goods. This point illustrates efficiency in production.
- Over time, new technology and innovation may shift the curve outward resulting in production of more of both goods – point X_2.

This is also referred to as **long-term economic growth**.

THE ECONOMIC PROBLEM

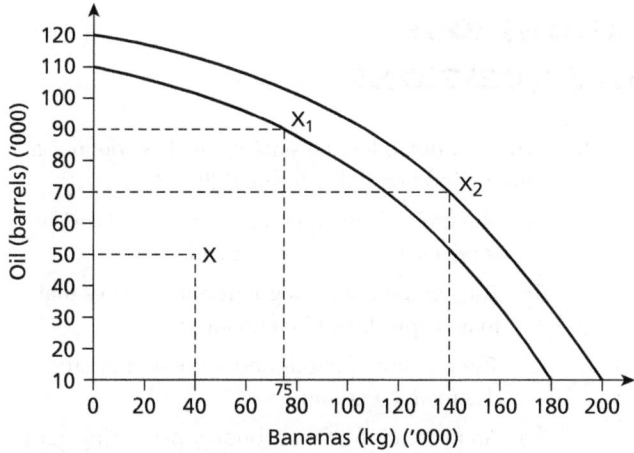

Figure 1.4 Combinations showing points within and outside of the production possibilities frontier

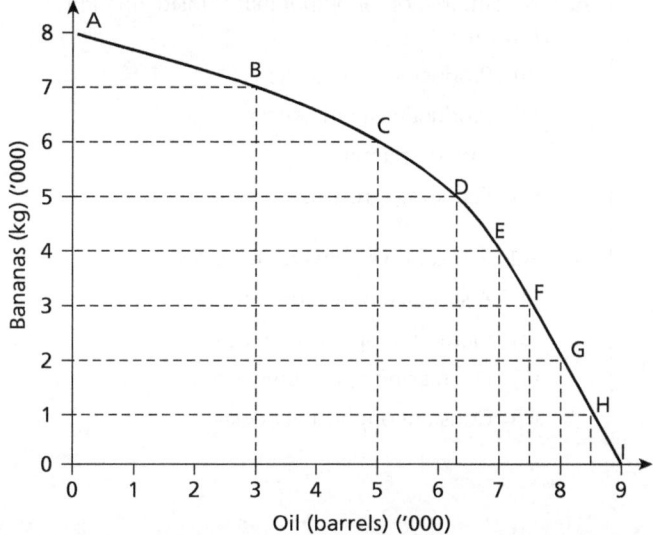

Figure 1.5 Possibilities curve showing Pareto optimality

Pareto optimality

- Pareto optimality or Pareto efficiency is achieved when it is impossible to allocate resources to improve the position of some persons without reducing the position of others.
- Pareto optimality exists on all points on the PPF.
- In Figure 1.5, for example, changing combination B to combination C makes oil producers better off by 2000 bpd of oil but at the loss of 1000 kg of bananas to banana producers.
- Pareto optimality therefore implies the very best possible outcome for the efficient use of resources.

TEST YOUR KNOWLEDGE
MULTIPLE CHOICE QUESTIONS

1. Which of the following BEST defines the concept 'scarcity'?
   (a) Goods and services to consumers are in short supply;
   (b) There are not enough resources available at present;
   (c) The excess of human wants over the economy's resources;
   (d) The wants of society are greater than the supply of goods.

2. A potter can make any combination of items using the following options:

Cups	Saucers
85	13
70	16

   What is the opportunity cost of making one saucer?
   (a) 1 cup
   (b) 5 cups
   (c) 7 cups
   (d) 8 cups

   Hint: Draw a PPF and use the change from 85 to 70 to show that 3 saucers gained = 15 cups given up.

3. Which of the following statements BEST defines a 'production possibility frontier' (PPF)?
   (a) The limit of the combinations of goods and services that can be produced;
   (b) The combinations of goods and services that may be produced in a country;
   (c) The mixture of goods and services that are desired by a country;
   (d) An illustration of an economy producing goods and services for its citizens.

   Hint: A boundary is a limit.

4. A combination of output that is inside the PPF indicates:
   (a) Productive efficiency;
   (b) Productive inefficiency;
   (c) Pareto optimality;
   (d) Economic growth.

5. A PPF that bows outward indicates:
   (a) A shortage of resources;
   (b) Increasing opportunity costs;
   (c) Decreasing opportunity costs;
   (d) Constant opportunity costs.

Chapter 2: Economic Systems

Learning Objectives

By the end of this chapter you should be able to:
- Describe the main economic systems
- Explain the 'what, how, for whom' issues
- Distinguish between the different systems
- Identify the advantages and disadvantages of each system

Introduction

An economic system is one which is designed to solve the economic problem of scarcity. The choice of any such system is determined by the following factors:

- Ownership of resources – Should there be private or public ownership of resources?
- Profit – Should private individuals and firms retain the profit they earn?
- Role of government – How much government economic activity should exist?
- Freedom to choose – Can producers and consumers exercise choice in their decision-making?

There are four economic systems that try to solve the problem of scarcity: a subsistence economy; a market economy; a planned economy; and a mixed economy.

Economic systems attempt to address the following issues:

- Freedom for all participants in the chosen system with respect to choice;
- The degree of competition and control of monopoly elements;
- The amount of power given to consumers or producers;
- The quality, availability and affordability of goods and services;
- Protection for consumers and producers;
- The employment of all citizens;
- The rate of growth of the economy;
- Control of price level increases;
- The standard of living of the general citizens;
- Self-sufficiency and economic independence;
- Preservation of the environment;
- Quality and quantity of public and merit goods.

Economic systems

The subsistence economy

A subsistence economy is one in which man provides for his own needs – known as 'direct', 'subsistence' or 'traditional' production. When specialization developed, barter became the accepted practice of satisfying wants known as 'indirect production'.

The failure of barter to satisfy wants stemmed from the problems of double coincidence of wants, rate of exchange disagreements, indivisibility and store of value – all of which were eventually overcome with the introduction of money.

Recognized economic systems are:

- Free market, capitalist, laissez-faire or unplanned economy;
- Command, planned or collectivist economy;
- Mixed economy.

The free market/market economy

A free market system is 'free' from government ownership and has the following features:

- A limited role for the government – e.g. law, order;
- Households and firms make decisions based on self-interest – e.g. profit for the producers and satisfaction for the consumer;
- Privately owned resources;
- Allocation of resources and distribution of output are achieved through the price mechanism, and determined by the forces of demand and supply;
- Complete freedom of choice for producers and consumers with respect to production and consumption;

Exam tip

Look out for questions asking you to compare and contrast economic systems.

- Consumer sovereignty which indicates that consumers have power since they possess the ability to use money to 'vote' for products, which acts as a signal to producers. The USA and Hong Kong have been cited as free market economies.

Market economy evaluated

Table 2.1 Positive and negative aspects of a market economy

Positive	Negative
Freedom of choice for producers and distribution to consumers	Income and wealth in this system are not evenly distributed, creating few rich and many poor
Consumer sovereignty	Factor owners earn more income than workers
Profit-driven enterprises encourage lower costs and keep prices and the rate of inflation low	High income earners dictate choice of goods and services produced through their buying power
Competition promotes high quality and efficiency, and weak firms are eliminated from an industry	Monopolies as sole producers may not act in the public interest e.g. raising prices
Resources are allocated to where there is high demand and where the rewards are high	Public goods are not provided because there is no incentive for profit
	Prices may be too high (shortages) or low (bumper crop) affecting consumers and producers
	Fluctuation in economic activity leads to boom or recession
Unregulated market forces of demand and supply set prices when they are in equilibrium	Inflation and unemployment normally results from an expanding or a contracting economy
	Pollution, environmental degradation and exhaustion of non-renewable resources inhibit sustainable development
	Over-consumption of demerit goods (e.g. alcohol) and under-consumption of merit goods (e.g., education and health) may occur

Planned, collectivist or command economy

A planned economy is managed by a central planning committee. There is no role for private enterprise.

Cuba is a country that has a planned economy.

The following are the features of a pure planned economy:

- All economic decisions are undertaken by a central planning authority.
- There is no role for private enterprise.
- There is no private ownership of resources.
- What to produce is determined by the central planning authority and therefore there is no freedom of choice.
- Any profit earned by state controlled companies is shared with all citizens.
- There is, therefore, no competition.
- Prices are set for all goods and services by the central planning authority.
- The level of wages is determined by the central planning authority.
- Self-interest is replaced by the national interest.
- Apart from price setting, distribution is also determined by a quota system, queuing for items in short supply, a merit and voucher system for food and other basic necessities, such as transport.

Planned economy evaluated

Table 2.2 Positive and negative aspects of a planned economy

Positive	Negative
The goal of this system is the welfare of all citizens	Decision-making is inhibited by bureaucratic procedures and bottlenecks
Government possesses the information to direct resources to their best use	There is no freedom of choice for consumers and producers
Wasteful competition is avoided	The system is rigid and not adaptable to change; shortages frequently occur
The government can choose priorities (e.g. to emphasize equality for all citizens with respect to education)	Specific production targets and lack of incentives lower worker morale leading to poor productivity
The government can ensure greater protection for the environment under this system	Goods and services are poor in quality due to lack of competition
	Queuing is commonplace when shortages occur

A mixed economy

A mixed economy is managed by private individuals, firms and the government. Both the planned economies and market economies have given way to mixed economies so as to capture the strength and eliminate the weaknesses of each system.

The state attempts to regulate the free market price system via subsidies (e.g. food, transport), taxes (indirect), e.g. VAT to discourage consumption of harmful products, such as alcohol and tobacco.

Regulation may also take the form of zoning for traffic congestion, a prices commission to set minimum and maximum prices, and ombudsmen for insurance and banking.

ECONOMIC SYSTEMS

TEST YOUR KNOWLEDGE
MULTIPLE CHOICE QUESTIONS

1. Which of the following is an advantage of a planned economy?
   (a) Decisions are based on social costs and benefits;
   (b) A balanced budget;
   (c) Production reflects consumer wants;
   (d) Producers are free to set prices.

2. Which of the following is a disadvantage of a planned economy?
   (a) Bureaucratic decision-making;
   (b) Freedom of choice;
   (c) Lack of competition;
   (d) Surplus production of goods.

3. Which of the following is a distinguishing feature of a mixed economy?
   (a) A well-balanced industrial structure;
   (b) Imported goods are banned;
   (c) Part of the economy is controlled by the government;
   (d) The state provides public and merit goods;

4. Prices are determined in a mixed economy by:
   (a) Producers only;
   (b) Consumers only;
   (c) Producers and consumers only;
   (d) Producers, consumers and the government.

5. Direction satisfaction of wants is provided by a:
   (a) Market economy;
   (b) Planned economy;
   (c) Mixed economy;
   (d) Subsistence economy.

Chapter 3: Theory of Demand

THEORY OF DEMAND

Factors which influence demand

Demand is influenced by price and non-price factors.

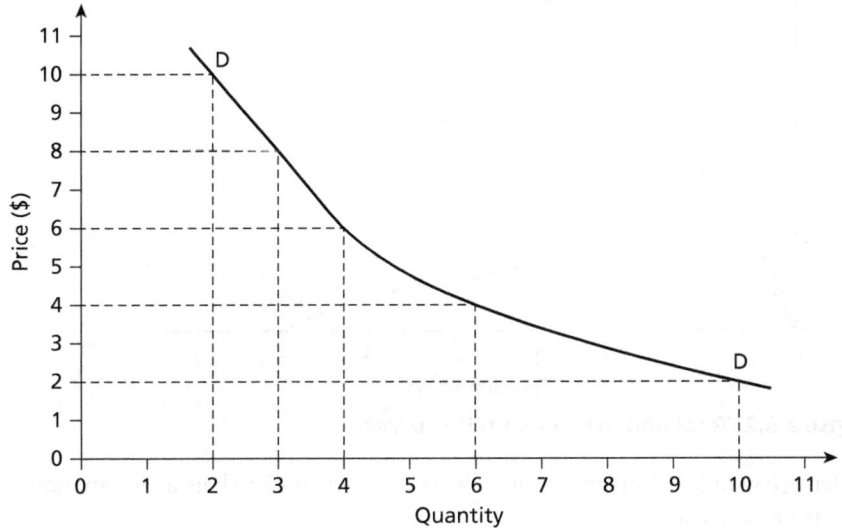

Figure 3.1 A demand curve

Price factors and non-price factors

Price factors: Many people are influenced by the price of a good when they make a purchase. The non-price factors are:

- Level of income;
- Prices of related goods – e.g. substitutes and complements;
- Advertising;
- Fashion and taste, and habit;
- Time;
- Seasonal changes;
- The structure of the population;
- Durability of a good.

Non-price factors are also called the **conditions of demand**. When price changes are analysed, the non-price factors are held constant.

The cardinalist theory of consumer demand

The cardinalist theory of demand assumes that satisfaction can be measured by using numbers. Other assumptions of this theory are:

- Prices of other related goods are unchanged;
- Incomes are fixed;
- The consumer is rational – i.e. is able to make a decision based on self-interest;
- Consumers aim to maximize satisfaction;
- Consumer tastes are unchanged.

Utility

Total utility and marginal utility. Total utility is the total satisfaction or usefulness received from consuming one or more of a good or service.

Learning Objectives

By the end of this chapter you should be able to:

- Explain the first law of demand
- Define effective demand
- Identify the conditions of demand
- Differentiate between total and marginal utility
- Explain the law of diminishing marginal utility
- Explain consumer equilibrium
- Explain the optimal purchase rule
- Differentiate between the income and substitution effect for normal, inferior and Giffen goods
- Explain and differentiate between change in quantity demanded and change in demand
- Explain price, income and cross elasticity of demand
- Use formulae to calculate the value of the three elasticities
- Interpret the values of elasticity
- Understand the implications of elasticity for total spending

Definition

Demand is the willingness and ability to pay for a good or service at a given price over a given period.

Exam tip

Both concepts are frequently tested in **module 1**.

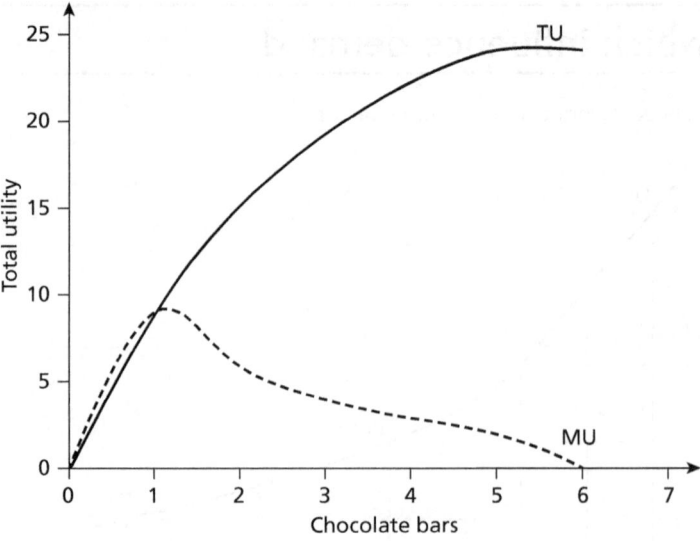

Figure 3.2 Total and marginal utility curves

Refer to Figure 3.2. Note that total utility is rising when more bars are consumed and peaks at 6 bars.

- **Marginal utility** measures the satisfaction from consuming one more good and is measured by $\dfrac{\text{Change in TU}}{\text{Change in Q}}$.

For instance, if 3 chocolate bars yield 19 units of satisfaction and 4 bars 22 units, the marginal utility of the fourth bar is 3 units.

> **Exam tip**
> This law is tested in MCQs.

- **The law of diminishing marginal utility** states that 'as increasing units of a good are consumed, the marginal utility of each additional unit consumed diminishes until it reaches zero'.
- **The first law of demand** The first law of demand states that more of a good will be demanded at lower prices and less at higher prices if non-price factors are held constant.
- **Consumer equilibrium** is achieved when consumers equate satisfaction with price. If satisfaction falls as more is consumed, consumers will be only willing to pay less.

> **Exam tip**
> Frequently tested by CAPE.

The optimal purchase rule/law of equi-marginal returns

The optimal purchase rule states that consumers allocate their expenditure on several purchases to ensure that the ratio of satisfaction per dollar spent (Mu/p) is the same for all goods.

Expressed in formula it is: $\dfrac{MUX}{PX} = \dfrac{MUY}{PY} = \dfrac{MUZ}{PZ}$

where Mu/x is the marginal utility of good x and Px the price of good x.

The same applies to goods y, z. For example, Adam has $50 per month to spend on snacks and fruits. Snacks cost $10 each and fruits cost $10 each. Follow the worked example in Table 3.1 and the simple steps to apply the optimal purchase rule.

Step 1: Calculate marginal utility for snacks – e.g. 1 snack = 15 mu. (0 to 15);

Step 2: Calculate MU/p – e.g. 15/10 and 5/10 for units 1 and 2 of snacks;

Step 3: Calculate marginal utility for fruits in the same manner – e.g. 15 and 4 for units 1 and 2 of fruits;

Step 4: Calculate MU per dollar – e.g. for 1 snack it is 15/10 × $1.00 = $1.50;

Step 5: Identify ratios MU per dollar that are the same – e.g. 4 snacks = 0.30 and 3 fruits = $.30 but 4 snacks and 3 fruits = $70 so this is incorrect.

Note that 3 snacks and 2 fruits together cost $50 and therefore the correct combination where the MU per dollar spent is the same (40 cents).

Table 3.1

Quantity	Total utility from snacks	Total utility from fruits	Marginal utility/price		Marginal utility (per $)	
			Snacks	Fruits	Snacks	Fruits
0	0	0	0	0		
1	15	15	15/10	15/10	$1.50	$1.50
2	20	19	5/10	4/10	0.50	0.40
3	24	22	4/10	3/10	0.40	0.30
4	27	24	3/10	2/10	0.30	0.20
5	39	25	2/10	1/10	0.20	0.10

Consumer surplus

Consumer surplus is the difference between the market price of a product and the price consumers are willing to pay.

Note:

- In Figure 3.3, a consumer is willing to pay $6.00 for the first orange but the actual price is $2.00.
- Consumer surplus for the first orange is equal to $4.00 and the shaded area for 4 oranges.
- Diagrammatically, consumer surplus is identified as the area to the left of the demand curve and above the price line.

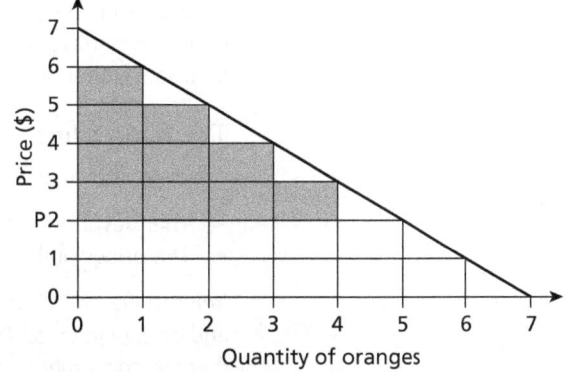

Figure 3.3 Consumer surplus

Indifference curve theory of demand

An indifference curve is one which shows different combinations of two goods which yield the same level of satisfaction.

> **Exam tip**
>
> This definition is a popular CAPE – MCQ.

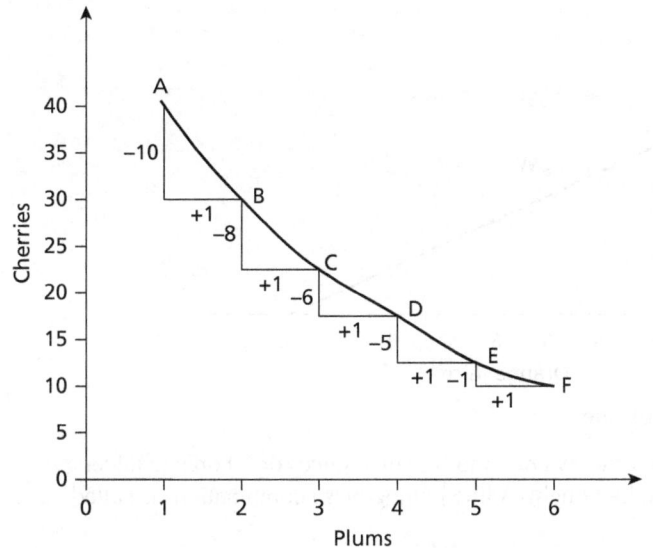

Figure 3.4 Indifference curve and marginal rate of substitution

An indifference curve is illustrated in Figure 3.4. Basic assumptions are:

- There are only two (2) goods to choose from – cherries and plums.
- The consumer is rational and a utility maximizer.
- Income, prices and demand factors of the items are fixed.
- Combination A of 40 cherries and 1 plum yields the same satisfaction as combination D – i.e. 16 cherries and 4 plums.
- This rate of exchange that cherries are given up for plums is called the **Marginal Rate of Substitution (MRS)**.

Other points about indifference curves to note:

- The curve normally slopes downward because to consume more of one good requires you to give up some of the other goods, since income is fixed.
- The curve is convex because the MRS is diminishing – i.e. more is given up on the vertical axis to make a gain of 1 on the horizontal axis.
- They do not intersect since they will then represent two different levels of satisfaction, which is contradictory.
- They cannot slope upward because more of both goods are being consumed, contradicting the rationale of the indifference curve.

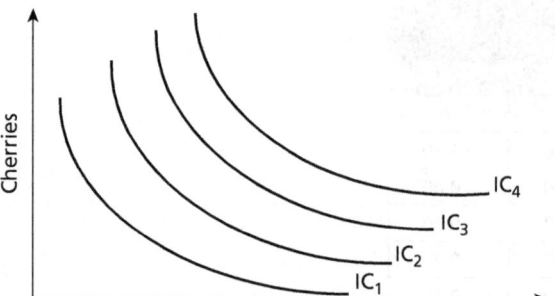

Figure 3.5 An indifference map

An indifference map, as illustrated in Figure 3.5, consists of several indifferent curves extending outward from the origin indicating increasingly higher levels of total satisfaction and what consumers wish for.

The budget line

A budget line is drawn to show what a consumer can afford to buy based on:

- Their level of income;
- The prices of the two goods in question.

Refer to Figure 3.6. If income is $20.00 per day and a sandwich costs $4.00 and orange juice $2.00, a budget line shows the combinations of two goods that the consumer can buy, given his level of income and the relative prices of the two goods.

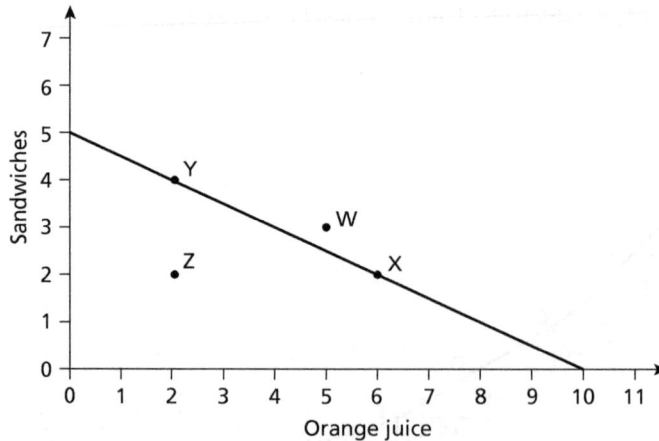

Figure 3.6 A budget line

Figure 3.6 shows that 5 sandwiches and 0 orange juices or 10 orange juices and 0 sandwiches can be bought. A line joining these combinations is called a 'budget line'.

Note:

- Any point on the line is affordable and total income is spent;
- Point X and Y are affordable;
- Point W is not affordable;
- Point Z is affordable and the cost is $12 but $8.00 remain.

See Figure 3.7. If sandwiches change from $4.00 to $2.00 and orange juice from $2.00 to $1.00, the budget line will shift outward from XY to X_1Y_1. With prices constant and a change in income to $40.00, then the curve would also shift outward by the same distance.

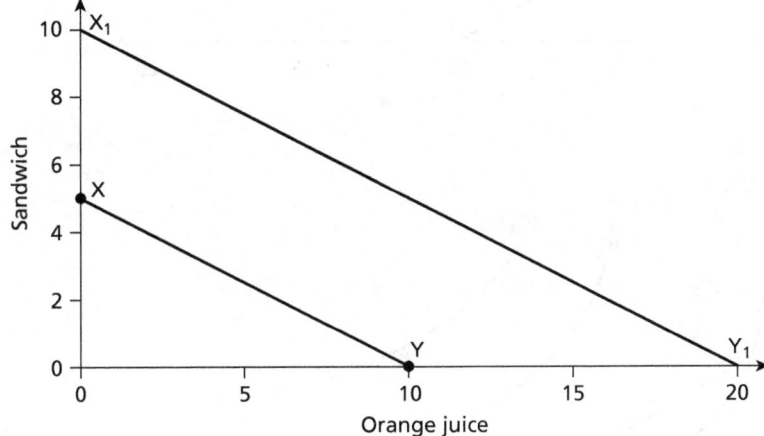

Figure 3.7 Shifts of the budget line

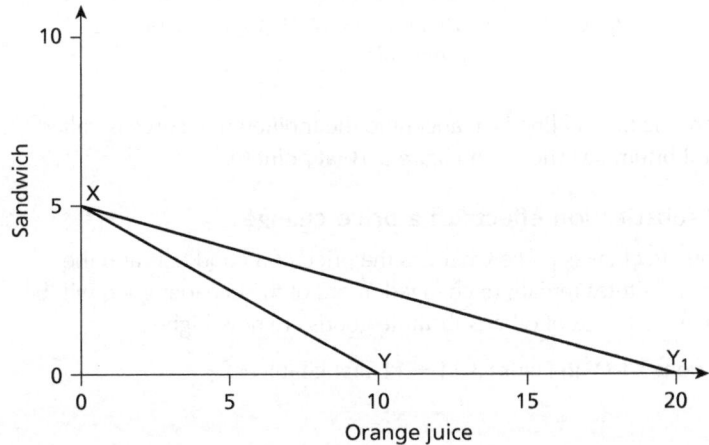

Figure 3.8 Budget line pivots (1)

If one price changes, however – e.g., orange juice from $2.00 to $1.00 – then the budget line would pivot as in Figure 3.8 from XY to XY_1.

Similarly, if the price of sandwiches changed from $4.00 to $2.00, the budget line would pivot as shown in Figure 3.9 from XY to X_1Y and the gradient or slope would reflect the change in relative prices from 1:2 to 1:1.

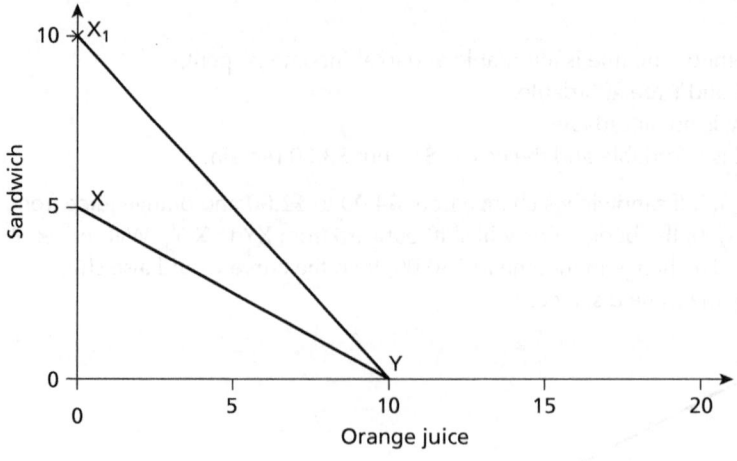

Figure 3.9 Budget line pivots (2)

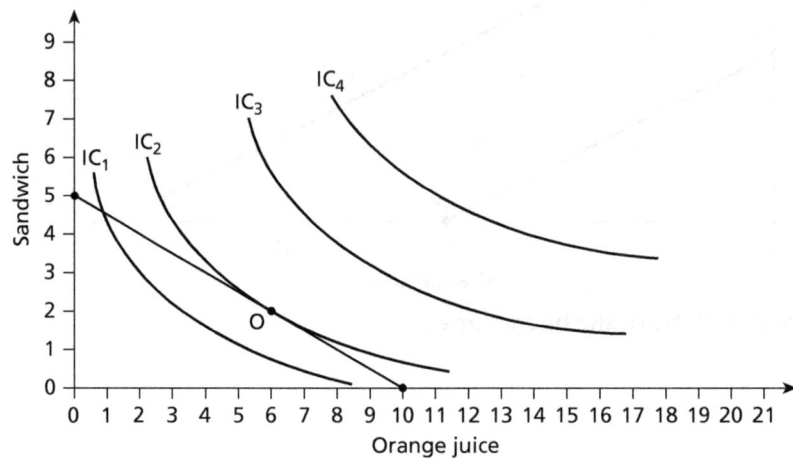

Figure 3.10 Consumer equilibrium

The point where the budget line is a tangent to the indifference curve is called 'consumer equilibrium', as shown in Figure 3.10 at point O.

Income and substitution effects of a price change

The substitution effect takes place when, as the price of a good falls and the prices of other substitutes remain unchanged, more of the cheaper good will be demanded since the prices of other substitute goods are now higher.

This is shown from X to Y in Figure 3.11 = 11 orange juices.

> **Exam tip**
>
> Frequently tested by CAPE as an MCQ.

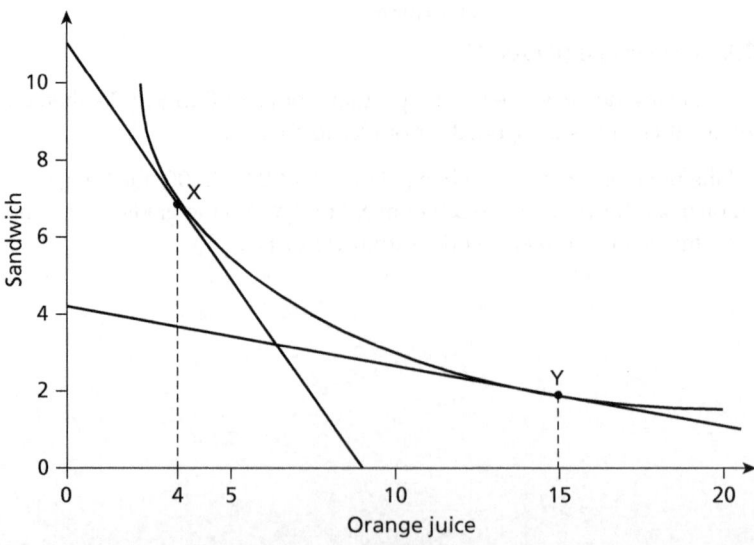

Figure 3.11 The substitution effect

THEORY OF DEMAND

Figures 3.11 and 3.12 illustrate a substitution effect. Note the direction of the arrow in Figure 3.12

Figure 3.12 also shows the income effect.

The income effect of a price change is the impact on the quantity of a good purchased due to a change in purchasing power brought about by a fall in price.

This effect may operate as an increase or decrease depending on the nature of the good. Figure 3.12 shows the income effect (Y to Z) of a price fall.

Both the substitution and income effects (indicated by the arrows) move in the same direction for a normal good, which is defined as one of which the quantity demanded increases as real income increases and, therefore, has a positive income effect.

Separating the substitution and income effects of a price fall for a normal good

> **Exam tip**
>
> This topic is often a question in **module 1**.

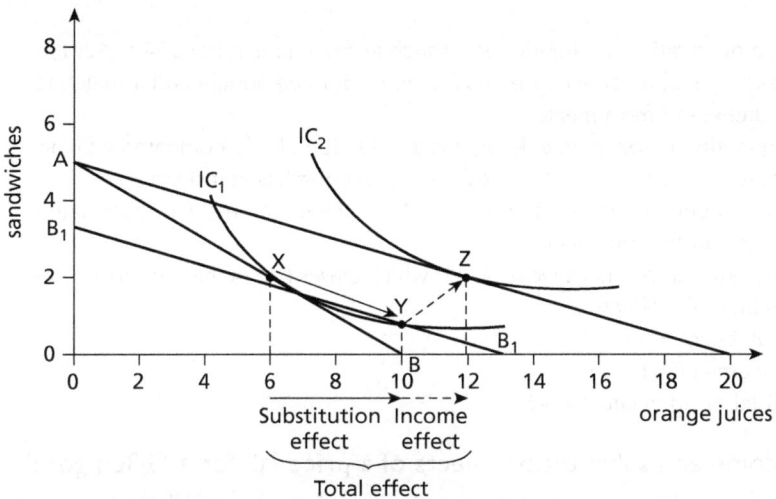

Figure 3.12 Income and substitution effects

To determine which effect is more powerful, it is possible to separate these two effects. Refer to Figure 3.12.

- AB is the original budget line. Point X denotes an equilibrium quantity 6 orange juices and 2 sandwiches. As a result of a fall in the price of orange juice from $2.00 to $1.00, the quantity demanded increases to 12. The new budget line pivots to the right with a new price ratio of 1:4.
- The previous ratio of prices was 1:2.
- A new budget line B_1B_1 tangential to the original indifference curve IC_1 isolates the substitution effect by changing the gradient of AB (1:2) to reflect the new price ratio of 1:4 on the original indifference curve IC_1.
- X to Y is the substitution effect, which is equivalent to 4 orange juices (6 to 10). Note the direction of the arrow.
- The income effect is therefore Y to Z and is equal to 2 orange juices. Note that where the substitution effect ends, the income effect begins.
- The substitution effect of 4 orange juices added to the income effect of 2 orange juices makes the overall total or price effect of 6 orange juices.

Inferior goods

An inferior good is one which experiences a fall in demand when real income increases and is therefore subject to a negative income effect. See Figure 3.13.

REVISION GUIDE TO ECONOMICS

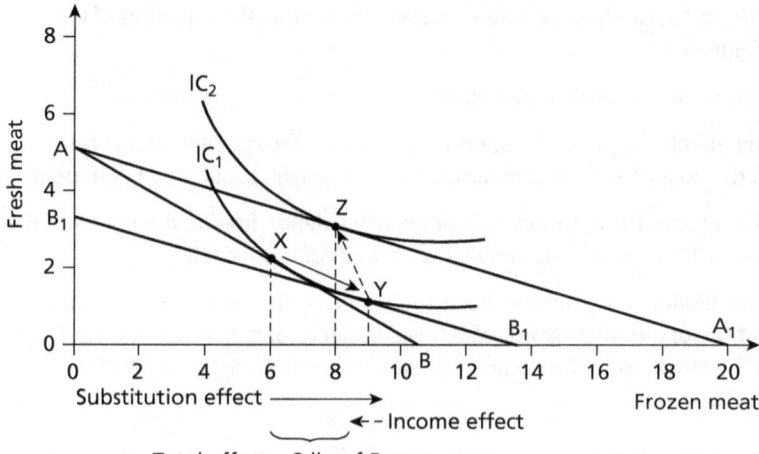

Figure 3.13 Income and substitution effect for an inferior good

Note:

- With a price fall for an inferior good such as frozen meat from $4 to $2, the increase in real income cause less frozen meat to be bought and a switch to the purchase of fresh meat.
- The quantity of frozen meat bought is a reduction of 1 lb compared with an increase from 2 lb to 3¼ lb of fresh goat meat purchased instead.
- The substitution effect is X to Y, or 3 lb. Note the increase always associated with the substitution effect.
- The income effect is negative – i.e. –1, which erases part of the substitution effect.
- The sum of the effects are:
   Sub effect = +3
   Income effect = –1
   Total or price effect = +2

The income and substitution effects of a price fall for a Giffen good

- A Giffen good is a type of inferior good with an extreme negative income effect.
- The income effect moves in the opposite direction to the substitution effect, completely erasing the increasing substitution effect (see Figure 3.14).
- Demand for the product falls considerably with a price fall and vice versa.

Note in Figure 3.14, the substitution effect is equal to 3 (6 to 9, or X to Y) but the negative income effect is equal to Y to Z, or –5. The total effect is equal to –2.

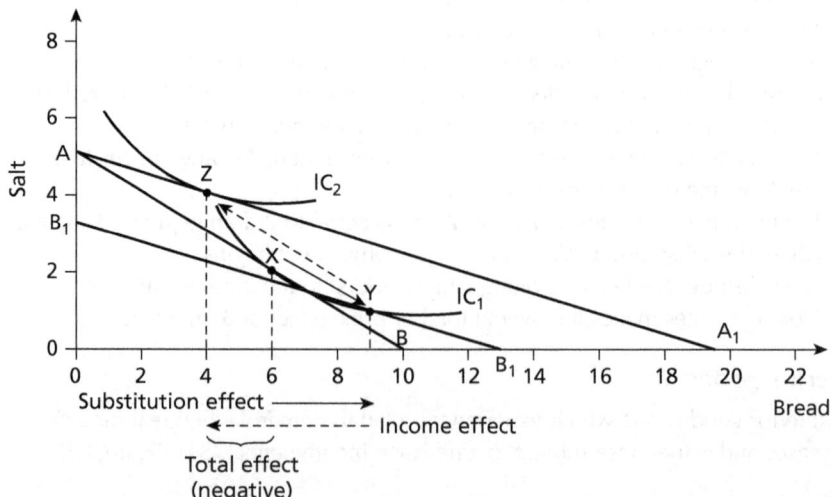

Figure 3.14 Income and substitution effects of a fall in price of a normal good

A change in quantity demanded (**Hint:** Do not confuse a change in demand with a change in quantity demanded.)

A change in the quantity demanded of a good refers to an extension or contraction of demand due to a price change assuming **that the conditions of demand remain fixed** (*ceteris paribus*).

An extension in demand takes place when the price of a good falls and there is an increase in demand, as illustrated in Figure 3.15 from $10.00 to $5.00. The quantity demanded extends from 6 to 14 units.

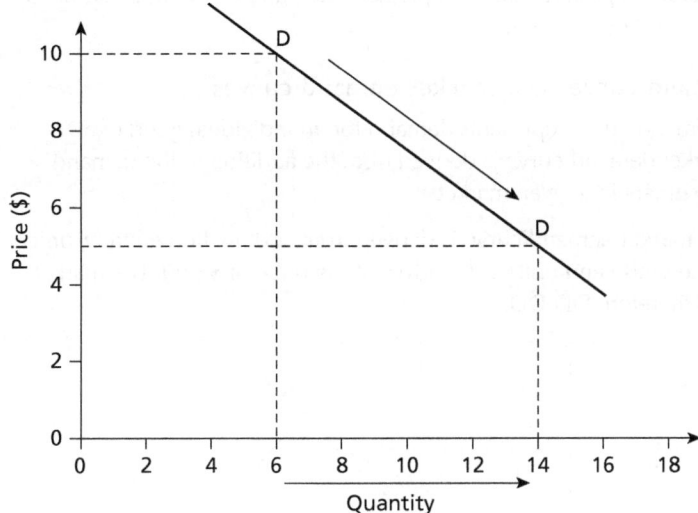

Figure 3.15 Movement along a demand curve

When the price of good X increases from $5.00 to $10.00, demand decreases (contracts) from 14 units to 6.

A change in demand

A change in demand is a result of a change in non-price factors. The demand curve will shift to the right or the left depending on the nature of the change.

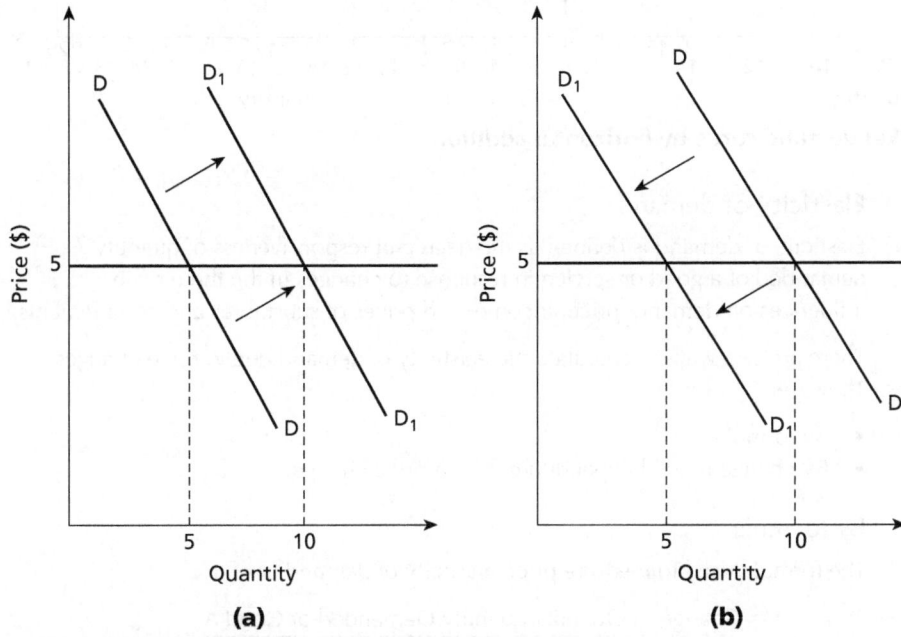

Figure 3.16 Shift in a demand curve

The following factors will cause a change in demand. The demand curve for a good such as cellular phones will shift to the right (Figure 3.16a) to a new position. More of the good would be demanded at each and every price. The non-price factors of demand are:

- An increase in income
- A change in taste from landlines towards cell phones.
- A rise in the price of a substitute – e.g. e-mail.
- A fall in the price of a complement good jointly used – e.g. phone cards.
- A longer time period will allow for better information to reach customers.
- Number of uses: If a product has multiple uses, demand would increase at all prices, at each and every price.

Individual demand curves and market demand curves

An individual demand curve represents demand for an individual good of a consumer. A market demand curve is derived from the addition of the demand curves of all consumers in a given market.

In Figure 3.17, a market demand curve is derived from adding, horizontally, units 3, 5 and 9 at price $5.00 and units 5, 9 and 15 at the price of $2.00. The market demand curve is therefore DD DD.

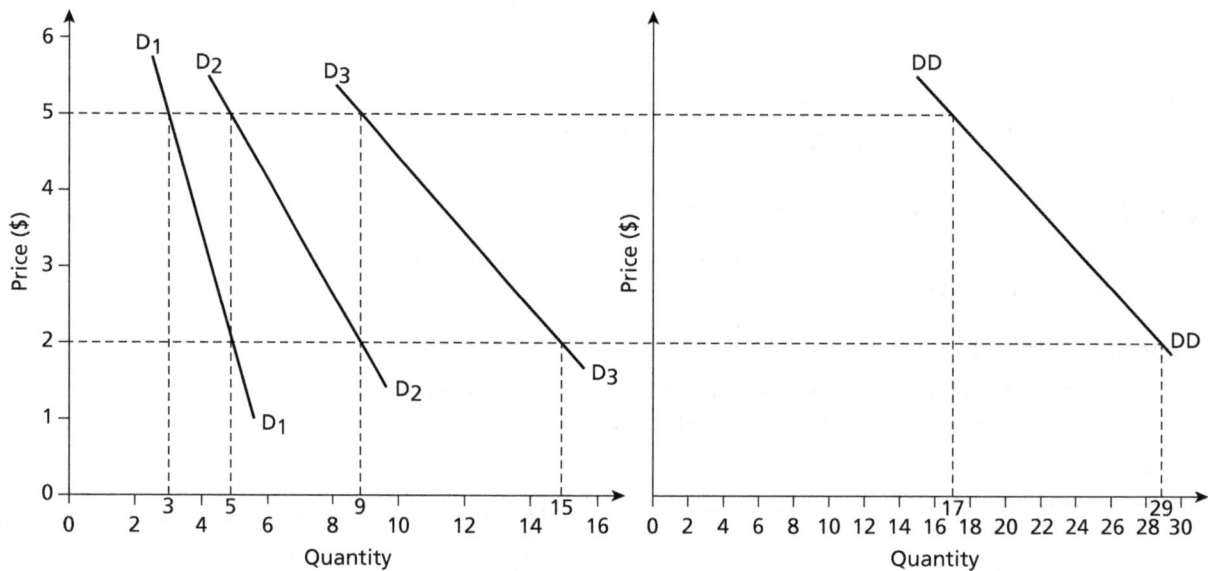

Figure 3.17 Deriving a market demand curve by horizontal addition

Elasticity of demand

Elasticity of demand is defined as the degree of responsiveness of quantity demanded of a good or service in response to changes in the three main influences on demand: price, income, and prices of substitutes and complements.

There are two ways to calculate the elasticity of demand due to price changes. They are:

- By formula;
- By change in total expenditure from a price change.

By formula

The formula used to measure price elasticity of demand is:

$$\frac{\text{Change in Quantity/quantity Demanded of Good A}}{\text{Change in Price/price of Good A}} \times 100$$

This is also known as the 'percentage change' in quantity to changes in price.

An elastic response

(See Figure 3.18.) Applying the formula, a price rise from $4 to $5 is (5 − 4/4 × 100) = 0.25

A change in quantity from $3 to $2 = 1 (1/3 × 100) = −0.33

Price elasticity of demand therefore = −0.33 / 0.25 = −1.33

The size refers to the value −1.33. If the value is greater than 1, it is called an 'elastic response'.

An inelastic response

(See Figure 3.19.) When the elasticity value is less than 1, the price elasticity of demand is inelastic. In Figure 3.19, a fall in price of good X from $10 to $5 induces a quantity change of 1(4 to 5). Applying the formula will give the following:

Figure 3.18 An elastic response measured

$$\frac{\text{\% Change in Qd}}{\text{\% Change in Price}} = \frac{(Q_2 - Q_1/Q_1) \times 100}{(P_2 - P_1/P_1) \times 100} = \frac{(5 - 4/4) \times 100}{(5 - 10/10) \times 100} = \frac{(+1/4) \times 100}{(-1/2) \times 100} = \frac{+0.25}{-0.5}$$

$$\text{PED} = +0.25/-50 = -1/2 \text{ or } -0.5$$

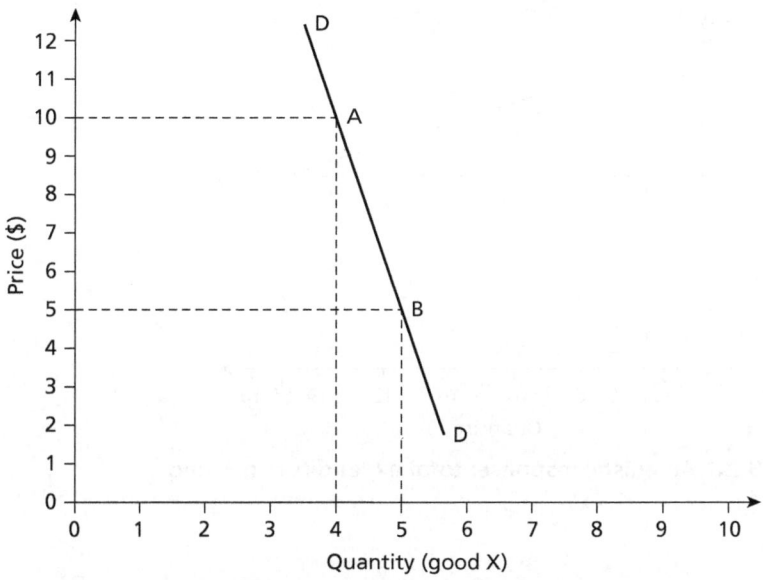

Figure 3.19 An inelastic response measured for good X

For the same segment A B, there are different measures of elasticity.

To get around this problem, the **average** or **midpoint** price elasticity of demand formula is applied by dividing formula (1) and formula (2) as follows:

1. $\dfrac{\text{Change in quantities} \times 100\%}{\text{Sum of quantities}}$

2. $\dfrac{\text{Change in price} \times 100}{\text{Sum of prices}}$

3. Divide formula 1 by formula 2 to find point elasticity.

Important points

- Elasticity of demand measures the responsiveness of quantity demanded to changes in price.
- Values greater than 1 are elastic responses, while values less than 1 are inelastic.

- Since a rise and fall in price over a segment of the curve yield two different values, this is solved using the midpoint or average formula.
- The sign preceding the coefficient is important because it reflects the type of good.
- A negative sign implies a normal good according to price, while a positive sign implies a Giffen good.
- The size refers to the degree of responsiveness.

The total expenditure method of estimating price elasticity of demand

For a price rise, a decrease in expenditure indicates that price elasticity of demand is elastic. See Figure 3.20. A price rise from $5.00 to $8.00 yields a fall in total expenditure as follows:

15 × $5 = $75
4 × $8 = $32

From a price rise of $5 to $8 the fall in total expenditure = $43

A price fall is just the opposite – i.e. from $75 to $32 indicating an elastic response.

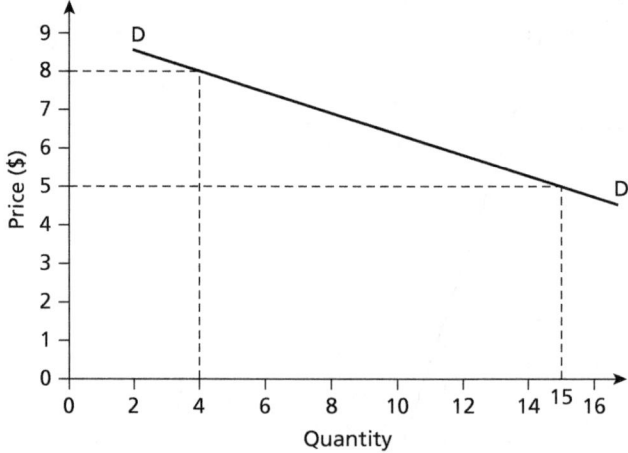

Figure 3.20 An elastic response: total expenditure method

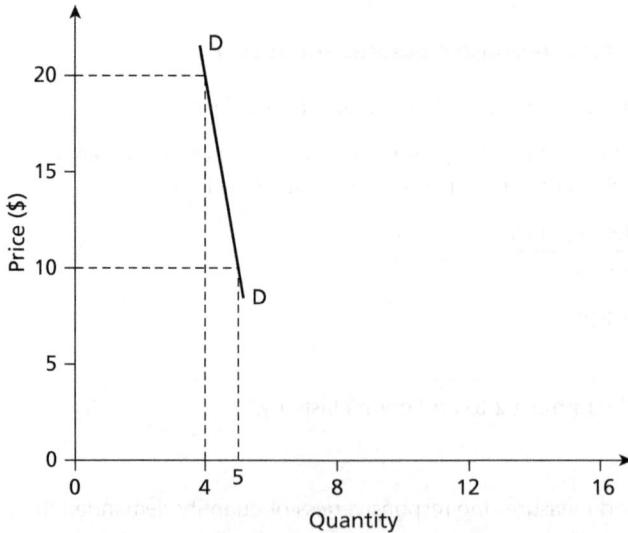

Figure 3.21 An inelastic response: total expenditure method

THEORY OF DEMAND

Refer to Figure 3.21. When price elasticity of demand is inelastic, a fall in price from $20 to $10 will cause total expenditure to fall by $30.00; for a price rise from $10 to $20, total expenditure will rise by $30.

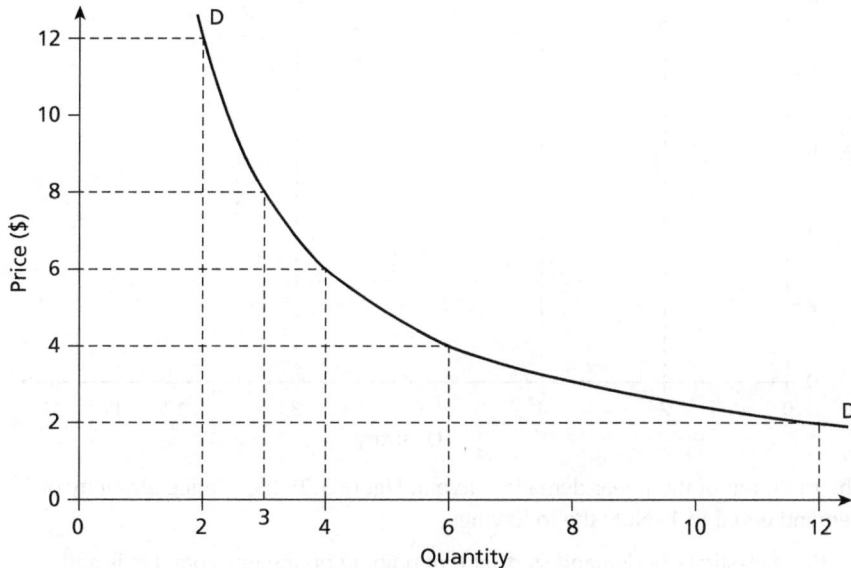

Figure 3.22 Unitary elasticity – total revenue method

In Figure 3.22, any price multiplied by quantity would yield a total expenditure of $24.00 whether prices are rising or falling. Price elasticity of demand is therefore equal to one or unitary.

Extremes in elasticity

Two extremes in price elasticity of demand are 0, or **perfectly inelastic demand**, and **perfectly elastic demand**.

Perfectly inelastic demand

Figure 3.23 shows that a rise or fall in price will yield an elasticity value of 0 because any change in price divided by a quantity change of 0 will be equal to 0.

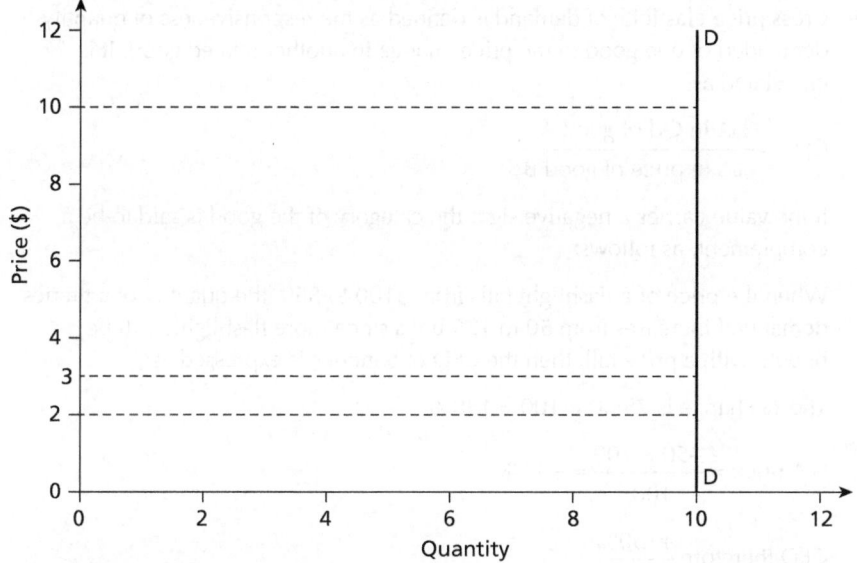

Figure 3.23 Perfect inelasticity

In the case of perfect elasticity, the price does not change but quantity does change. In fact, at a price of $10.00 an unlimited amount is demanded.

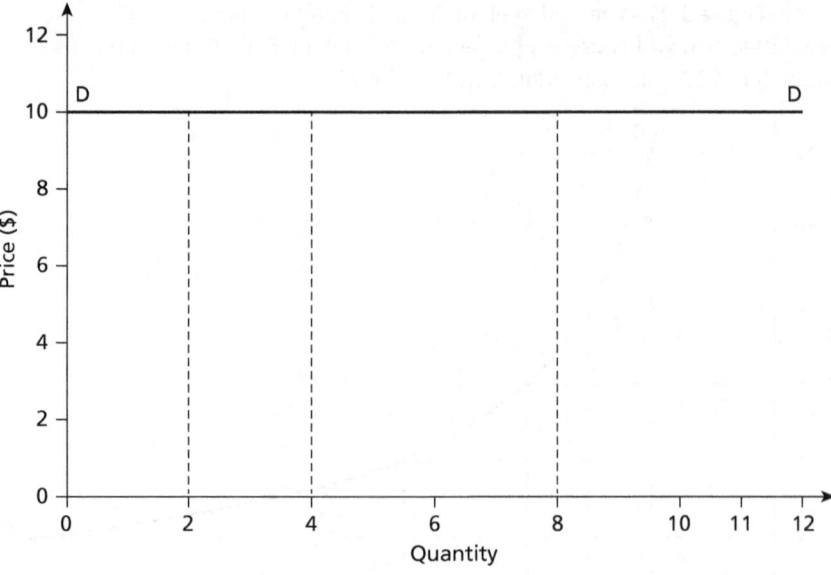

Figure 3.24 Perfect elasticity

The midpoint of the linear demand curve in Figure 3.25 has a price elasticity of demand equal to 1. Note the following:

- Price elasticity of demand starts at 0 at point D on the horizontal axis and increases in value to point A on the vertical axis.
- Points to the right of B above have a value of less than 1, while to the left of B, values are greater than 1.
- At point B, the value is equal to 1.

The factors that affect price elasticity of demand are:

- The availability of substitutes;
- The proportion of income spent on the good;
- Habit;
- The absolute price level of the good;
- Time;
- The usefulness of the good.

Cross elasticity of demand (CED)

- Cross price elasticity of demand is defined as the responsiveness of quantity demanded of one good to the price change in another related good. It is calculated as:

$$CED = \frac{\%\Delta \text{ in Qd of good A}}{\%\Delta \text{ in price of good B}}$$

- If the value carries a negative sign, the category of the good is said to be a complement, as follows:

When the price of a flashlight falls from $100 to $50, the quantity of batteries demanded increases from 50 to 125 units since more flashlights will be bought with a price fall, then the CED of batteries is expressed as:

The % change is $75/50 \times 100 = 150\%$

$$\%\Delta \text{ price} = \frac{-50 \times 100}{100} = -50\%$$

$$\text{CED therefore } \frac{+150\%}{-50\%} = -3$$

Substitutes

- Wheat flour and cornmeal flour are considered substitutes.

THEORY OF DEMAND

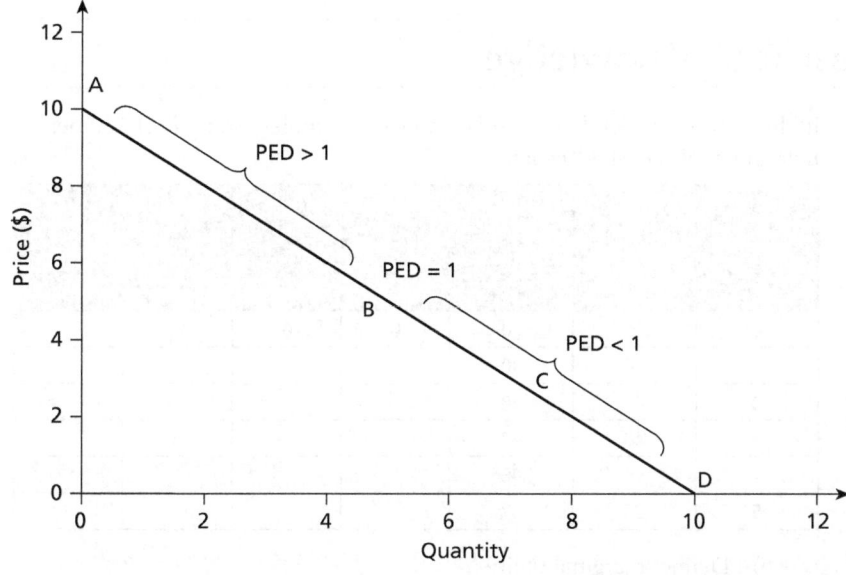

Figure 3.25 Changing elasticity values

- If wheat flour prices rise from $10 to $15 per bag, the demand for wheat flour will fall.
- The demand for a substitute, cornmeal flour, will rise from 10 to 20 lb.
- The CED of cornmeal = %Δ in Qd of cornmeal = 20 − 10/10 × 100 = +100%
  %Δ in price of wheat flour = 15 − 10/10 × 100 = +50%

$$CED = \frac{+100\%}{+50\%} = +2$$

The positive sign is associated with price and quantity changes for substitutes, such as whole wheat and cornmeal flour.

The size denotes how responsive cornmeal is as a good substitute for wheat flour.

Independent goods

When goods are not related in any way, they are said to be independent and carry a coefficient of 0.

The value of cross elasticity of demand to a firm

- Cross elasticity of demand for complements – e.g. hot dog sausages and hot dog bread – is valuable to a grocer because if there is a price rise for hot dog sausages, firms may counteract the fall in demand for hot dog sausages by offering hot dog bread on sale, or by selling them together at a bargain price.

Income elasticity of demand

- Income elasticity of demand (YED) measures the percentage change in quantity demanded to changes in income. Expressed in formula it is:

$$\frac{\%\Delta \text{ in Qd}}{\%\Delta \text{ in Income}}$$

- A coefficient greater than 1 is said to be elastic, less than 1 inelastic and 0 elastic if there is no change in quantity demanded when income changes.
- A positive sign indicates a normal good according to income. (See Figure 3.19.) A negative sign indicates an inferior good in Figure 3.19.

The value of income elasticity of demand and decision-making

- A firm may benefit from a knowledge of income elasticity of demand when economic conditions are positive. Cars, foreign travel, upscale dining and real estate markets record high profit levels. Caribbean hotels target markets in foreign countries whose incomes are rising.
- In a recession when incomes are falling, firms may sell inferior goods – e.g. basic goods and services.

REVISION GUIDE TO ECONOMICS

Test Your Knowledge

1. Jill has $100 per month to spend on shoes and apples. Shoes cost $20 per pair and apples cost $20 each.

Quantity	Utility from shoes	Utility from apples	Marginal utility		Marginal utility per dollar	
			Shoes	Apples	Shoes	Apples
0	0	0	0	0		
1	30	30				
2	40	38				
3	48	44				
4	54	46				
5	58	47				

(a) (i) Define 'marginal utility';
   (ii) Calculate Jill's marginal utility from:
       (1) Shoes;
       (2) Apples.
(b) Draw a diagram showing Jill's budget constraint.
(c) (i) Calculate the marginal utility per dollar of Jill's consumption choices;
   (ii) State the optimal number of shoes and the optimal number of apples that Jill can purchase given her income and the relative prices of the two goods.

MULTIPLE CHOICE QUESTIONS

1. The price elasticity of demand of good X is 0.5. If the price of the good changes by 10%, what is the corresponding percentage change in quantity?
   (a) 10%;
   (b) 20%;
   (c) 5%;
   (d) 15%.

2. The price elasticity of demand for good X is perfectly elastic; 50 units are sold at bds $3.00 per unit. If the price is raised to $4.00, expenditure on good X will be:
   (a) $150.00;
   (b) $200.00;
   (c) $600.00;
   (d) $0.00.

3. The price elasticity of demand of a good is unitary. When the price of the good is $3.00, the quantity demanded is 40 units. If the price of the good increases to $6.00, what will be the change in quantity demanded?
   (a) 24;
   (b) 20;
   (c) No change;
   (d) 80.

4. The price elasticity of demand of good B is unitary. What will increase if the price is reduced?
   (a) Total expenditure;
   (b) Expenditure on substitutes;
   (c) Quantity demanded;
   (d) Expenditure on the good.

5. The midpoint of a linear demand curve has a price elasticity of demand that is:
   (a) Inelastic;
   (b) Perfectly elastic;
   (c) Unitary;
   (d) Perfectly inelastic.

Chapter 4: Theory of Supply I

Learning Objectives

By the end of this chapter you should be able to:
- Identify the factors of production
- Define and explain the term production function
- Calculate and explain the relationship between total, average and marginal product and the costs related to each concept
- Explain short and long run supply and their upward slope
- Explain the law of variable proportions and returns to scale and economies of scale

Production

Production is the act of converting inputs into output – e.g. baker + flour + yeast + oven = bread. Production ends when the good reaches the customer.

Production function

The production function expresses the maximum output produced by a number of combinations of inputs as shown in Table 4.1.

Table 4.1 A production function

Labour (units)	Capital (units)	Output (kg)
40	10	2000
100	20	5000

In Table 4.1, note the ratio of labour to capital is 4:1 (40/10) and 5:1 (100/20) for the outputs 2000 kg and 5000 kg, respectively.

The periods of production

The periods of production explain the ability of a firm to increase output when inputs are changed. Production is achieved with fixed and variable input factors. A **fixed factor** is one which is long-lasting, not easily changed and is usually unchanged during the process of production – e.g. a stove in a restaurant. A **variable factor** changes as output changes, is easily changed and may also be altered during production – e.g. flour to bread.

There are four periods of production:

- The momentary or market period;
- The short-run period;
- The long-run period;
- The very long-run period.

The **momentary period** of production is a period during which output cannot be increased because there is no time to change the input factors – e.g. when products are sold out.

The **short-run period** is the period of production when output can be increased by changing the variable factor – e.g. raw materials and when at least one fixed factor cannot be changed.

The **long-run period** is the time taken to change both variable and fixed factors in order to increase production – e.g. expanding the premises.

The **very long-run period** is the period of production when output can be increased through invention or innovation – e.g. automation.

Table 4.2 Time allowed to change

Period of production	Fixed factor	Variable factor
1. Momentary	Cannot change	Cannot change
2. Short-run	Cannot change	Can change
3. Long-run	Can change	Can change
4. Very long-run	Can change easily	Can change easily

The short-run period

Table 4.3 shows:

- The input/output relationship of workers on a one hectare farm planting tomatoes in the short-run period.

Exam tip

Tabular calculations appear often in CAPE exams.

THEORY OF SUPPLY I

- The total physical product (TPP) refers to total output per time period – e.g. worker #1 plants 12 tomato plants per day.
- The marginal physical product (MPP) measures the change in TPP when one additional unit of labour is added. It is expressed as $\Delta TPP/\Delta input$.
- The average physical product (APP) is the TTP divided by the quantity of inputs: TPP/q.

Table 4.3 TPP, MPP and APP

No. of workers	Total physical product	Marginal physical product	Average physical product
1	12	12	12
2	27	15	13.5
3	44	17	14.7
4	58	14	14.5
5	69	11	13.8
6	77	8	12.8
7	82	5	11.7
8	82	0	10.25

The short-run period is influenced by the law of variable proportions which comprises two laws:

- The law of increasing returns to the variable factor;
- The law of diminishing returns to the variable factor.

Both laws explain the relationship between the total physical product (TPP), marginal physical product (variable proportions MPP) and average physical product (APP).

The law of variable proportions states that as increasing amounts of a variable factor – e.g. labour – are combined with a fixed amount of a fixed factor – e.g. land, returns to the variable factor will initially increase at an increasing rate (law of increasing returns) until they peak and thereafter fall to 0 (law of diminishing returns).

Observations

In Table 4.3 note that:

- the change from 1 worker to 2 workers yields an MPP of 15 units of output as TPP increases *from 12 to 27 units*;
- the total physical product is rising throughout from 1 worker to 7 workers, levelling off at 82 units;
- the MPP is rising by increasing amounts – i.e. 12, 15, 17, and so on, (increasing marginal returns) then declining to 14, 11, 8, and so on. This is called 'diminishing returns to the variable factor';
- the APP is also rising and falling from 12 to 14.6 and 14.6 to 10.25, respectively.

The marginal and average product are related to **productivity**, which is the rate of production given by the formula, output/input per hr. Production is the total output per time period.

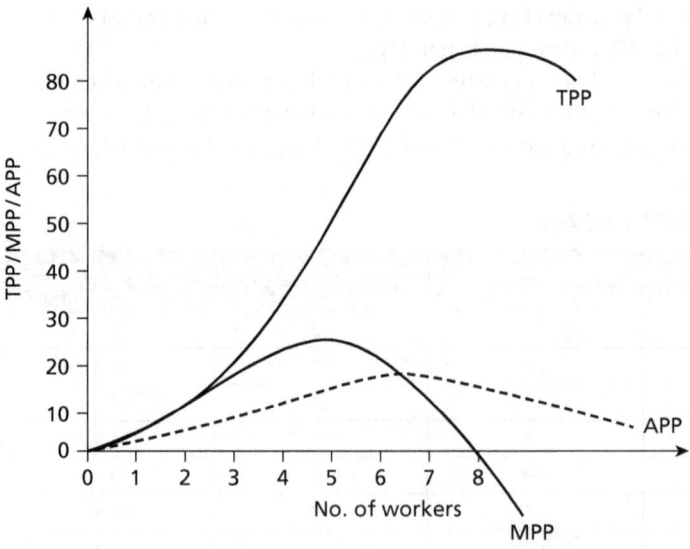

Figure 4.1 Total, marginal and average physical product

Observe in Figure 4.1 that TPP, MPP and APP all rise and fall. Note also:

- Even if MPP is declining but greater than APP, APP is rising.
- When the MPP curve intersects the APP, the APP immediately declines but remains positive until it reaches worker #8, when it becomes negative.

Reasons for increasing returns to the variable factor

- From worker #1 to worker #3, each has more of the fixed factor (land) with which to work.
- Specialization – also called 'division of labour' – may increase output.

Reasons for diminishing returns to the variable factor

- The fixed factor becomes overcrowded as the ratio of workers to land changes (variable proportion);
- The monotony of repetitive work, worker apathy, disruption in production on the assembly line if one worker is absent or injured.

Assumptions of the law of diminishing returns

- Technology is fixed.
- All variable inputs are equally efficient.
- The short-run period is the period of production in question.
- Factors of production are mobile.

Note also: Mathematically, when a marginal value is higher than an average value, the average value would be rising. When the marginal value is lower than the average value, the average will be falling.

The stages of production

There are three stages of production:

Stage 1: Lies between A and B on the TPP curve.

Stage 2: Lies between B and C on the TPP curve; APP is at a maximum when marginal physical product is declining to 0.

Stage 3: Lies between C and D where TPP is declining, and APP and MPP is positive.

- An entrepreneur would not produce at Stage 3 because the TPP is declining and the MPP is negative.
- Instead, a producer would produce at Stage 1 (best returns) or Stage 2 (where TPP is still increasing between Stages 2 and 3; additional workers increase the total product until it declines).

THEORY OF SUPPLY 1

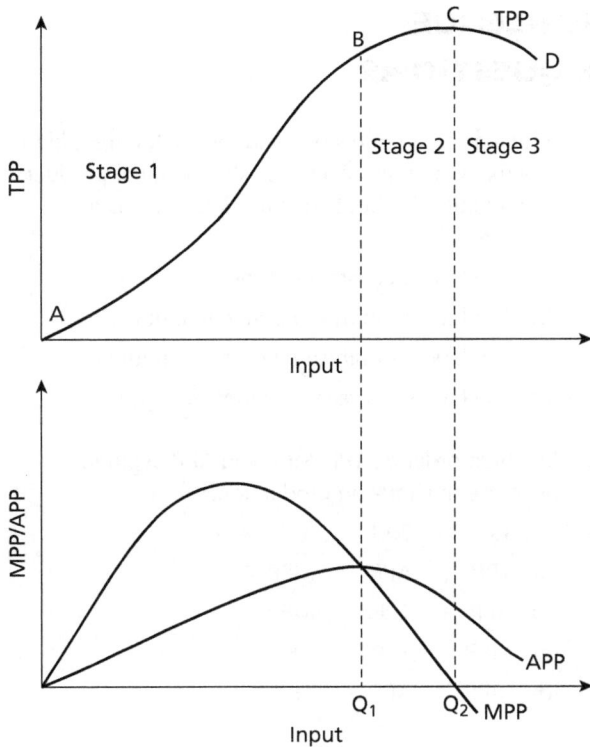

Figure 4.2 The stages of production

A firm handicapped by diminishing returns to the variable factor in the short run will increase its capacity in the long run by changing its scale of production.

Long run production

Table 4.4 Increasing returns to scale

Capital (ovens)	Labour (bakers)	Output (loaves)
2 ovens	4 bakers	500
3 ovens	6 bakers	1,250

The long run production function shown in Table 4.4 shows that when the percentage change in output is greater than the percentage in inputs this is called **increasing returns to scale**. A change in capital and labour of 50% (2 to 3 ovens and 4 to 6 bakers) increases output by 150% (500 to 1250 loaves).

If a percentage change in output is less than the percentage change in input, this is called **decreasing returns to scale** as shown in Table 4.5.

Table 4.5 Decreasing returns to scale

Capital (ovens)	Labour (bakers)	Output (loaves)
2	3	500
4	6	600

Notes:
- A 100% change in capital and labour yields an output change of only 20%. This is called **decreasing returns to scale**.
- When the percentage change in input yields the same percentage change in output this is called **constant returns to scale**. These three returns to scale are referred to as the **long-run law of returns to scale**.

TEST YOUR KNOWLEDGE
MULTIPLE CHOICE QUESTIONS

1. Diminishing returns are caused by:
   (a) Some inputs being less efficient than others;
   (b) Too much of the fixed factor with which to operate;
   (c) Overcrowding of the fixed factor;
   (d) Specialization.

2. In the short run:
   (a) All factors are variable;
   (b) All fixed factors can be changed;
   (c) At least one factor cannot be changed;
   (d) The variable factors cannot be changed.

3. Which of the figures below illustrates short-run output?

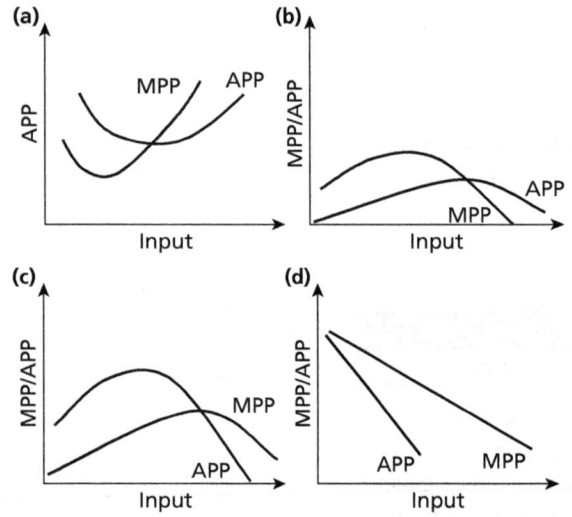

4. If increasing amounts of a variable factor are added to a fixed quantity of a factor, the marginal product will initially rise but thereafter decline. This is a statement of:
   (a) The law of constant returns;
   (b) The law of diminishing marginal utility;
   (c) The law of diminishing marginal returns;
   (d) The law of decreasing returns to scale.

5. In which order do TPP, MPP and APP begin to decrease in short-run production.

	1st	2nd	3rd
(a)	TPP	APP	MPP
(b)	APP	TPP	MPP
(c)	MPP	TPP	APP
(d)	MPP	APP	TPP

Chapter 5: Theory of Supply II

REVISION GUIDE TO ECONOMICS

Learning Objectives

By the end of this chapter you should be able to:
- Explain the shape of the supply curve for a firm and industry
- Explain extension and contraction of supply
- Demonstrate and explain shifts of the supply curve
- Explain and calculate price elasticity of supply (PES)
- Calculate and interpret supply elasticities
- Demonstrate extension and contraction of supply
- Explain shifts in the supply curve

Introduction

Supply is defined as the quantity of goods or services that firms offer for sale at different prices per time period.

As Figure 5.1 illustrates

Supply curves slope upward left to right, since more of a good is supplied at higher prices and less at lower prices due to the following:

- Higher prices induce producers to produce more;
- Firms who cannot survive at low prices enter with increased quantity when prices are higher.

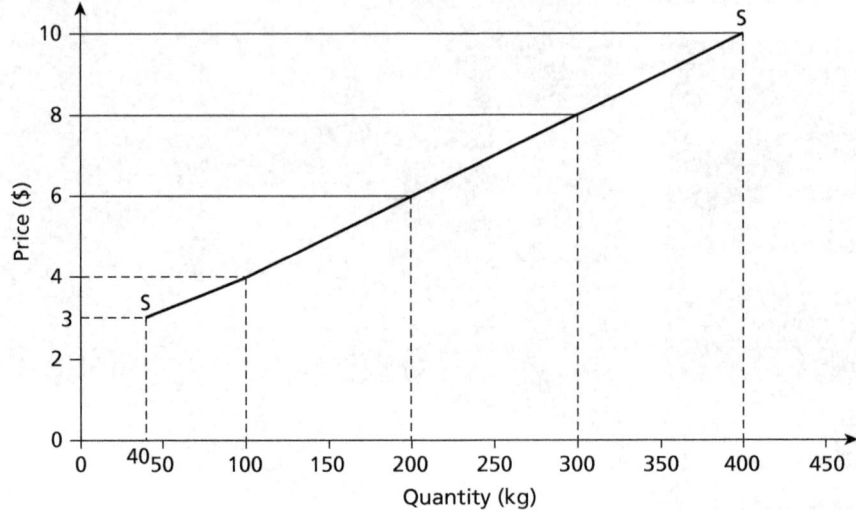

Figure 5.1 A supply curve

Factors affecting supply

Factors which affect the supply of a good or service are:

- Price factors;
- Non-price factors.

The price factor refers to the prevailing price of a good, which affects the incentive to produce.

Non-price factors are also called the **conditions of supply**, which include the following:

- The cost or prices of the inputs of production – e.g. raw materials;
- Good or bad weather (for agricultural goods);
- Disease, pests or drought (for agricultural goods);
- Changes in technology;
- Changes in the prices of other related commodities;
- The economic objectives of a firm;
- Government indirect taxes, subsidies, regulations;
- Time.

Exam tip

Tested at CAPE – Papers 1 and 2.

Movements along a supply curve

Extension of supply

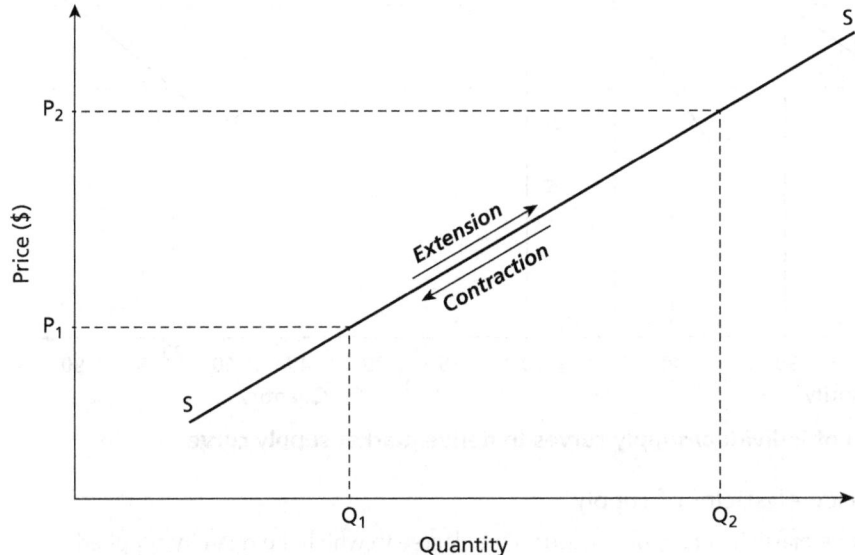

Figure 5.2 Movements along a supply curve

In Figure 5.2, an extension of supply is a movement from left to right, Q_1 to Q_2, along the supply curve in response to a price rise from P_1 to P_2.

Non-price factors are assumed to remain fixed when prices change. Note the change from Q_1 to Q_2 when prices rise.

A contraction of supply occurs when prices fall from P_2 to P_1 and supply falls from Q_2 to Q_1. (Non-price factors remain fixed.)

A change in supply

A change in supply refers to a shift of the supply curve to the right or left. This shift may be caused by a change in any of the following non-price factors as shown in Table 5.1.

Table 5.1 Factors that cause a shift in the supply curve

Non-price factors	Direction of shift
An increase in the cost of the factors of production. Output is reduced.	Shift to the left
Adverse weather conditions for agricultural produce. If drought affects crops, supply will decrease.	Shift to the left
Government indirect taxes – e.g. VAT will raise supply costs and negatively affect profit. Output is reduced.	Shift to the left
Aim of producers: A firm plans to restrict supply to obtain a high price – e.g. the OPEC cartel.	Shift to the left
If a substitute good becomes cheaper to produce, firms will switch away from the original product – e.g. from oranges to grapefruit if sold at the same price.	Supply of oranges shifts to the left
New technology, innovation or invention and increased productivity – e.g. microchip revolution.	Shift to the right
Government subsidies cause supply costs to fall. Firms raise output.	Shift to the right
Goods in joint supply – e.g. beef and leather. The production of beef invariably coincides with the production of leather.	Supply curve of leather shifts to the right if beef production increases

Figure 5.3 shows the horizontal addition of individual supply curves to derive the market supply curve.

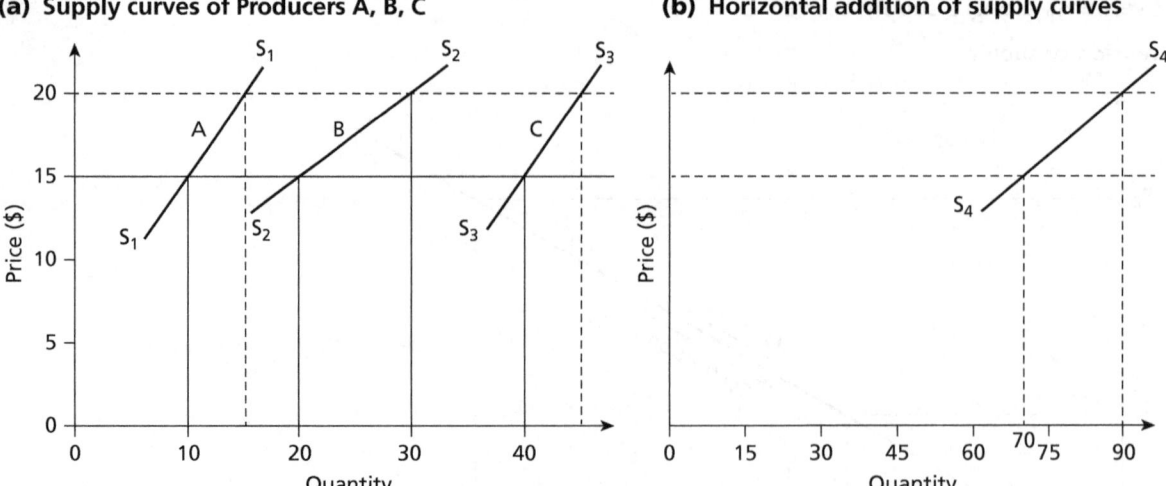

Figure 5.3 Horizontal addition of individual supply curves to derive market supply curve

Price elasticity of supply

Price elasticity of supply measures the degree to which the quantity supplied changes as prices change. It is expressed by formula as:

$$\frac{\% \text{ change in quantity}}{\% \text{ change in price}}$$

Elastic and inelastic supply

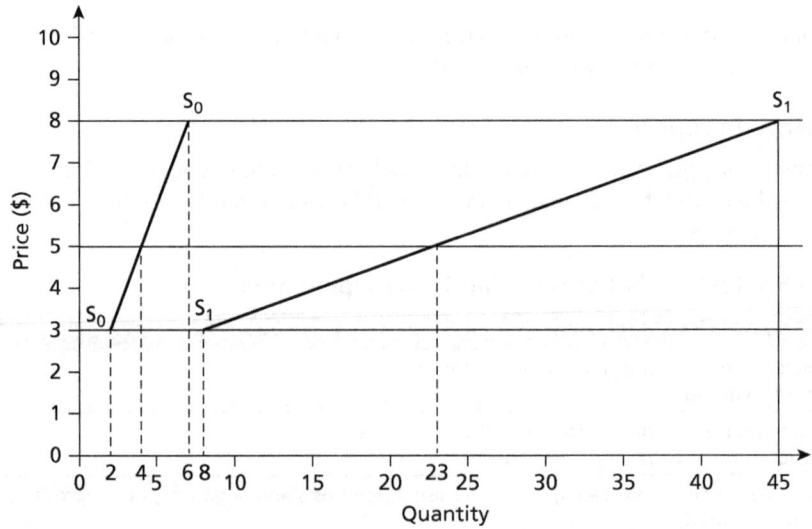

Figure 5.4 Changes in supply curve based on price changes

Figure 5.4 shows two different quantity changes when price changes from two different supply curves – e.g.:

% Price change from $5 to $8 on S_0 = 3/5 = 0.6 or 60%

% Quantity change from 4 to 6 on S_0 = 2/4 = 0.50 or 50%

Therefore, PES = 0.5/0.6 = 0.83 PES is inelastic because the value is less than one.

Price change from $5 to $8 on S_1 = 0.6

Quantity change from 23 to 45 on S_1 = 22/23 = 0.96

PES of price change $5 to $8 on S_1 = 0.96/0.6 = 1.6 PES is elastic since the value is greater than one

Determining price elasticity of supply other than by formula

Where the supply curve intersects the two axes, x and y, determines the price elasticity of supply (PES). If the supply curve intersects the vertical y axis, the PES > 1. (fig 5.6) If the supply curve intersects the horizontal x axis PES < 1, (fig 5.6) and if it intersects the point of origin, PES = 1 (fig 5.5)

However, if a supply curve is non-linear, PES is determined by a tangent to the point on the supply curve. (See Figure 5.5.)

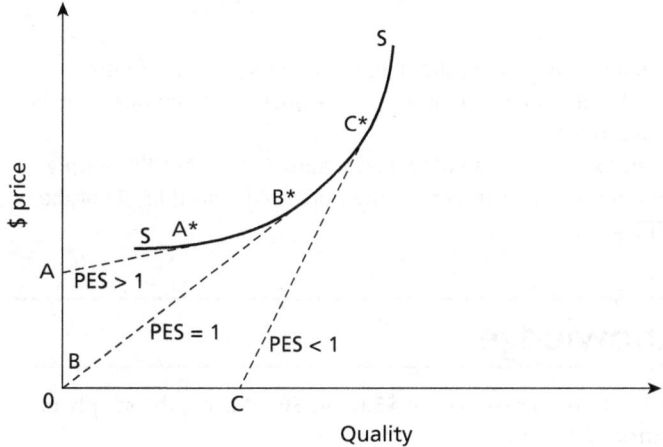

Figure 5.5 Point elasticity of supply

Note:

Tangent A* intersects the vertical axis; therefore, price elasticity of supply > 1. Tangent B* reflects price elasticity of supply = 1 at point B. At point C tangent C* reflects price elasticity of supply < 1.

Determinants of price elasticity of supply

The time period In the **momentary period**, it is not possible to change the output and price elasticity of supply is perfectly inelastic, as shown in Figure 5.7.

In the short-run period, price elasticity of supply may be less than one because in the short run there is time to change the variable factors to increase output, while the fixed factor is unchanged as shown in Figure 5.7.

In the long run, all factors can be altered and price elasticity of supply is very elastic and new firms may enter the industry to capitalize on profit opportunities (See Figure 5.10.)

The supply curve pivots to the right as more time allows for the changing of variable and fixed factors. (See Figure 5.7.)

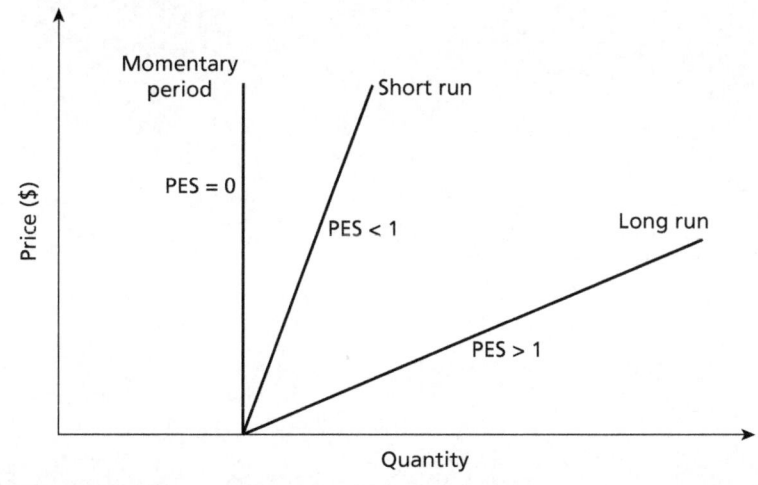

Figure 5.7 Price elasticity of supply in the three time periods of production.

Other determinants of price elasticity of supply

- The existence of stock when prices rise: if prices rise, firms can easily supply when they have stock; therefore, price elasticity of supply is greater than 1.
- Spare capacity: price elasticity of supply is greater than 1 if a firm has spare raw materials, labour and machines.

Important points

Price elasticity of supply measures the change in quantity supplied in response to changes in price.

- Price elasticity of supply may be elastic, inelastic, unitary, 0, or infinite.
- One of the most influential factors that determine price elasticity of supply is the time periods of production.
- Price elasticity of supply is also calculated according to whether the supply curve intersects the vertical axis (PES > 1), the horizontal axis (PES, 1) or the point of origin (PES = 1).

Test Your Knowledge

1. When the price of shirts increases from $5.00 to $6.00 each, the supply of shirts increases from 20 to 25.

2. Calculate the price elasticity of supply based on the information in Q1.

THEORY OF SUPPLY II

MULTIPLE CHOICE QUESTIONS

1. A car park filled to capacity has a price elasticity of supply that is:
   (a) Inelastic;
   (b) Perfectly elastic;
   (c) Perfectly inelastic;
   (d) Unitary.

2. The supply curve has a unitary elasticity when it is:
   (a) Vertical;
   (b) Horizontal;
   (c) Passes through the point of origin;
   (d) Downward sloping.

3. Identify the figure which illustrates a contraction of supply.

4. More is supplied at a higher price because:
   (a) High prices are an incentive to supply more;
   (b) Raw materials are always plentiful;
   (c) Firms like to keep goods in case of extra demand;
   (d) Workers are well-trained.

5. Which of the following will cause a shift of the supply curve?
   (a) Changes in income;
   (b) Advertising;
   (c) Changes in preferences and taste;
   (d) Productivity.

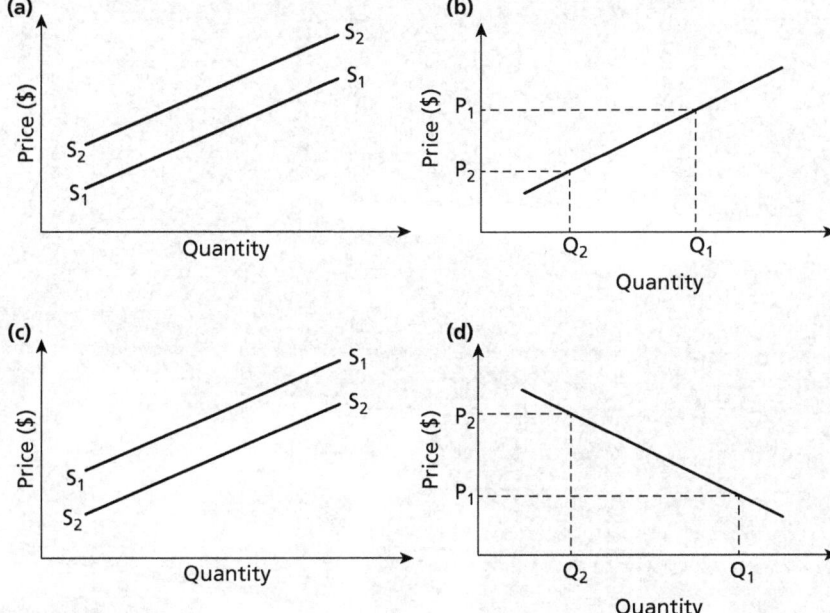

Chapter 6   Market Equilibrium

Market equilibrium

Market equilibrium is achieved at the intersection of the demand and supply curves, which indicates an equilibrium price and quantity.

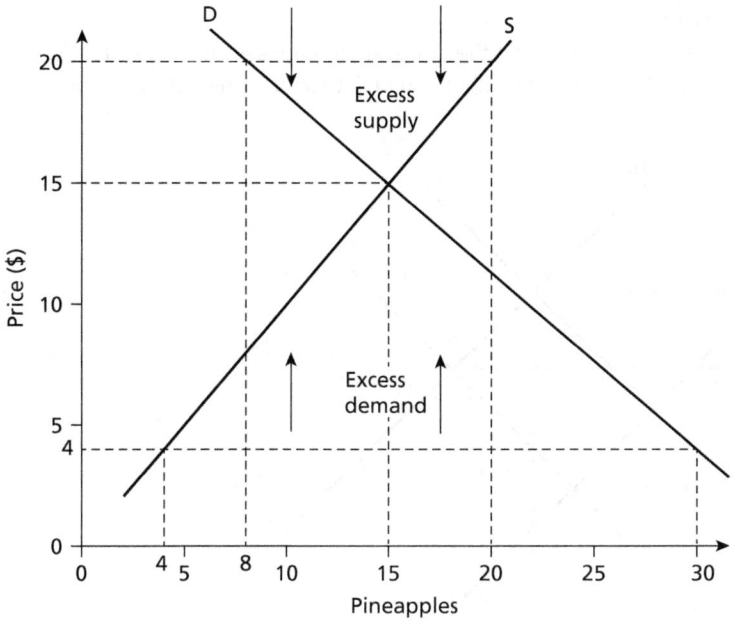

Figure 6.1 Market equilibrium

Observations on Figure 6.1:

- $15 is the equilibrium price and the equilibrium quantity is 15 pineapples.
- At the price of $20, the quantity demanded is 8 pineapples, while the quantity supplied is 20. Excess supply of 12 pineapples will exert a downward pressure on the price leading to a price fall to $15.
- At price $4, quantity demanded (Qd) = 30, while quantity supplied (Qs) = 4. A market shortage of 26 pineapples would cause prices to rise, encouraging suppliers to supply a greater quantity at $15.
- Equilibrium price is reached at $15, where Qd = Qs.

An increase in equilibrium price

A rise in equilibrium price may result from:

- A change in conditions of demand shifting the demand curve to the right – e.g. a change in household incomes; as in Figure 6.2 from DD to D_1D_1.
- A shift in the supply curve to the left due to a change in conditions of supply (Figure 6.2)

A fall in equilibrium price

A price fall may result from:

- A change in demand shifting the demand curve downward and to the left: D_1D_1 to DD in Figure 6.2;
- The shift of the supply curve downward and to the right, S_1S_1 to SS.

Learning Objectives

By the end of the chapter you should be able to:
- Explain equilibrium price
- Explain changing equilibrium price
- Explain and calculate price elasticity of supply
- Explain and illustrate change in demand and supply
- Explain functions of the price mechanism
- Define, illustrate and explain price ceiling, floors, and consumer and producer surplus
- Illustrate the incidence of a tax

Exam tip

This concept is regularly tested – Module 1.

Exam tip

This concept is regularly tested in CAPE – Module 1.

Changes in demand and supply

Case 1

Refer to Figure 6.2.

- Change in demand to the right – e.g. a successful promotion and advertising by the pineapple company. The demand curve shifts to the right from D to D_1. The price rises to P_2.
- A change in supply – e.g. when the government imposes an indirect tax (VAT) on pineapples. This causes the supply curve S to shift to the left to S_1, and price to P_3.

Exam tip

This concept is regularly tested in CAPE – Modules 1 and 2.

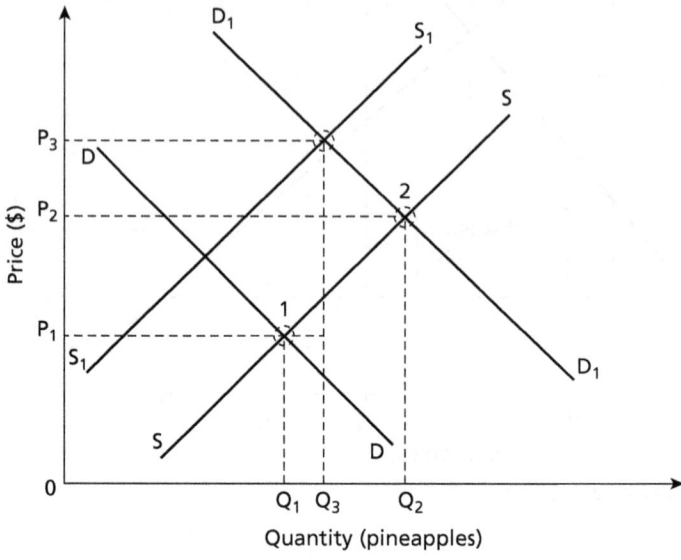

Figure 6.2 Change in both demand and supply

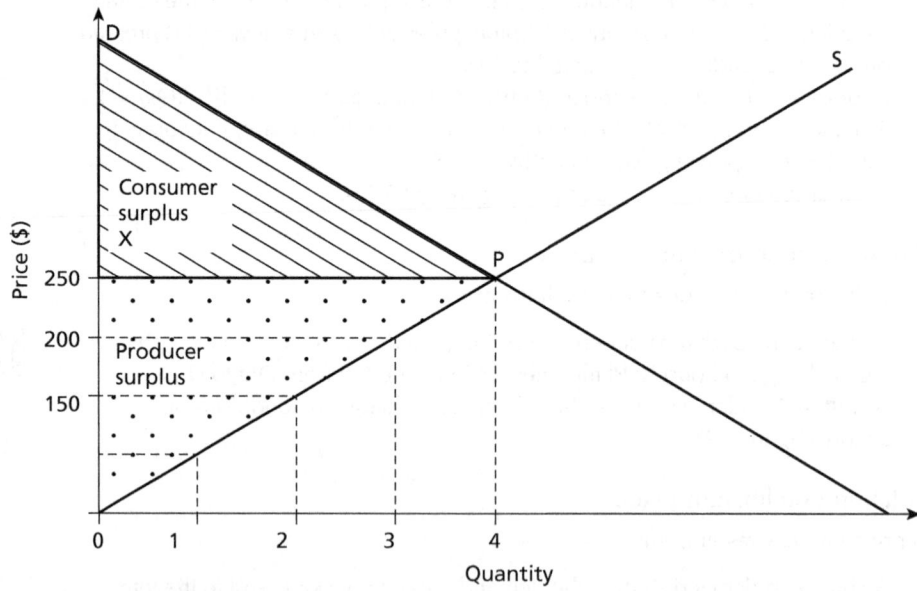

Figure 6.3 Producer surplus

Observations on Figure 6.3:

- Producer surplus is the difference between the market price of a good and the supply price of the producer.
- In Figure 6.3, the supply price of camera #2 is being supplied at a cost of $150, but the market equilibrium price is $250.

Exam tip

This concept is regularly tested in CAPE – Modules 1 and 2.

MARKET EQUILIBRIUM

- Producer surplus for camera #2 is therefore $250 − $150 = $100.
- Producer surplus for 4 cameras is the shaded area OPX.
- Total producer surplus is therefore equal to the area under the price line (XP) and to the left of the supply curve – i.e. triangle OPX.

Price control

Government regulation, subsidy, or other forms of state intervention serve to reduce the impact of high prices on low-income earners for basic food items such as milk and flour.

> **Exam tip**
>
> This concept is regularly tested in CAPE – Modules 1 and 2.

Price ceiling

Observations on Figure 6.4

- A price ceiling or maximum price is the highest price a consumer can be charged for a good or service by law.
- Ceiling prices are a form of income redistribution and poverty reduction, as illustrated in Figure 6.4.
- A maximum price is set at $7.00, which is below the free market equilibrium price of $10.00.

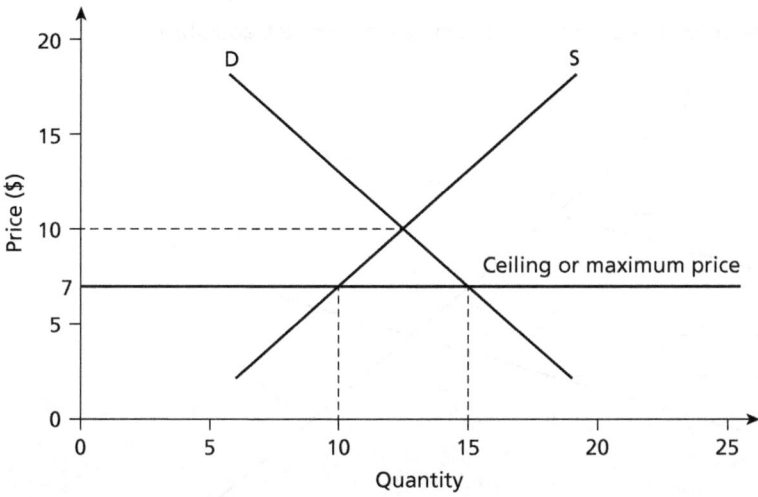

Figure 6.4 A price ceiling

- Shortages are associated with maximum prices, which can lead to 'black market' prices that may go above the ceiling price.
- Rent control is an example of a ceiling price.
- Governments who set ceiling prices resort to rationing the low quantity supplied.

Price floor: minimum price

A price floor is the minimum price that can be legally charged for a good or service.

> **Exam tip**
>
> This concept is regularly tested in CAPE – Modules 1 and 2.

- It is meant to protect a producer from the adverse effects of low prices caused when supply and demand are unstable.
- An example of a minimum price is minimum wage.
- In Figure 6.5, the equilibrium wage rate of labour is $5.00 per hour.
- The government sets a minimum wage of $10.00 per hour.
- Minimum prices create a surplus (Q_1Q_2).
- The government is then obliged to intervene and finance the purchase and stocking of such surpluses to maintain high prices.

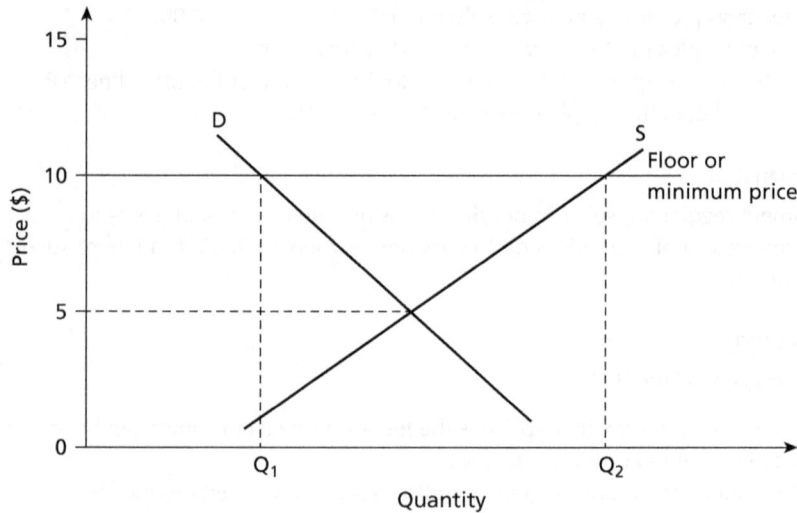

Figure 6.5 A price floor

The effects of taxes and subsidies on market equilibrium

The incidence or impact of an indirect tax on market equilibrium

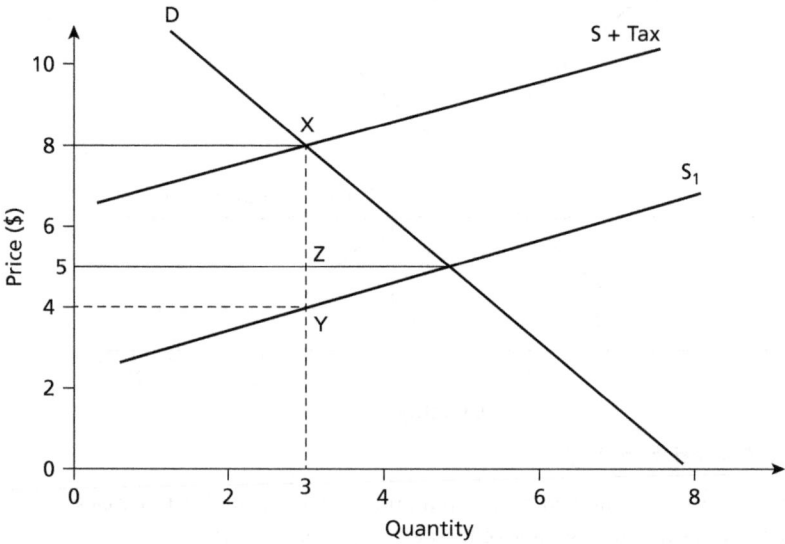

Figure 6.6 Incidence of tax

- An indirect tax is levied on consumer expenditure, the impact of which can be passed on to consumers by the producer.
- An example is a specific tax which is imposed on the sale of alcohol and tobacco.
- An indirect tax may create an incidence (impact or burden). For example, if the government imposes a specific tax of $4.00 on a pack of cigarettes, the burden/incidence is the proportion of the $4.00 that consumers and producer pay. Refer to Figure 6.6 and note the following:
- The imposition of the tax causes the supply curve S_1 to shift upward and to the left by the total amount of the tax YX to a new equilibrium X.
- The price of the pack of cigarettes to the consumer increases from $5.00 (old equilibrium) to $8.00 (the new equilibrium).
- The buyer pays $3.00 out of the $4.00 tax (ZX).
- The producer only plays $1.00 – i.e. $4.00 to $5.00 (YZ), which is the difference between the $4 tax and what the consumer pays, $5.
- ZX + YZ = XY

MARKET EQUILIBRIUM

Note:

Consumers pay ZX of the total tax while the producers pay YZ. ZX and YZ are referred to as the **incidence of the tax**.

The effect of a subsidy on price equilibrium

Refer to Figure 6.7.

> **Exam tip**
>
> This concept is regularly tested in CAPE – Modules 1 and 2.

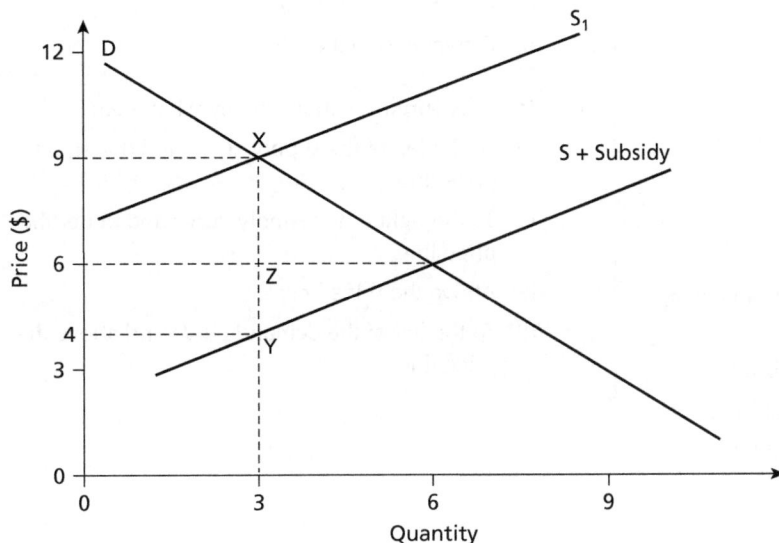

Figure 6.7 Effect of a subsidy

Note:

- The government grants a subsidy of $5.00 per gallon on gasoline ($9 to $4).
- The supply curve S_1 shifts downward and to the right (S + Subsidy).
- XY represents the extent of the subsidy.
- The equilibrium price falls from $9.00 to $6.00.
- The benefit to the consumer is therefore $3.00 (ZX).
- The benefit to the producer is $2.00 (ZY).

Test Your Knowledge

1. The government has decided to put a ceiling on the price of milk. What effect will this have on the following?
   (a) The demand for milk;
   (b) The supply of milk;
   (c) The quantity of milk sold.

2. Define the following concepts:
   (a) Consumer surplus;
   (b) Producer surplus.

3. (a) Draw a carefully labelled figure to show equilibrium in the market for compact discs.
   (b) On the figure in (a) above, show how an improvement in technology is likely to affect the supply of compact discs all other things being equal (*ceteris paribus*).
   (c) State how an increase in population is likely to affect the market for compact discs.

MULTIPLE CHOICE QUESTIONS

1. An indirect tax causes the:
   (a) Supply curve to move to the right;
   (b) Demand curve to move to the left;
   (c) Supply curve to move to the left;
   (d) Demand curve to move to the right.

2. A rise in equilibrium price will cause:
   (a) A reduction in consumer surplus;
   (b) A reduction in producer surplus;
   (c) An increase in consumer surplus;
   (d) No change in producer surplus.

3. If a government wishes to prevent rent from rising, what action should it take?
   (a) Set a price ceiling above the equilibrium;
   (b) Set a price ceiling below the equilibrium;
   (c) Set a price floor above the equilibrium;
   (d) Impose a tax on landlords.

4. A positive change in consumer income will shift the demand curve (*ceterus paribus*) in which direction?
   (a) Upward to the right;
   (b) Upward to the left;
   (c) Downward to the right;
   (d) Downward to the left.

5. Producer surplus is indicated by what area?
   (a) To the left of the supply curve and under the price line;
   (b) To the right of the supply curve and under the price line;
   (c) Above the price line;
   (d) To the left of the demand curve and above the price line.

Chapter 7: The Cost of Production

REVISION GUIDE TO ECONOMICS

Learning Objectives

By the end of this chapter you should be able to:
- Identify total costs
- Identify short run costs
- Identify and explain total fixed and variable costs
- Identify and explain average fixed and variable costs
- Calculate marginal costs
- Explain long run costs
- Explain and identify economies and diseconomies of scale (internal and external)

A firm's costs are the payments it makes for the use of factors of production, land, labour, or capital. A firm may incur the following costs:

- Opportunity costs;
- Social or external costs;
- Explicit costs.

Note:

- Social costs are the costs imposed on society by firms which they ignore – e.g. pollution costs.
- Explicit costs are fixed, variable, average, marginal, and total costs.
- Fixed costs are independent of production and do not change when production changes – e.g. interest on bank loans.
- Variable costs change as production increases – e.g. cost of raw materials.

Figure 7.1 represents fixed cost (FC), variable cost and total costs of production.

Note:

- At output 0, FC is $50 and does not change as output changes.
- It is therefore a horizontal line.
- Total variable cost curve (TVC) varies directly with production.
- It has a gradual, then a steeply sloping segment which reflects the law of diminishing returns.
- Total costs of production = Total Fixed Costs + Total Variable Costs, expressed in formula as: TFC + TVC = TC

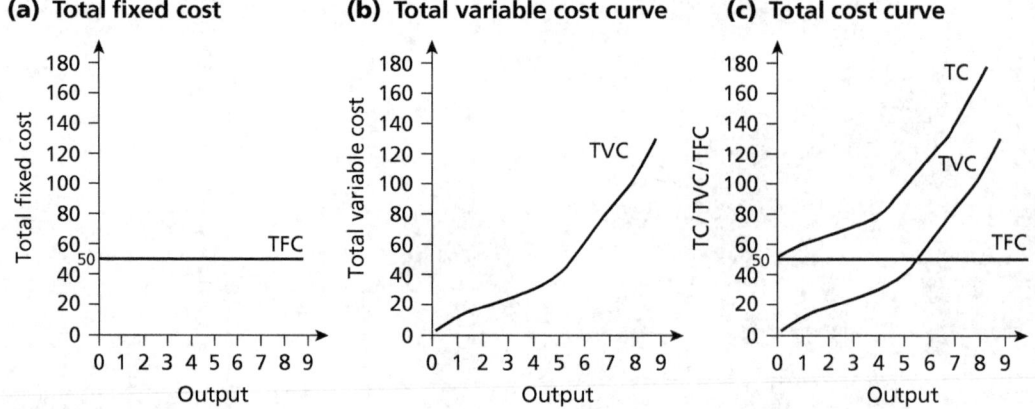

Figure 7.1 Costs of production

Average total cost

Note:

- The average total cost (ATC) or average unit cost (AC) may be calculated as:
  (1) Total cost/total output.
  (2) Average fixed cost + average variable cost – i.e. AFC + AVC = ATC

If the fixed cost of a cake of 50 slices is $25, then AFC = TFC/q or $25/50 = 0.50 cents. If the TVC is $75, then AVC = TVC/q or $75/50 = $1.50.

Therefore, AFC + AVC = ATC or $0.50 + $1.50 = $2.00.

These simple cost concepts are graphically presented in Figure 7.2.

THE COST OF PRODUCTION

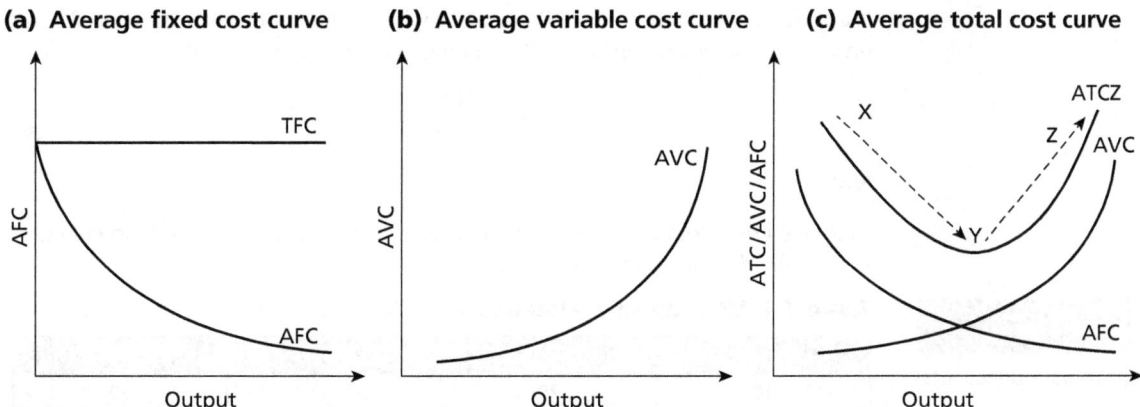

Figure 7.2

In Figure 7.2a, note the relationship between TFC and AFC:

- AFC falls evenly because it is a fixed dollar value divided by increasing output in the short run.
- AVC is derived by dividing TVC by Q.
- When AFC is vertically added to AVC in Figures 7.2a, 7.2b and 7.2c, an ATC curve is derived.
- The ATC curve is usually U-shaped because the downward segment XY in Figure 7.2c is influenced by the downward segment of AFC above AVC.
- The upward segment YZ is influenced by the AVC curve.
- The average cost curve shows the lowest cost of production for any given level of output.

> **Exam tip**
>
> Questions in cost theory are usually presented in tables. You will be required to calculate costs such as FC, VC, TC, ATC and MC.

Marginal cost

Marginal cost is the change in total cost of producing one more or one less unit and is expressed as change in TC/change in Q.

If the cost of 10 pens is $100 and 11 pens cost $105, then the marginal cost of the 11th pen is $5. It is expressed as:

$$\frac{\Delta TC}{\Delta Q} = \frac{\$100 \text{ to } \$105}{10 \text{ to } 11} = \frac{\$5}{1} = \$5$$

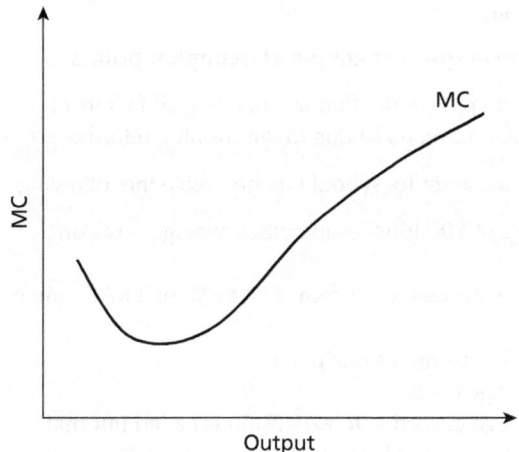

Figure 7.3 Marginal cost curve

Note that in Figure 7.3 the marginal cost curve is easy to recognize. It resembles the NIKE logo, or a fish hook.

If the change in total cost is $100 to $120 when output changes from 10 to 20 units, then the change in TC is $20 and the change in output = 10.

$$MC = \frac{\$20}{10} = \$2.00$$

Note:

Marginal cost is directly related to changes in total variable costs NOT to changes in total fixed costs. Refer to Table 7.1.

Table 7.1 MC is directly related to TVC

Output	TFC ($)	TVC ($)	TC ($)
10	20	30	50
11	20	40	60

> **Exam tip**
>
> This concept is often tested at CAPE.

Note that the marginal cost curve cuts both AVC and ATC at their minimum points.

Note also that as soon as MC is greater than AC, AC immediately starts to increase so the point of intersection of AC and MC must mathematically be the minimum point.

> **Exam tip**
>
> Observe that MC MUST intersect both AVC and ATC at their minimum points.

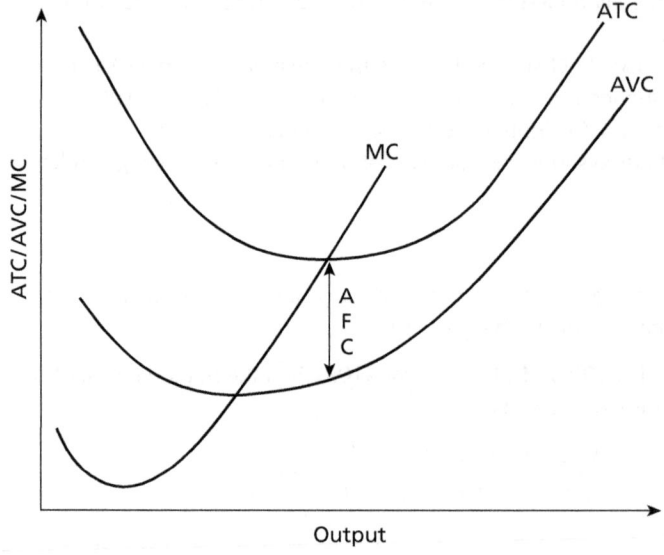

Figure 7.4 Marginal cost cuts average cost curves at minimum points

In Figure 7.5, a firm could enter long-run production by changing all factors of production when short-run costs start to increase due to diminishing returns.

Figure 7.5 shows the cost curve of a caterer for school lunches. Note the following:

- Increasing production in excess of 100 lunches increases average costs on $SRAC_1$.
- Expanding to 200 boxes reduces average costs from $12 to $7 on $SRAC_2$ when the caterer expands his plant.
- An output of 200 increases to $12 using his first plant.
- Expansion has reduced his average costs.
- This reduction in long-run average costs due to expansion is called **internal economies of scale**, or the cost savings of large-scale production.

THE COST OF PRODUCTION

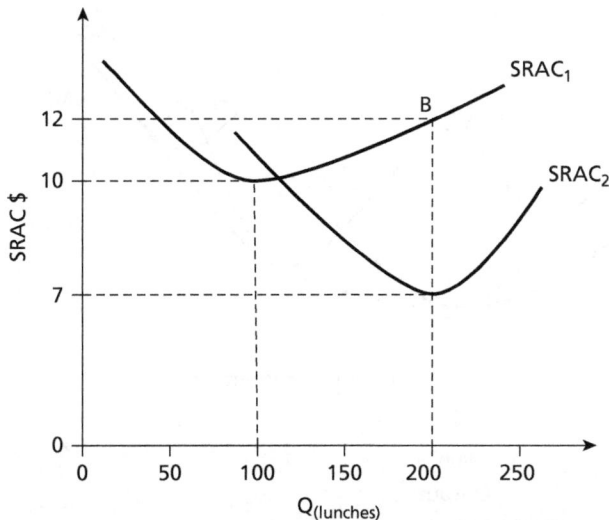

Figure 7.5 Increase in demand for school lunches

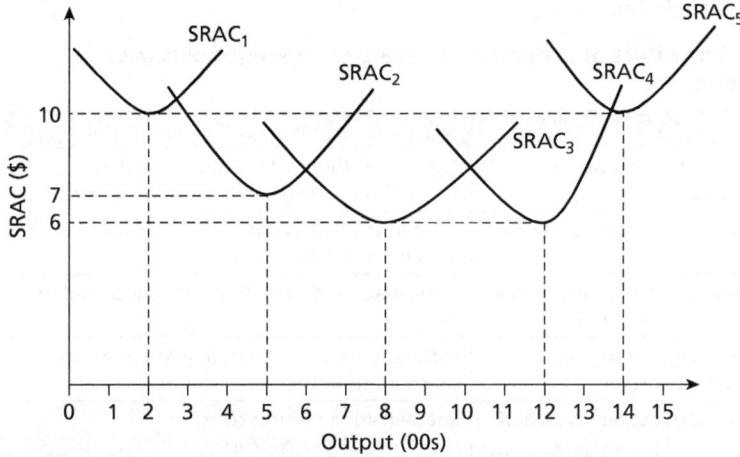

Figure 7.6 Reduction in average costs in the long run

Notes for Figure 7.6:

- Increasing returns to scale from 200 to 800 reduces the long-run average cost (LRAC) from $10 to $6. This cost reduction is called 'internal economies of scale'.
- In further expansion from 800 to 1200 units, LRAC is constant. This is referred to as constant economies of scale.
- From output 1200 to 1500, LRAC has risen – this is called 'internal diseconomies of scale'.
- The least cost of output, 800 units, is called the **minimum efficient size of production**, where all economies of scale have ended.

Table 7.2 The effect of returns to scale and LRAC

Returns to scale	Effects on LRAC
Increased returns to scale	Economies of scale (falling LRAC)
Constant returns to scale	Constant long-run costs
Decreasing returns to scale	Diseconomies of scale (rising LRAC)

- The long-run average cost curve is a curve tangent to all the short-run average cost (SRAC) curves and is also U-shaped, similar to the SRAC curves.
- This shape is due to economies and diseconomies of scale.
- This curve represents the lowest cost of producing any given level of output.

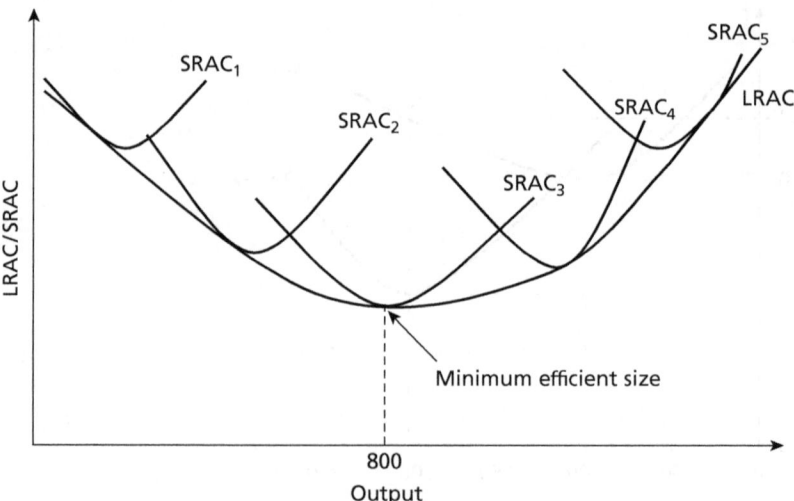

Figure 7.7 Long-run average cost

Internal economies of scale

Table 7.3 The effect of economies of scale on average costs (AC) of production

Level of economy of scale	Example	Reason AC falls
Indivisibilities	A large construction firm uses a tractor more often than a small company.	The cost of the tractor is the same if used 3 or 8 times. If frequently used, average costs fall.
Increased dimension	A 9-ton truck's capacity is three times that of a 3-ton truck.	A 9-ton truck does not cost three times the amount of a 3-ton truck.
Linked process	Bringing together many stages of production in one plant reduces costs – e.g. oil refinery.	Same place and same time production reduces AC.
Principle of multiples	A soft drink factory uses large integrated machinery operating at one speed.	Different machines operating at same speeds cause AC to fall.
Division of labour	An auto plant uses mass production division of labour.	Specialization reduces costs.
Purchasing	Large firms buy in bulk quantity.	Bulk buying of raw materials is done at discounted prices.
Financial	Raising capital by selling company stock or raising cheaper loans from banks due to the asset value of a large firm.	Raising capital this way is inexpensive. Borrowing is at a low rate of interest. Large assets enable financing and borrowing at reduced interest rates.

Internal diseconomies of scale

The output expansion of a firm beyond the maximum efficient plant size will cause LRAC to rise, causing internal diseconomies of scale (DOS).

Examples:

- Coordination and control of a large work force are difficult for managers. Efficiency falls and long-run costs rise.
- Internal communications are also not easily achieved, although information technology has minimized this problem.
- Overspecialization reduces productivity and increases long-run unit costs.
- Workers feel distanced from managers, and interpersonal relations tend to lower worker morale and create poor industrial relations. Work stoppages increase costs.

THE COST OF PRODUCTION

External economies of scale

A firm may indirectly benefit from actions outside its control. These are called **external economies of scale**.

Examples are:

- Improved infrastructure – e.g. road networks, power, water and telecommunications improvements by government and existing firms benefit new firms;
- Skilled labour pool – through siting of training schools in close proximity to industrial centres, or hiring skilled professionals from nearby firms;
- Agglomeration – which is the entry of new large firms to process waste, provide technical support – e.g. machine shops, catering, cleaning and security.

The above external economies of scale will cause the LRAC to shift vertically downward.

Large scale expansion may also lead to external diseconomies of scale – i.e. a vertical rise in the LRAC curve.

Examples are:

- Pollution;
- Prices rise as firms compete with one another for services, labour, raw materials, and land space;
- Traffic congestion causes distribution delays.

Test Your Knowledge

1. Complete the table by filling with appropriate data.

Output	FC	TVC	Total cost	AFC	AVC	MC
0			10			
1			18			
2			24			
3			33			
4			48			
5			65			

2. Answer the following questions.
   (a) State the law of diminishing returns and the law of returns to scale.
   (b) Explain with the aid of figures how the two laws in (a) may cause both SRAC and LRAC to be U-shaped.

3. Define each of the following or write the formula for calculating it:
   (i) APP;
   (ii) MPP;
   (iii) AVC;
   (iv) MC.

MULTIPLE CHOICE QUESTIONS

1. A steel band craftsman produces 5 tenor steel pans at an average cost of TT$3000 per pan. When he produces the 6th tenor pan, the average cost falls to TT$2900. What is the marginal cost of the 6th tenor pan?
   (a) $1900;
   (b) $600;
   (c) $2400;
   (d) $483.

2. Diseconomies of scale start when output is:
   (a) Before the minimum point on a U-shaped average cost curve;
   (b) Beyond the minimum point on a U-shaped long run average costs curve;
   (c) At the end of a rising U-shaped long run average costs curve;
   (d) At the beginning of long run average costs curve.

3. In the short run which is affected by variable costs:
   (a) Opportunity costs;
   (b) Marginal costs;
   (c) Average fixed costs;
   (d) Fixed costs.

4. Marginal cost must mathematically intersect ATC and AVC at which point?
   (a) Minimum ATC and AVC;
   (b) Before minimum ATC and AVC;
   (c) After minimum ATC and AVC;
   (d) Minimum ATC but beyond minimum AVC.

5. Marginal cost is the cost of producing one extra unit of output and is directly related to which costs?
   (a) Total fixed costs;
   (b) Total variable costs;
   (c) Average fixed costs;
   (d) Average total costs.

Chapter 8: Price, Revenue and Profit Concepts

REVISION GUIDE TO ECONOMICS

Learning Objectives

By the end of the chapter you should be able to:

- Explain and illustrate total, average and marginal revenues in different market structures
- Explain revenue concepts in different markets: total, marginal, and average revenue
- Explain exit conditions of a perfect competitor
- Explain profit maximization, normal and above normal (economic) profit

Revenue concepts in perfect and imperfect competition (monopoly)

The main types of revenue related to a firm's operations are:

- Total revenue;
- Average revenue;
- Marginal revenue.

Total revenue (TR) is the total sales of the firm per time period calculated as price multiplied by quantity: TR = P × Q

Average revenue (AR) is the revenue per unit sold, calculated as TR/Q – e.g. 1 day's sales of $200 divided by quantity sold 50 units = $200/50 = $4.00

(AR is always mathematically equal to price.)

Marginal revenue (MR) is the revenue realized from the sale of an additional unit of output – e.g.:

TR from 10 oranges @ $2.00 = $20

TR from 11 oranges @ $2.00 = $22

$$\text{Change in TR} = \frac{\$2.00}{\text{Change in quantity sold} = 1}$$

Therefore, MR = $2.00

Revenue and output in perfect and imperfect markets structures (e.g. monopoly)

Note:

- Perfect markets and imperfect markets are discussed in greater detail in chapter 9.
- In a **perfect market** each firm's output is so small that supply is unaffected if firms enter or leave the market.
- Each firm is a price taker.
- In Figure 8.1, the price line taken from the market equilibrium is the demand curve, which is horizontal and perfectly elastic.
- For a perfectly competitive firm, average revenue is shown in Figure 8.1.
- Total revenue is shown in Figure 8.2

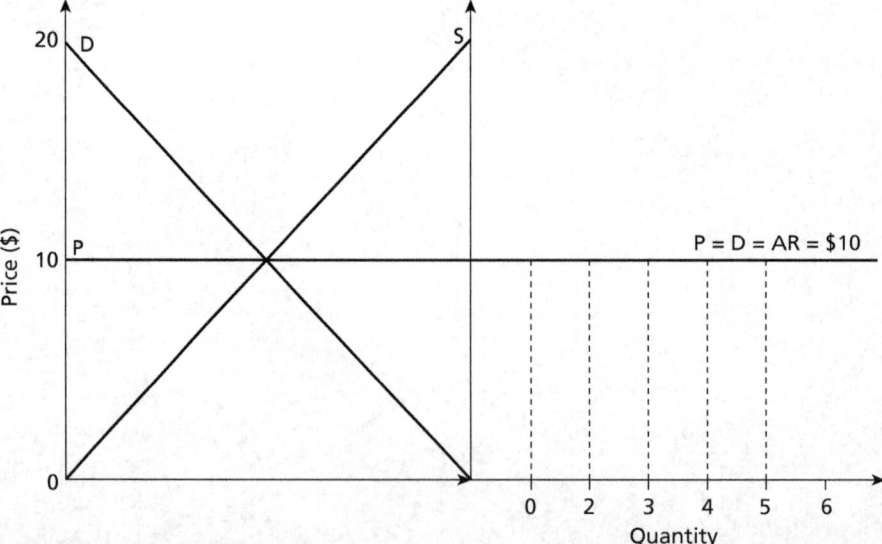

Figure 8.1 Price in a perfect market (price taker)

PRICE, REVENUE AND PROFIT CONCEPTS

Note in Figure 8.1:

- The firm is a price taker;
- An infinite number of products can be sold at the ruling market price.

Since the price is the same for every quantity, total revenue is a 45 degree line through the point of origin

The AR for the first unit is $10/1 = $ 10. AR for unit 2 = $10 x 2 = 20/2 = $10. For units 3 through 6, AR is the same. Hence price, average revenue and demand are the same. Thus, in a perfect market P = AR = D (i.e. horizontal line as shown in Figure 8.1).

Marginal revenue in a perfect market

- Since marginal revenue is the additional revenue gained from one more unit sold, the extra revenue gained from the sale of the 3rd, 4th, 5th or 6th unit is also $10.
- Since the demand curve is horizontal or perfectly elastic in a perfect market, the price (AR) and MR will be the same.
- The demand curve may be written as P = D = AR = MR for any firm in a perfectly competitive market.

Total revenue in a monopoly market structure

Note:

- A monopolist controls supply but not demand.
- A greater output will be bought by consumers at lower prices than at higher prices.
- This single firm therefore faces a downward sloping demand curve.

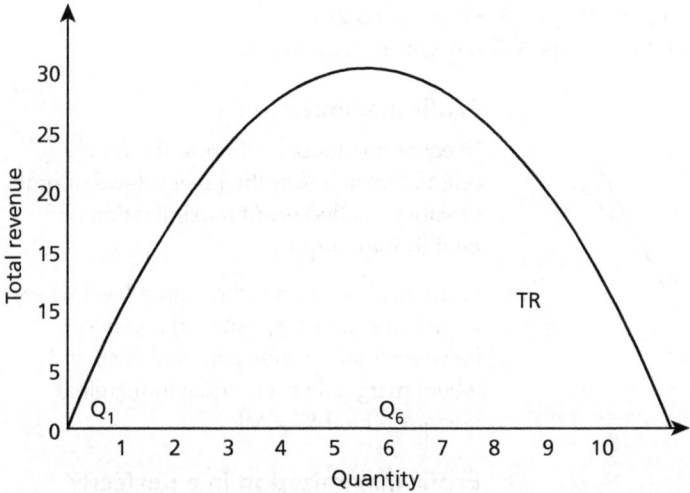

Figure 8.2 Total revenue curve (that is when the MR and AR curves cut the x axis)

Note: As shown in Figure 8.2, Total revenue will rise, but (when MR < 0) it will then start to fall to 0 (when AR also < 0).

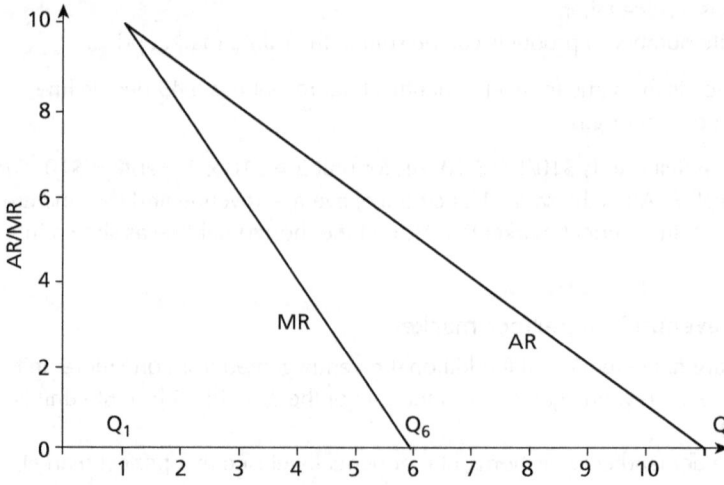

Figure 8.3 MR < AR for a monopoly

In Figure 8.3, note:

- Both AR and MR are falling.
- However, MR is falling faster than AR.
- If AR (AR = D) is a linear curve, the MR curve will bisect the horizontal axis.

In summary (refer to Figures 8.2 and 8.3):

- AR = D = P is downward sloping (Figure 8.3).
- TR rises, peaks at Q_6, then declines to 0 (Figure 8.2).
- MR falls more quickly than AR and is less than AR from Q_1 to Q_6 (Figure 8.3).
- When TR is highest at Q_6, MR = 0 (Figure 8.2).
- From output 6 to 11 units, MR is negative (Figure 8.3).

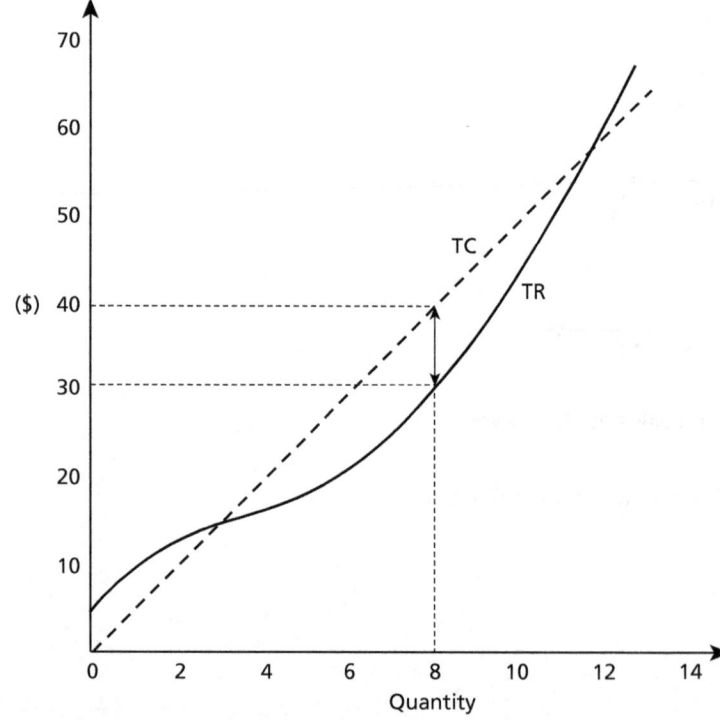

Figure 8.4 Total revenue/total cost short run profit maximization analysis for a perfect competitor

Profit maximization

In economic theory, all firms aim for an output that achieves the highest level of profit possible – called **profit maximization** or **equilibrium output**.

Profit maximization is the output level where there is the greatest positive difference between total revenue and total cost, and where marginal cost is equal to marginal revenue – i.e. MC = MR.

Profit maximization in a perfectly competitive firm

In Figure 8.4, note that TR = Total Revenue and TC = Total Cost.

Observations on Figure 8.4:

- Profit maximization is achieved at an output where TR exceeds TC by the greatest positive margin and also where MC = MR (where MC must intersect MR from below).
- TR exceeds TC by the greatest amount at output 8 units, where TR = $40 and TC = $30.
- The highest level of profit equals $10.00.

Other observations:

- Between output level 1 to 3, there is a loss (TC > TR in Figure 8.4).
- At output level 3, TC = TR, this is called the **break-even point**. There is neither profit nor loss at this level of output.
- Between output levels 3 to 12 units, the perfectly competitive firm is making a profit. (TR > TC).
- At output level 12, the firm is making 0 profit, which is also called the 'break even' point (TR = TC).
- At output levels beyond 12, the firm is making a loss (TC > TR).

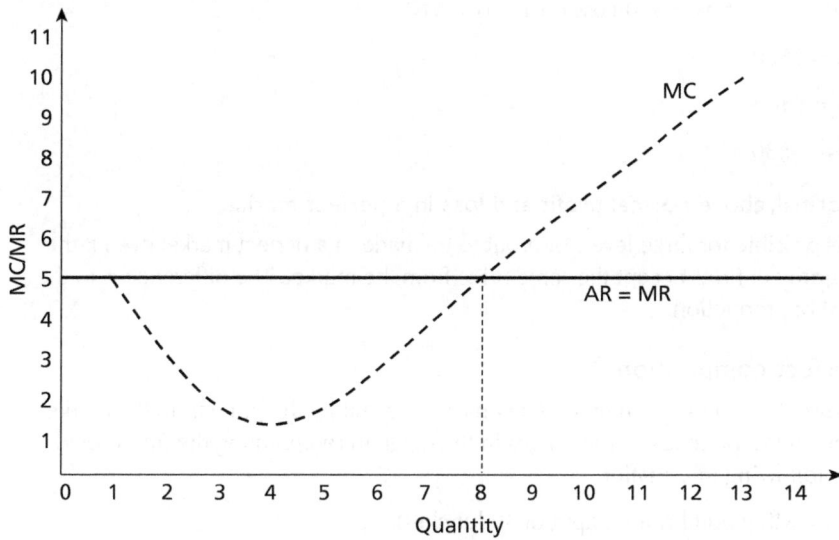

Figure 8.5 Profit maximization by MC/MR analysis for a perfect competitor

Notes on Figure 8.5:

- Observe that MC = MR at output 1 and 8 units but profit maximizing output is not at output 1 because MC is falling at this level of output.
- At output 8 units, MC is rising. Profit maximization therefore occurs where MC cuts MR from below (at output 8).
- Profit is being made on each successive unit from unit 1 to 8.
- As long as an extra unit of output adds more to revenue than to cost, a firm would increase output until the cost of 1 extra (MC) is equal to MR.
- At output 9 units, MC > MR so the firm should reduce output to 8 to profit maximize.

Profit in the short run

Normal profit, above normal profit and loss

Profit is determined by the difference between total revenue and total cost (TR − TC).

Normal profit or zero economic profit

Normal profit is achieved when average cost = average revenue (AC = AR), or total cost = total revenue – e.g.:

- Average cost of a lunch = $20.00
- Average price of a lunch = $20.00
- Normal profit is being made although the cost and price are the same because part of the cost of providing the lunch is a profit of $5.00 which is included as a fixed cost of production.

Above normal profit or positive economic profit

Above normal profit is made when AR is greater than AC – e.g.:

AC of 1 lunch = $20

AR (price) of 1 lunch = $30

Average profit = $10 per box

Loss

Average cost (AC) is greater than price (AR), or TC > TR – e.g. (AR) of 1 box = $10 and AC of 1 box = $20 Loss on 1 box = $10

TC = $600

TR = $300

Loss = $300

Normal, above normal profit and loss in a perfect market

It is possible for three levels of profit to be made in a perfect market even if the majority of firms accept the same price from the market. The difference is in the cost of production.

Perfect competition

Figure 8.6 shows a firm in a perfect market accepting the price from the market since it is a price taker. The curves in the diagram representing the firm provide the following information:

MC = MR (equilibrium output of 30 lunches).

ATC = AR (the information needed to calculate the profit of 30 lunches).

On the vertical axis, note the letters CPR for cost, price and revenue. To determine whether profit is normal, above normal or negative, follow these three simple steps:

1. Identify profit maximization (equilibrium output) MC = MR at 30 lunches.
2. Identify the price of 1 lunch by drawing a line connecting 30 lunches on the horizontal axis up to the demand curve (AR) and it will reveal a price of $20 per lunch (the dotted line).
3. Find the cost of 1 lunch (AC) by connecting a line from equilibrium output (30 lunches) to the AC curve. Note the AC is also $20; therefore, if AR = AC, then the firm is making normal profit.

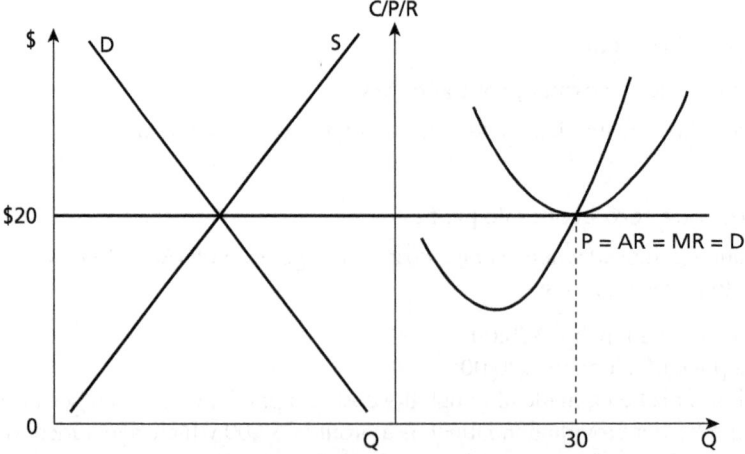

Figure 8.6 Normal profit for a perfect competitor

PRICE, REVENUE AND PROFIT CONCEPTS

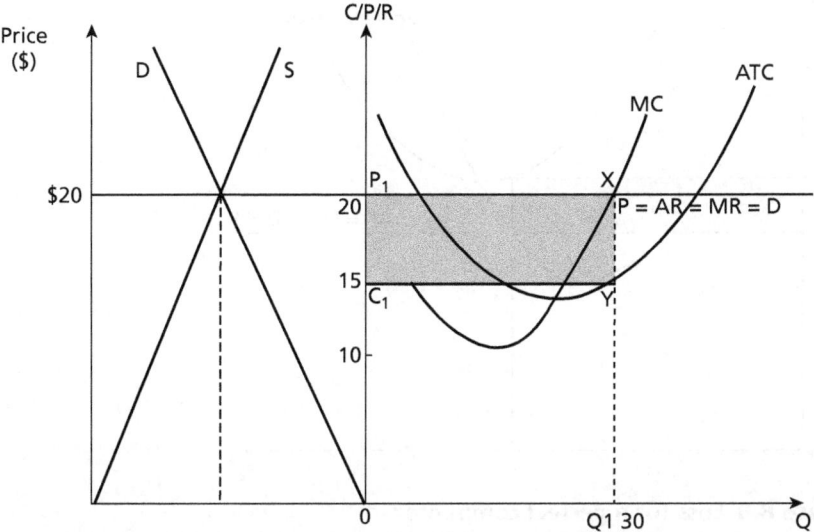

Figure 8.7 Above normal profit for a perfect competitor

In Figure 8.7, normal profit for a perfect competitor is calculated as outlined below:

1. Identify profit maximization (equilibrium output) MC = MR (at X) = 30 lunches.
2. Identify the price of one lunch (AR) by connecting q(30) to the AR or demand curve = $20
3. Identify unit cost (AC) C_1 of 1 lunch by connecting q(30) to AC curve = $15 per lunch.

Total revenue = 30 x $20 = $600($P_1XQ_10$)

Total cost = 30 x $15 = $450($C_1YQ_10$)

Profit on 30 lunches = $150, or the shaded area P_1XYC_1

Loss

See Figure 8.8.

Note that at profit maximization output of 30 lunches, the AC of $25 is greater than the price of $20. The firm is making a loss.

1. Identify profit maximization output = 30 lunches
2. Identify price of 1 lunch (AR) by connecting q(30) to the AR curve (D) price therefore = $20.
3. Identify unit cost (AC) of 1 lunch by:

Connecting (q)30 lunches to the AC curve = $25

Loss on 1 lunch = $5 (loss)

Therefore, loss on 30 lunches = $150 (loss) or shaded area.

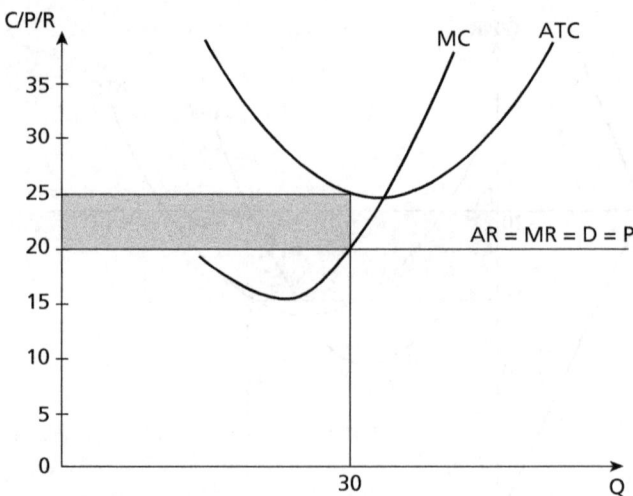

Figure 8.8 Loss for a perfect competitor

Note that at output = 30 units the firm's losses are the least. MC = MR is also **loss minimization output**.

The long-run equilibrium of perfect competition

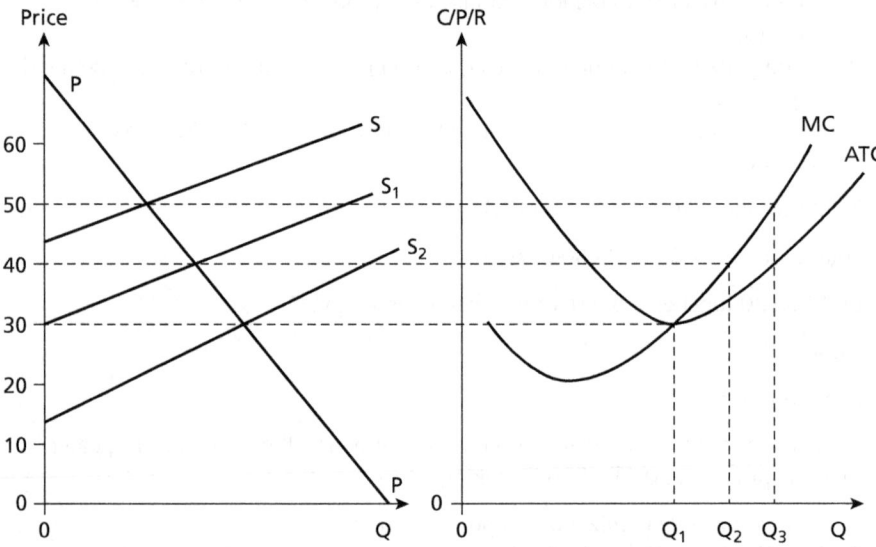

Figure 8.9 New entrants entering the industry (perfect competition)

Positive economic profit attracts other firms into the industry because it is assumed that firms outside the industry will already be earning a normal profit. It is easy for new firms to enter another industry because:

- There are no barriers to entry;
- The resources of new entrants are mobile (easily moved and set up);
- Knowledge of the market is perfect.

What happens when new entrants enter the market is shown in Figure 8.9.

In the transition from the short to the long run, new entrants enter the industry because there are no barriers to entry. Increased output by new entrants causes the supply curve to shift along the demand curve from S to S_1 to S_2.

- As a result, the price falls from $50 to $30;
- Output is reduced from Q_3 to Q_1 and above normal profit is competed away;
- All firms initially earning above normal profit may make only normal profit;
- All firms will have to exit the industry in the long-run period if they are making a loss.

Shut down or exit conditions

Any firm making a loss may remain in the industry in the short run but must cover its variable costs of production, since it still has to pay its fixed costs whether leaving or staying. Variable costs will be 0, since there is 0 production.

Consider the following example:

Note:

Figure 8.9 reveals the following:

- Price is falling as a new firm enters the industry;
- The price has fallen to P_5;
- The firm is covering AVC at P_4;
- The firm is not covering AVC at P_5.

If the price falls to P_4, the firm may stay and not exit the market in the short run.

If the price falls to P_5, the firm will have to exit in the short run because it cannot cover AVC.

The short-run supply curve

Observe that in Figure 8.10 the supply curve shifts downward along the demand curve as new firms enter the industry.

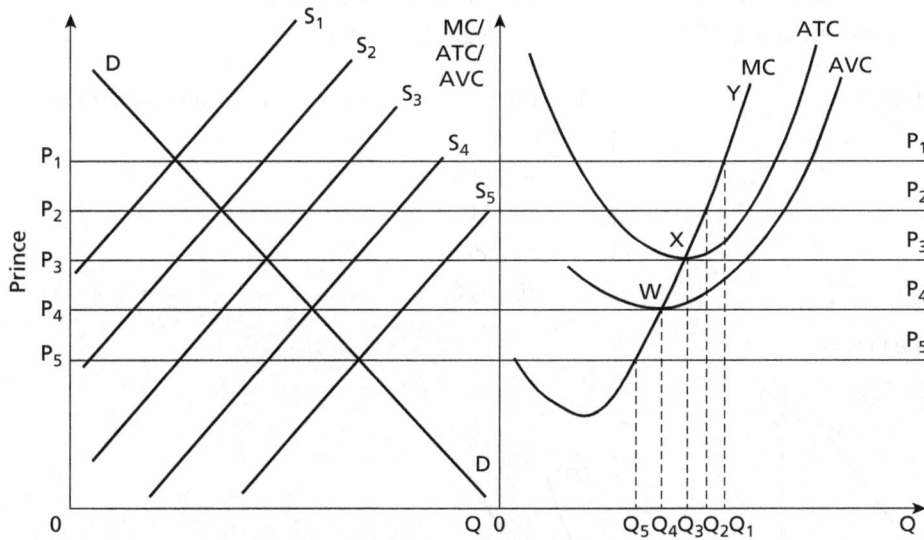

Figure 8.10 Short-run supply curve in a perfectly competitive firm

Observations on Figure 8.10:

- As price falls from P_1 to P_5, quantity falls from Q_1 to Q_5 in the manner of a supply curve.
- The marginal cost curve is effectively the **supply curve of the firm** since it links price with quantity supplied in a perfectly competitive market.
- The supply curve of a perfectly competitive firm is therefore **MC above AVC (W to Y) in the short run**.
- The firm will not produce at a point where price (AR) is below AVC because, at that point, it cannot cover AVC.
- Since all costs must be covered in the long run, the long-run supply curve is **MC above the long-run average total cost (LRATC) (X to Y)**.
- By this reasoning, the firm's supply curve in a perfect market is **its MC curve above AVC in the short run**, but **MC above LRATC in the long run** as shown in Figure 8.10.

Test Your Knowledge

1. (a) Define the term 'market structure'.
   (b) List any two market structures and state one way in which they are different.
   (c) In which market would you place gasoline stations in your country?

2. Write the formulae for equilibrium output, profit maximization, the shut-down point, normal, and above normal profit and loss.

MULTIPLE CHOICE QUESTIONS

1. Profit maximization is indicated where:
   (a) AC = AR;
   (b) MC = AVC;
   (c) MC = MR;
   (d) AVC = AR.

2. Short-run supply curve of a competitive firm is indicated where:
   (a) ATC above AFC;
   (b) MC above AVC;
   (c) MC above ATC;
   (d) AR above ATC.

3. Normal profit is indicated where:
   (a) ATC = MC;
   (b) ATC = AR;
   (c) AR = MC;
   (d) AR above ATC.

4. A perfectly competitive firm making short-run above normal profits can only make normal profits in the long run mainly due to:
   (a) Strong barriers to entry;
   (b) No barriers to entry;
   (c) Imperfect knowledge;
   (d) Imperfect mobility.

5. The exit conditions of a firm require the firm to cover:
   (a) AFC;
   (b) ATC;
   (c) MC;
   (d) AVC.

6. The figure indicates that the firm is:

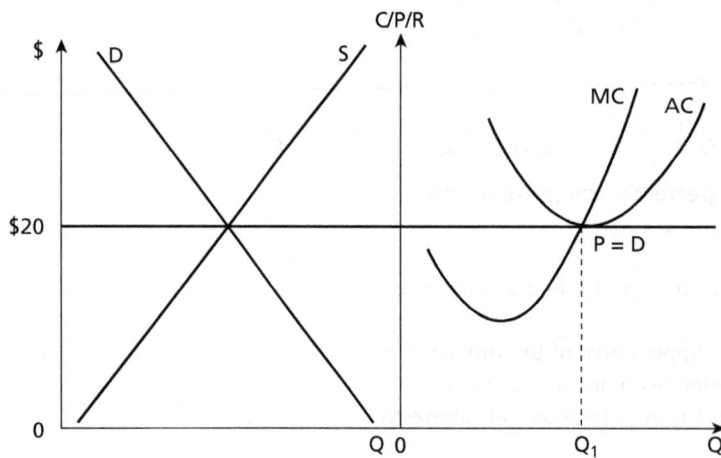

(a) Earning above normal profits;
(b) Earning normal profits;
(c) Making a loss;
(d) Covering average variable costs.

Chapter 9

Imperfect Competition: Monopoly and Monopolistic Competition

Learning Objectives

By the end of this chapter you should be able to:
- Define monopoly
- Define monopolistic competition
- Explain short-run and long-run equilibrium of both markets
- Explain price discrimination
- Explain effect of taxes and subsidies on monopoly market structure

Introduction

A monopolist is a sole supplier with the following characteristics:
- The ability to set price;
- Very strong barriers to entry;
- A differentiated product;
- A downward sloping demand curve in the market in which they operate;
- One firm as opposed to many in a perfectly competitive market.

Short-run equilibrium

In the short run, a monopolist may earn normal profit, above normal profit or loss according to their efficiency.

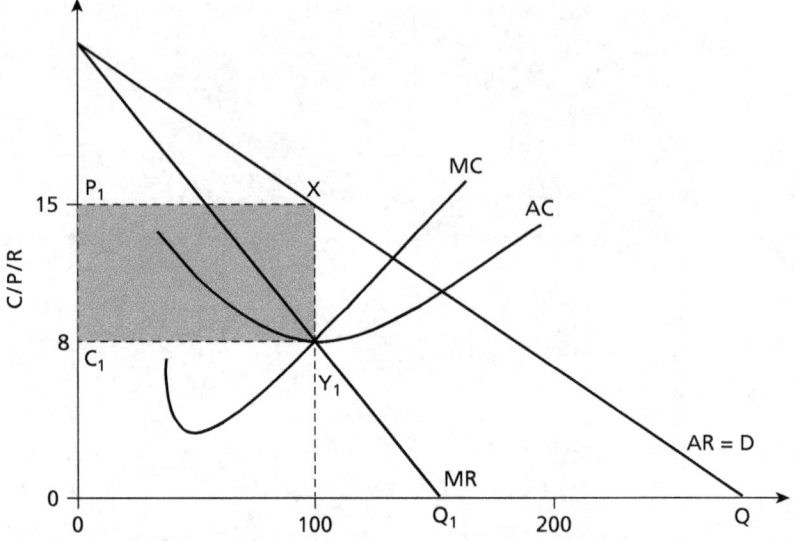

Key: C = costs, P = price, R = revenue.

Figure 9.1 Monopolist making above normal profit

Above normal profit is earned when TR is greater than TC, or when AR is greater than AC.

In Figure 9.1, the monopolist is making above normal profit according to the following steps:

- Step 1: Profit maximization output (MC = MR) at equilibrium output of 100 units;
- Step 2: The price of one unit (connect Q_1 100 to AR curve) = $15 × 100 = $1500 = TR;
- Step 3: The cost of 1 unit (connect Q_1 100 to AC curve) = $8 × 100 = $800 = TC;
- Step 4: Profit on 100 = $700

   or

   Above normal profit = Rectangle $P_1 X Q_1 O$ − Rectangle $C_1 Y_1 Q_1 O$ = $P_1 X Y_1 C_1$ (the shaded area).

In Figure 9.2, the monopolist is making normal profit. Note AR = $15 and AC = $15 (follow Steps 1 through 4).

or

TR = 1500 (15 × 100) TC = 1500 (15 × 100)

Therefore, profit = normal.

IMPERFECT COMPETITION: MONOPOLY AND MONOPOLISTIC COMPETITION

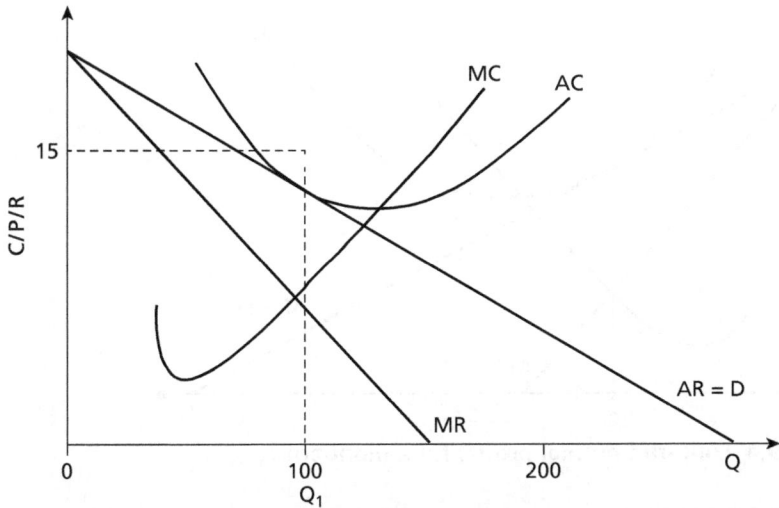

Figure 9.2 Monopolist making normal profit

A monopoly may incur a loss if it is inefficient, as shown in Figure 9.3 (follow the steps).

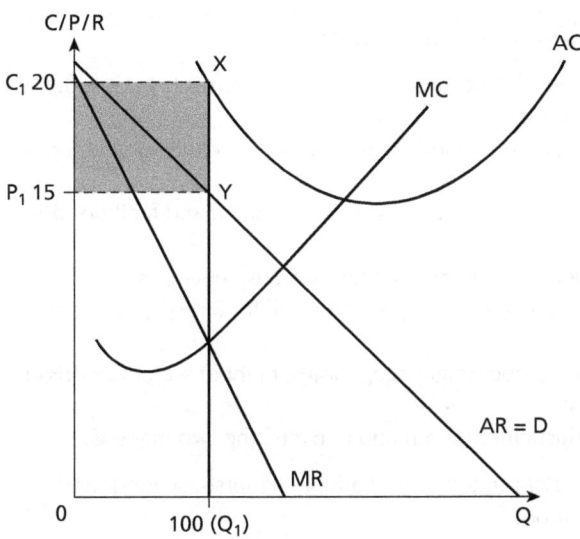

Figure 9.3 Monopolist making a loss

Observations on Figure 9.3:

- Loss is represented by the shaded area C_1XYP_1

$TR = P_1YQ_1O$

$TC = C_1XQ_1O$

$Loss = C_1XYP_1$

Long-run equilibrium

Note the following:

- For monopolists, in the long run, strong barriers to entry exclude new competitors.
- As a result, above normal profit persists in the long run (see Figure 9.1).
- The firm will benefit from economies of scale.
- All firms in all markets must cover long-run costs or exit the industry.

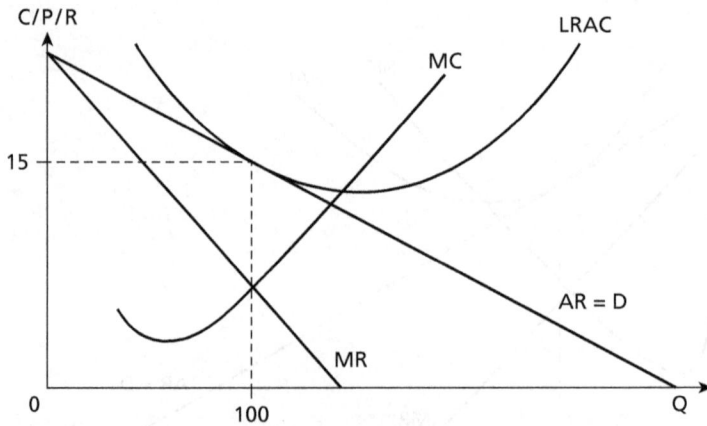

Figure 9.4 Long-run normal profits for a monopolist

Price discrimination

Price discrimination is the charging of different prices for the same good or service to different customers. The difference in prices must not be due to differences in costs of production – e.g. students paying a lower price than adults at a soccer match when all are seated in same area.

Price discrimination requires the following conditions:

- The seller must be a monopolist because, if not, and he raises his price, fellow competitors may take profit away from him.
- Two distinct markets must be identified – e.g. children or adults for a cinema show.
- The good or service must be the same – e.g. football match and facilities the same for everyone.
- There must be barriers between the two markets because enterprising individuals may purchase the good cheaply and resell for a profit, taking away the monopolist's profit.
- Barriers may be related to gender (e.g. cheap ladies' night in a club) or origin (foreign versus local cars).
- There may be differing elasticities of demand between the two markets.

There are three different types of price discrimination – i.e. first-, second- and third-degree price discrimination.

First-degree price discrimination

The seller can charge every customer a different price – e.g. a doctor in a small community who knows everyone and knows what each person can afford to pay.

Second-degree price discrimination

This may take place in utilities where a higher price can be charged for the first quantity of units of a service, then a lower price for any amount beyond this quantity.

The first 1000 units of a service – e.g. electricity – are sold at $10 per unit and beyond 1000 units at $5 per unit.

Third-degree price discrimination

The monopolist aims to sell his profit maximizing output in two well-separated markets with different elasticities – i.e. charging a high price in the more inelastic market and a low price in the more elastic market. Combining both markets earns higher revenue than operating as a single firm.

IMPERFECT COMPETITION: MONOPOLY AND MONOPOLISTIC COMPETITION

Natural monopoly

A natural monopoly is one in which the scope for economies of scale is so vast that it is possible for one firm to service the entire market more efficiently than two or more firms together. Refer to Figure 9.5.

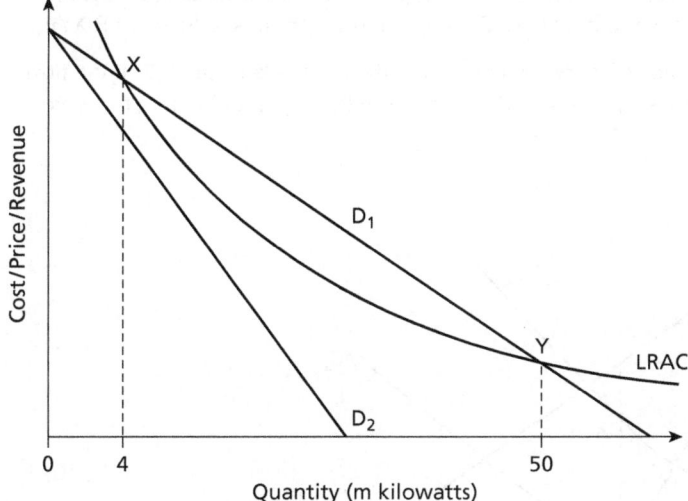

Figure 9.5 A natural monopoly

Note the following:

- Demand curve D_1 represents the demand curve of the electricity industry.
- Economies of scale between 4 and 50 million kilowatts of power enable the LRAC to be less than average revenue.
- If another company were to enter to provide half of the industry's needs, the LRAC would be greater than D_2, which is the demand curve facing two firms.
- Both firms would experience a loss at all levels of output.

A natural monopolist's LRAC reflects falling long-run average costs. Firms of this type incur very high fixed costs. At high levels of output, these costs are reduced due to economies of scale.

Effect of taxes and subsidies on monopoly profits as a form of regulation

A lump sum tax is a tax equal to a fixed sum. A lump sum tax will affect fixed costs and, hence, average cost, which will shift vertically upward reducing the firm's level of profit. Refer to Figure 9.6.

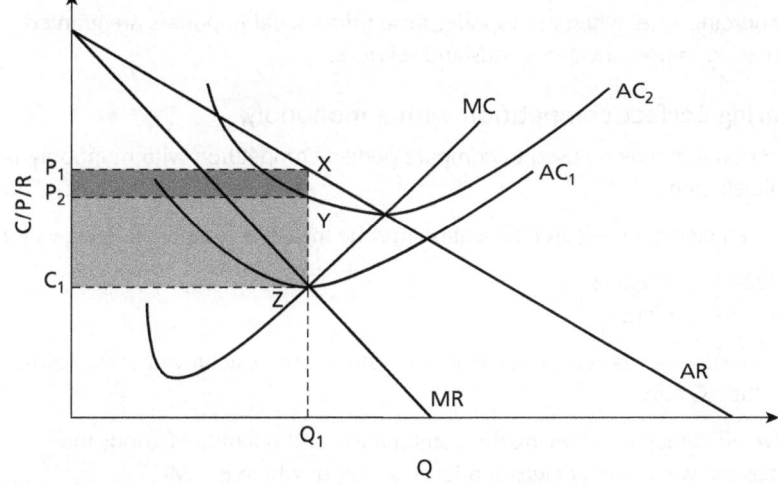

Figure 9.6 A lump sum tax

Note the following:

In Figure 9.6, a lump sum tax shifts AC_1 vertically upward to AC_2.

- Profit maximization is at Q_1 and above normal profit the rectangle P_1XZC_1.
- AC_1 rises to AC_2 and profits are now represented by the rectangle P_1XYP_2.
- The tax reduces profit by P_2YZC_1 and abnormal profit is reduced to P_1XYP_2.

A subsidy shifts the MC curve downward to the right. See Figure 9.7. If the firm is a profit maximizer, price would change from P_2 to P_1 if an indirect tax were imposed.

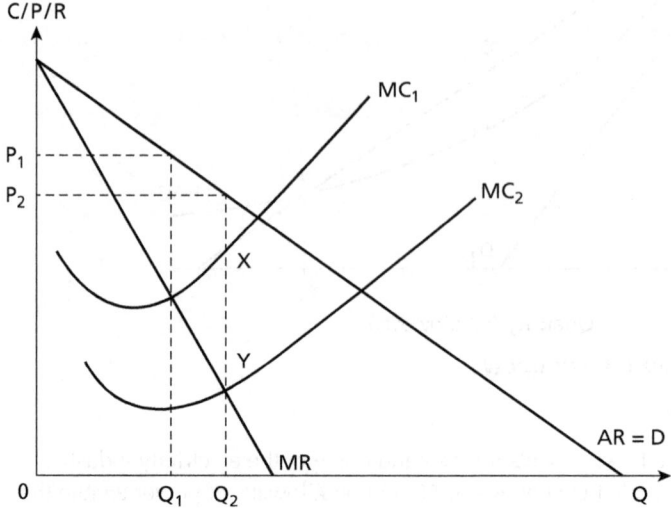

Figure 9.7 Effect of a subsidy

Effect of a subsidy

Note in Figure 9.7 that profit maximization output is Q_1 and at price of P_1. If the government wishes to regulate prices to a low of P_2, it must grant a subsidy equal to XY. Profit maximization is now at output Q_2.

Apart from taxes and subsidies, monopolies may be regulated in the following ways:

- Price controls;
- Nationalization;
- Privatization and deregulation for state-owned monopolies;
- Disintegration – i.e. breaking up a large monopoly into smaller units;
- Reducing entry barriers by inviting competition from abroad;
- Outsourcing – i.e. when monopolies raise prices local importers are granted licences to import cheaper goods and services.

Comparing perfect competition with a monopoly

One criterion that may be used to compare perfect competition with monopoly is economic efficiency.

Economic efficiency in resource allocation may be measured in the following ways:

- Productive efficiency;
- Allocative efficiency.

Productive efficiency is achieved where the output level is achieved at the lowest point on the AC curve.

Allocative efficiency is achieving the combination and quantity of goods that maximizes the welfare of society at a level of output where P = MC.

> **Exam tip**
>
> This concept is often tested by CAPE.

IMPERFECT COMPETITION: MONOPOLY AND MONOPOLISTIC COMPETITION

Criteria that may be used to compare both market structures should be:

- Price;
- Output;
- Consumer surplus;
- Efficiency.

Note what happens when thousands of small firms either merge or are taken over by a monopoly.

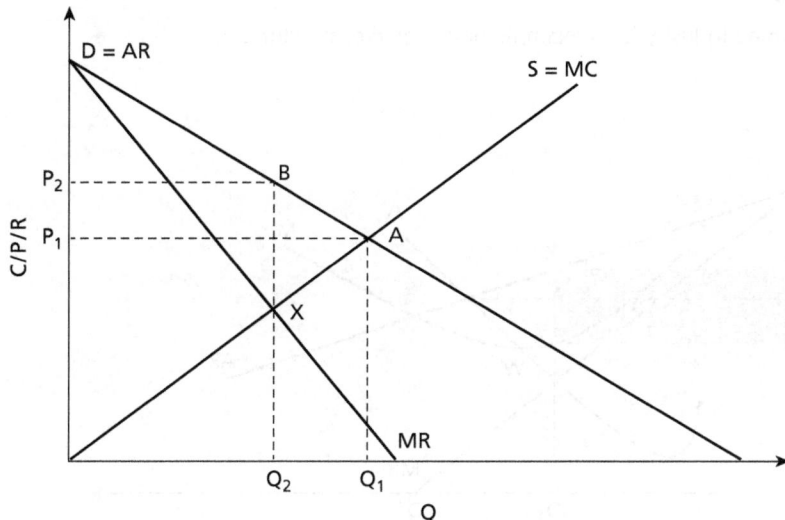

Figure 9.8 Comparing perfect competition with monopoly

Refer to Figure 9.8, which converts perfect competition to a monopoly. The following curves need to be identified for a monopoly: MC, MR, AR. Since S = MC and D = AR, MR is drawn intersecting the mid-point of the horizontal axis. Note that the demand curves AR and supply curves S = MC reflect perfect competition. There are no economies of scale in this analysis.

The changes are:

- Equilibrium output of perfectly competitive industry = Q_1
  Equilibrium of monopoly = Q_2
  Therefore a loss of Q_1Q_2 in output.
- Price under perfect competition = P_1
  Price under monopoly = P_2
  Conclusion: a monopoly charges higher prices
- Consumer surplus in perfectly competitive industry = Triangle DAP_1
  Consumer surplus under monopoly = DBP_2
  Reduction in consumer surplus (welfare) = P_2BAP_1
- Output Q_2 is not technically and cost efficient. A perfectly competitive industry produces where P = MC. A profit maximizing monopolist produces where P is greater than MC, hence allocatively inefficient.

Monopolistic competition

Monopolistic competition has some similarities with both perfect competition and monopoly.

The main features of this market are:

- Many buyers and sellers;
- Some ability to set price;
- Product differentiation (branding);
- Promotional advertising to establish brand loyalty;
- Three forms of profit are possible – i.e. short-run normal, above normal profit, and loss;
- Long-run normal profits.

The clothing industry is an example of this market structure.

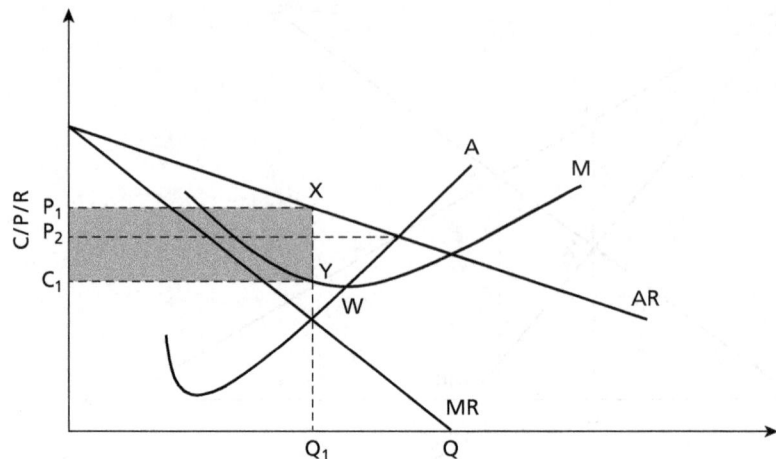

Figure 9.9 Monopolistic competitor earning above normal profit in short run

Figure 9.9 represents a monopolistic competitor earning above normal profit (P_1XYC_1) in the short run. Other firms in the industry, as in other market structures, may also make normal profits and losses.

Note:

- Equilibrium or profit maximization output is Q_1 where MC = MR.
- Above normal profit is P_1XYC_1.
- Output Q_1 is not cost efficient as production is taking place to the left of minimum average cost. There is therefore excess capacity of Y to W. This is an inefficient use of resources.
- The firm is not allocatively efficient since output is sold at P_1 and not where P = MC at P_2.

The long run

Note the following:

- New firms easily overcome entry barriers to compete profits away from profit-making firms in the transition to the long-run period in a similar manner to perfect competition.
- The demand curve shifts to the left as firms lose market share.
- This leftward shift in the demand curve brings the demand curve tangential to the LRAC.
- Only normal profits are earned in the long run.

Refer to Figure 9.10 on the long run.

Exam tip

This concept is often tested by CAPE.

IMPERFECT COMPETITION: MONOPOLY AND MONOPOLISTIC COMPETITION

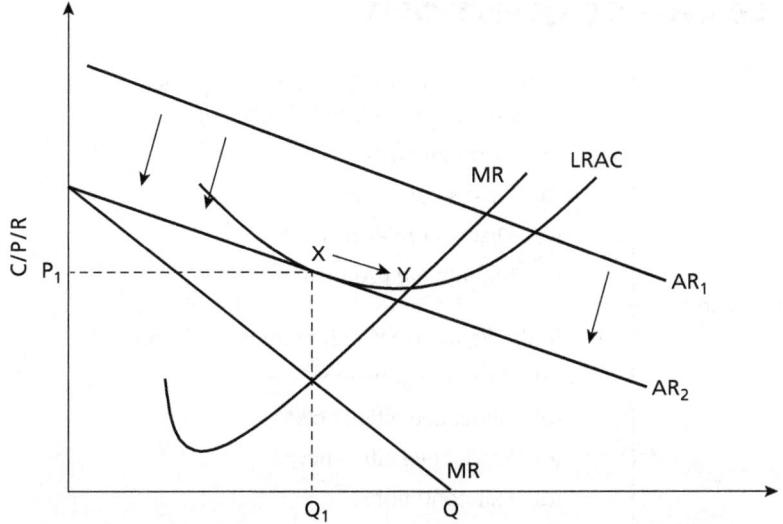

Figure 9.10 Long-run equilibrium of a monopolistic competitor

In Figure 9.10, note:

- Profit maximizing output Q_1;
- Normal profit (AR_2 = LRAC);
- Excess capacity of X to Y (see arrow);
- The firm is both technically and allocatively inefficient;
- The demand curve AR has shifted to the left due to the entry of new firms competing with existing ones;
- Long-run equilibrium is at Q_1 where LRAC is tangential to AR_2;
- Normal profit is earned at price P_1.

Test Your Knowledge

1. (a) Define the term 'price discrimination'.
   (b) Define the term 'normal profit'.
   (c) Can a firm in perfect competition make above normal profit in both the short- and long-run periods?

2. (a) Define the term 'monopoly' and give an example of a monopoly in your country.
   (b) How does output and price of a firm under a monopoly differ from output and price of a firm under perfect competition?
   (c) What problems will the firm experience if the price is equal to its marginal cost?

MULTIPLE CHOICE QUESTIONS

1. The demand curve facing a monopolist is:
   (a) Upward sloping;
   (b) Downward sloping;
   (c) Vertical;
   (d) Horizontal.

2. The demand curve of a monopolist is different to a monopolistic competitor because it is:
   (a) More demand elastic;
   (b) Less demand elastic;
   (c) Unitary;
   (d) Perfectly inelastic.

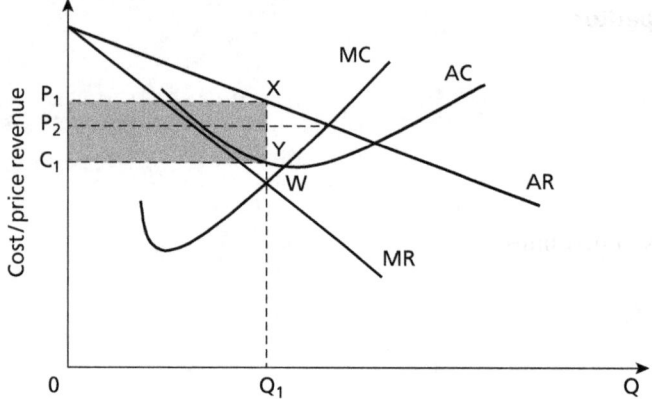

3. In the figure in MCQ2, of a monopolistic competitor, points Y to W indicate:
   (a) Constant costs;
   (b) Excess capacity;
   (c) Diseconomies of scale;
   (d) Incomplete production.

4. In the figure in MCQ2, point W indicates:
   (a) Profit maximization;
   (b) Allocative efficiency;
   (c) Productive efficiency;
   (d) Exit conditions.

5. In the figure in MCQ2, price P_2 indicates:
   (a) Allocative efficiency;
   (b) Productive efficiency;
   (c) Dead weight loss;
   (d) Least cost combination.

6. In the figure in MCQ2, Q1 indicates:
   (a) Equilibrium output;
   (b) Optimum output;
   (c) Marginal cost pricing;
   (d) Average cost pricing.

Chapter 10

Oligopoly and Contestable Markets

Learning Objectives

By the end of this chapter you should be able to:

- Define oligopoly
- Distinguish between different types of oligopolies
- Explain price rigidity and non-price competition
- Define and explain collusion
- Explain interdependence, collusion and price rigidity
- Describe when firms tend to engage in non-price competition

Introduction

An oligopoly is a market structure dominated by a small number of large firms.

Examples of oligopolistic firms are banks and insurance companies. There are four basic models of oligopoly. They are the:

- Sweezy kinked demand curve;
- Barometric leader;
- Dominant leader;
- Cartel.

Features of an oligopoly include:

- Few sellers but many buyers
- Each firm may sell differentiated products;
- There are strong barriers to entry.

Most models, however, exhibit the following behaviour:

Interdependence

Firms' decisions are based on how their rivals are likely to react.

Price stability/rigidity

Firms will not risk a price war that may adversely affect the few in the market.

Non-price competition

Firms compete with each other through non-price strategies such as advertising or promotions, giveaways, after-sales service, branding and credit.

Collusion

A few firms in an industry will cooperate directly (formally) or indirectly (informally). This behaviour is referred to as **formal collusion** and **informal collusion**.

Models of oligopolistic behaviour

The Sweezy model of oligopolistic behaviour explains two common features of oligopoly:

- Interdependence
- Price rigidity.

Figure 10.1 represents a firm in an oligopoly. The 'kinked' demand curve that the firm faces reflects how rigidly firms would react if prices were raised above or below point X of the demand curve.

If a firm raises its price above P_1 to P_2 other firms would not follow because there would be a loss of market share of Q_1Q_2. The curve above point X is price elastic for the firm raising its price.

If the price is lowered below P_1, other rivals will follow to prevent the firm from benefitting from the fall in price. The demand curve under P_1 is therefore price inelastic and price P_1 at point X remains 'rigid' or stable.

Price rigidity also occurs because the marginal revenue curve BAYW derived from the AR curve XQ has a vertical region of discontinuity (the dotted line). The oligopolist, as a profit maximize, sets output at MC = MR at Q_1 and price P_1 at point X on the demand curve.

OLIGOPOLY AND CONTESTABLE MARKETS

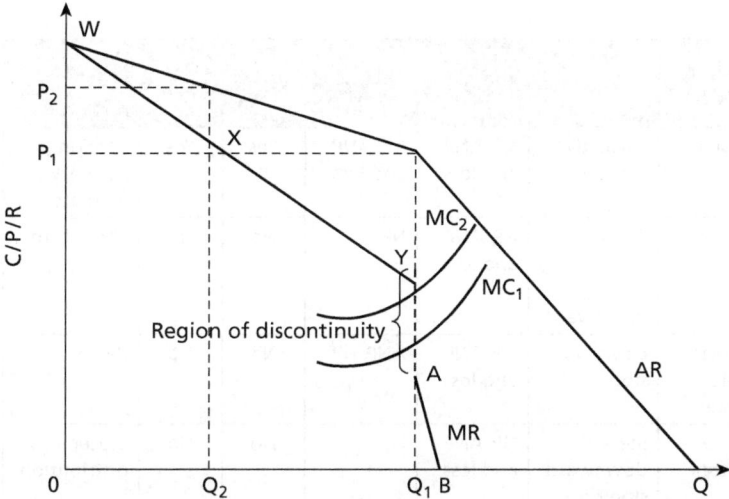

Figure 10.1 The Sweezy model of oligopolistic behaviour

If MC_1 increases to MC_2, the price will not rise because MC is moving along vertical line YA (= MR). Price and quantity are therefore unchanged as a result of the increases in costs.

The dominant price leader

The dominant price leader may be the largest, dominant or oldest firm in the industry. The sheer size of this firm enables it to vary output and be a dominant price setter. Other rivals not producing a matching quantity of supply, this supply influence may simply comply with this firm's price setting.

Barometric price leader

A barometric price leader is one who has the best knowledge of market conditions, especially demand. Out of a respect for this knowledge, other firms will follow its lead.

Cartel

When a few firms agree formally to limit competition between themselves, this is called a **collusive oligopoly**. Price fixing and quotas are formally agreed on. OPEC (Organization of Petroleum Exporting Countries) is an example of a cartel in oil production and distribution.

Contestable markets

W. Baumol, an American economist, developed a theory of contestable markets in the 1980s.

The main features of this market are:

- Ease of entry and exit plays a crucial role even if it is a monopoly.
- The threat of competition may act as actual competition, forcing a firm to keep its profit normal to discourage the entry of new firms.
- The cost of entry and exit is small compared with the profit they can all make.
- The threat of competition force existing firms to behave as if there were competition.
- This causes prices and profits to remain low.
- Perfect competition and monopolistic competition have elements of contestable markets, as do monopolies and oligopolies, because barriers are easily overcome.

REVISION GUIDE TO ECONOMICS

Table 10.1 Market structures compared

Market type	No. of firms	Barriers to entry and exit	Type of good or service	Control over price	Demand curve	Profit Short-run	Profit long-run	Efficiency Alloc.	Efficiency Tech.	Example
Perfect	Many	None	Identical	None	Perfectly elastic	NP, ANP and loss	NP, ANP and loss	Yes	Yes	Foreign currency markets
Monopolistic	Many	Very weak	Differentiated	Some	Fairly elastic sloping downward	NP, ANP and loss	NP	No	No	Shoe store
Oligopoly	Few	Strong	Similar or different	Mostly price taker	Downward sloping	NP, ANP and loss	ANP, NP	No	No	Banks
Monopoly	1	Very strong	Very differentiated	Price setter	Inelastic downward sloping	NP, ANP and loss	NP	No	No	Water distribution
Contestable	1–20	Very weak	Differentiated	None	Downward sloping	NP, ANP and loss	-	Yes	Yes	Airlines

Key: SR – Short-run; LR – Long-run; NP – Normal profit; ANP – Above normal profit; Alloc. – Allocative; Tech. – Technical

The strengths and weaknesses of the marginalist approach

The marginalist principle refers to economic decision-making at the margin – i.e. profit maximization (MC = MR), or where the wage or marginal input cost = the MRP (the producer), or where marginal utility = price (the consumer).

In practice, however, it is difficult to determine marginal product or marginal cost if factors of production are employed jointly – e.g. for a taxi and a taxi driver.

Making the highest level of profit in the short run will be the objective of a firm if ownership and control lie in the hands of the owner – e.g. a sole trader. There are other objectives of a firm (see Table 10.2).

Profit/consumer maximization

This is the objective of a producer or consumer cooperative whose primary objective remains the interest of members. Average cost pricing may be the preferred form of the firm's output.

Table 10.2 The different operating objectives of firms

Firm's objectives	Pricing/output
Profit maximization	To satisfy shareholders or owners of small enterprises MC = MR
Managerial utility	To satisfy shareholders or owners of small enterprises MC = MR
Growth maximization. Prestige status etc.	Setting a minimum target for competing groups in a firm (may also come close to MC = MR. (H. A Simon)
Conservation, survival	Normal profits so as not to attract new competitors; therefore AC = AR
Consumer/producer utility	The objective of consumers' and producers' cooperatives

Pricing and output strategies of multinational corporations

As the term suggests, multinational corporations (MNCs) operate in many countries at the same time.

Common features of MNCs are:

- Significant market power by their sheer size;
- The operations and decision-making of such firms are managed from a home country and are therefore centralized;

OLIGOPOLY AND CONTESTABLE MARKETS

- Financial strategies are geared towards tax avoidance and low cost;
- In recent times, especially through globalization, the world is regarded as a single market in which the same product is sold – e.g. KFC, Nestlé products, Macfoods Hamburgers, or oil companies such as BP/Amoco.
- Pricing and output strategies are geared naturally towards profit using a strategy called **transfer pricing**. This is achieved, for example, by setting prices above or below market prices to avoid paying taxes. If a country has a high corporation tax on profits, MNCs will set a low market price to achieve lower profits, and so less taxes.

MNCs may also overstate their costs in a high-tax country to raise their expenses artificially and avoid paying taxes. Equally, they may understate the price of a good in a high-tax country from which they import, to avoid paying tariffs on those imports. This is one way an MNC is able to earn very high profits while paying low taxes.

Multinational corporations

The advantages of producing in a foreign country are:

- A reduction in transport costs of inputs and of output distribution;
- Can deal with the threat of competition to their products better when in close contact with the market in a foreign country;
- Exploit low wages and low costs of inputs (raw materials);
- Avoidance of import restrictions – e.g. building a plant in a foreign country;
- Qualify for recognized assistance if they set up in grant-assisted locations;
- Exploit where employment legislation is less onerous/costly;
- Environmental health and safety standards are lower for MNCs;
- Government policy of industrialization by invitation offers benefits such as cheap sources of energy tax holidays.

Table 10.3 Effects of MNCs on host countries

Benefits for host country	Cost to host country
Employment	Elimination of domestic producers
New technology	Replacement of labour
New management techniques	Natural non-renewable resources are depleted
Export growth	Their sheer size insulates them from many government policies
Tax revenue	They may not strictly adhere to health or safety standards
Corporate sponsorship	They send their profits to their home countries
Good quality, low prices of products	They can shift production around the world and, in this way, exert influence on negotiations with unions or host governments

Market concentration and market structure

Concentration ratio

Note:

- A very concentrated market is dominated by industries where a few firms dominate the output or sales of the industry.
- A pure monopoly is considered totally concentrated because one firm accounts for total market share.
- Monopolistic competition is less concentrated than an oligopoly since the market share is divided up among many firms.
- The least concentrated market is a perfectly competitive industry.
- Market share is determined by the number of customers or clients which a firm serves as a percentage of the total market of customers.

In Table 10.4, the concentration ratio of the three largest firms would be 64% (28 + 20 + 16). This is a concentrated oligopoly market.

Herfindahl-Hirschman Index

The Herfindahl-Hirschman Index (HHI) is another measure of market concentration which gives a more accurate measure of market concentration than the concentration ratio. To calculate the index, the percentage of each firm is squared and added up.

A monopoly, for example, would control 100% of the market and so the HHI would be $= (100)^2$

$= 10,000$.

This is the highest value of the HHI and gives an indication of degree of equality or inequality in market share. A market is said to be unconcentrated if its HHI is less than 1000, but concentrated if the HHI is greater than 1800.

In Table 10.4, an HHI for the five firms would be:

$(28)^2 + (20)^2 + (16)^2 + (15)^2 + (14)^2$

$= 784 + 400 + 256 + 225 + 196$

$= 1861$

Table 10.4 Concentration ratios

Firm	Industry output (%)
1	28
2	20
3	16
4	15
5	14
All other	7

Test Your Knowledge

1. Compare the short-run and long-run situations of a monopolistically competitive firm with respect to the following:
   - Price;
   - Output;
   - Profit.

2. Define the following terms:
   - Cartel;
   - Natural monopoly.

3. Explain why the price in an oligopolistic industry might be sticky upward and downward.

OLIGOPOLY AND CONTESTABLE MARKETS

MULTIPLE CHOICE QUESTIONS

1. Firms are more likely to collude in an oligopoly if:
   (a) Products are very different;
   (b) Products are not branded;
   (c) There are few firms who dominate the industry;
   (d) There is a sudden change in demand.

2. Prices are sticky in the "kinked" demand curve because:
   (a) The AR curve is elastic above the kink and inelastic below it;
   (b) The AR curve is inelastic above the kink and elastic below it;
   (c) The MR curve is downward sloping;
   (d) The demand curve consists of two curves.

3. Which of the following is NOT a model of oligopoly?
   (a) Dominant price leader;
   (b) Barometric price leader;
   (c) Cartel;
   (d) Price discriminator.

4. Two measures of market concentration are:
   (a) Allocative efficiency;
   (b) Productive efficiency;
   (c) Concentration ratio and Lorenz curve;
   (d) Concentration ratio and Herfindahl-Hirchman index.

5. The three main features of an oligopoly are:
   (a) Price rigidity, interdependence and profit maximization;
   (b) Price rigidity, interdependence and marginal cost pricing;
   (c) Price rigidity, interdependence and non-price competition;
   (d) Managerial utility, interdependence and collusion.

6.

Firms	Market share (%)
1	40
2	30
3	10
4	5
5	3
6	2

What is the percentage of the four-firm concentration ratio?
   (a) 5%;
   (b) 90%;
   (c) 85%;
   (d) 24.1%.

Chapter 11 Market Failure

MARKET FAILURE

Economic efficiency

Economic efficiency consists of:

- Productive efficiency
- Allocative efficiency.

Productive efficiency

Productive efficiency also called **cost efficiency**, and occurs when a firm can achieve its highest level of output at its lowest cost. This is achieved where MC = AC, or the lowest point on the AC curve.

Allocative efficiency

Allocative efficiency is achieved at the socially optimum output level where Price is equal to MC. When output is sold where Price = MC, society is paying just what the output costs in terms of alternative production.

Efficiency and Pareto optimality

When resources are allocated in such a way that no one loses, a Pareto improvement is achieved. When such improvements come to an end, this leads to Pareto optimality where it would only be possible to make someone better off by making someone else worse off.

Refer to the PPF in Figure 11.1.

Note:

- Point X yields 30 units of consumer goods and 20 units of capital.
- At point X_1, more of both is achieved. This is a Pareto improvement.

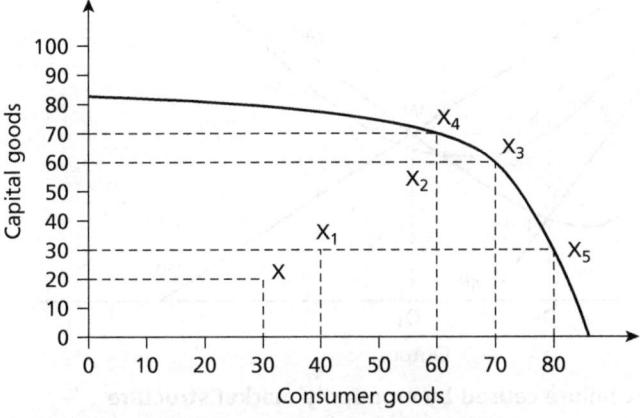

Figure 11.1 Efficiency and Pareto optimality

- Moving from point X_2 of 60 units of consumer goods and 60 units of capital goods to X_4 does not reduce the quantity of consumer goods but, instead, increases capital to 70 units. This is an improvement.
- However, trying to produce more consumer goods from X_4 to X_3 involves a loss of 10 units of capital goods but an increase of 10 units of consumer goods.
- From point X_4 to X_5, the same result is achieved, which is a loss of 40 units of capital goods to gain 20 units of consumer goods.
- All points on the PPF are Pareto optimal points because it is not possible to gain without losing.

Learning Objectives

By the end of this chapter you should be able to:

- Explain the concept of economic efficiency
- Distinguish among private goods, public goods and merit goods
- Distinguish between social costs and private costs and social benefits and private benefits
- Explain the concept of market failure
- Explain what is meant by deadweight loss
- Outline the causes of market failure

- Therefore, the link between Pareto optimality and efficiency is that efficiency leads to a Pareto optimal resource allocation.
- Allocative efficiency is also achieved on any point of the PPF.

Market failure is the inability to allocate resources to achieve allocative efficiency (P = MC) and productive efficiency (MC = AC), resulting in under-production, over-production, or 0 production of goods and services.

The causes of market failure

Market failure 1: imperfect market structure

Refer to Figure 11.2.

Market failure caused by a monopoly is due to:

- Incorrect output Q_2;
- The practice of profit maximization at MC = MR instead of P = MC;
- Price P_1 is higher than the efficient output price P_2;
- Consumer surplus is not maximized; it is YXP_1 instead of YWP_2;
- P_1XKP_2 is lost in consumer surplus;
- The firm/industry is also productively inefficient since output Q_2 cuts LRAC at K which is to the left of minimum LRAC (W); this represents excess capacity (Z to W);
- Triangle TXW represents loss of welfare to society, also called deadweight loss.

> **Exam tip**
> This concept is very popular with CAPE Examiners for Module 2.

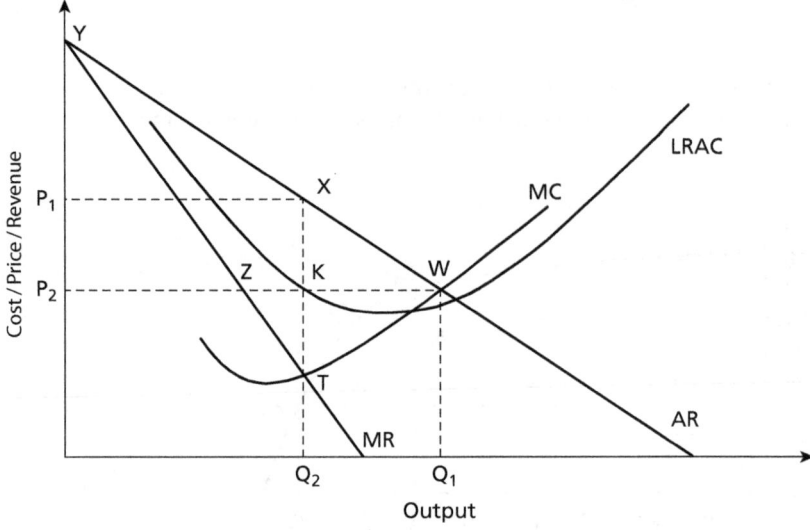

Figure 11.2 Market failure caused by monopoly market structure

Monopolistic markets and oligopoly are similarly market failures for the same reasons as for a monopoly.

Market failure 2: public goods
Note:

- A public good is one which is non-rivalrous and non-excludable – e.g. street lights.
- Non-rivalrous means that consumption of 1 unit does not leave 1 less for others since the supply is unlimited and the cost of providing an extra unit is 0.
- Non-excludable means that it is impossible to exclude others from consuming the good or service.

> **Exam tip**
> Regularly tested by CAPE.

MARKET FAILURE

- It is a market failure because there is 0 output from the free market because:
  1. there is no incentive for profit since it is difficult to exclude others from using the good free of charge. This is called the free rider problem;
  2. since the quantity consumed cannot be measured, pricing is difficult. There will therefore be no scope for profit.
- The government provide these goods in the public interest.

Private goods

A private good is one which is excludable and rivalrous – e.g. a soft drink. Consuming 1 unit leaves less for others to consume and others can be excluded from consuming it.

> **Exam tip**
> Regularly tested by CAPE.

Market failure 3: merit goods

A merit good is one which provides extended benefits to society beyond the benefit to the buyer – e.g. health and education. It is under-provided and under-consumed out of ignorance; hence, demand is weak. Market failure is due to information failure.

> **Exam tip**
> Regularly tested by CAPE.

Demerit goods

A demerit good is one which is harmful to the user and imposes negative effects on society. Alcohol and tobacco are commonly cited examples. These goods are over-provided by the free market and over-consumed out of ignorance. Output is beyond the efficient level where P = MC.

> **Exam tip**
> Regularly tested by CAPE.

Governments regulate the consumption of demerit goods, and provide education and information on the dangers of consuming the product.

Market failure 4: negative and positive externalities

Private, external and social costs

Merit goods provide extended positive benefits to society while demerit goods unintentionally impose negative costs to non-purchasers. These unintended effects are called **externalities**, **spillover**, or **third party effects**. Education is an example of a positive externality. Figure 11.3 shows the demand for education.

> **Exam tip**
> Regularly tested by CAPE.

Note:

- The demand curve reflects **private marginal benefit** (PMB).
- The spillover benefit of education to society is called **external marginal benefit** (EMB)
- When EMB is added to PMB, this will shift the PMB curve to the right by the amount of the EMB (as in Figure 11.3) to achieve **social marginal benefit** (SMB) to reflect the full benefit of the purchase.
- PMB + EMB = SMB

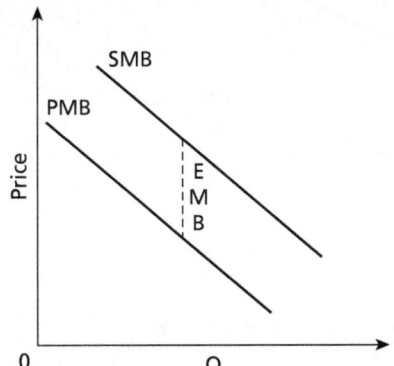

Figure 11.3 PMB + EMB = SMB

Figure 11.4 Positive externality of merit goods (education). The good is underproduced

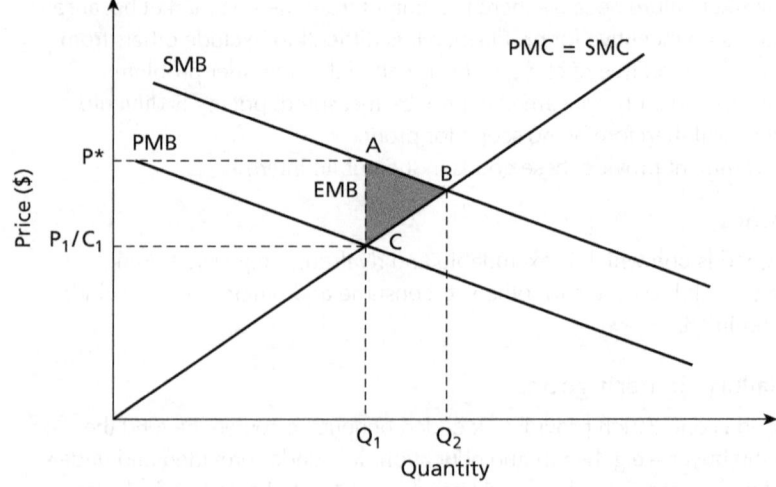

Figure 11.4 illustrates the extended benefit/externality of a merit good – e.g. education, – which is under-produced. The socially optimal level of output is Q_2 where SMB = SMC and not Q_1 where SMB > SMC.

Note the following:

- At Q_1, the benefit (P*) is greater than the cost to society (C_1).
- The extended benefit is denoted by the vertical distance of EMB which causes the PMB to diverge to the right to SMB (PMB + EMB + SMB).
- The correct or socially optimal quantity of education is Q_2, while the incorrect quantity is Q_1.
- The shaded area ABC is called **deadweight loss**.

Deadweight loss

Deadweight loss is the total loss of welfare to society when the level of output is not allocatively efficient – i.e. P = MC.

Costs to society

- The supply curve of a firm reflects PMC, such as marginal costs.
- Any spillover cost/externality from a transaction is called 'external marginal cost' (EMC) or a **negative externality**.
- The addiction of EMC to the PMC would shift the PMC to the left by the vertical distance EMC as shown in Figure 11.5.
- When a negative, spillover or third-party effect is imposed on society, the good will be over-produced and over-consumed.
- In Figure 11.5, SMC is achieved when EMC is added to PMC,

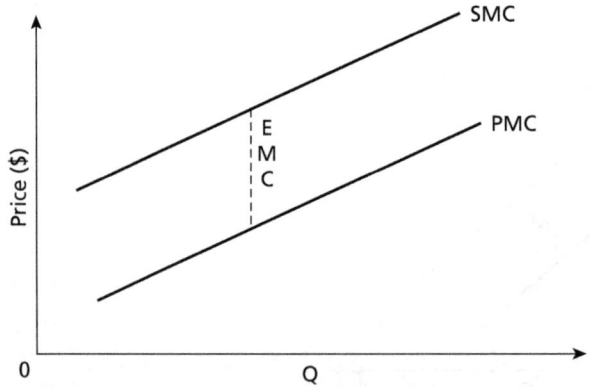

Figure 11.5 PMC + EMC = SMC (demerit goods: alcohol, tobacco)

MARKET FAILURE

Market failure 4: negative externality

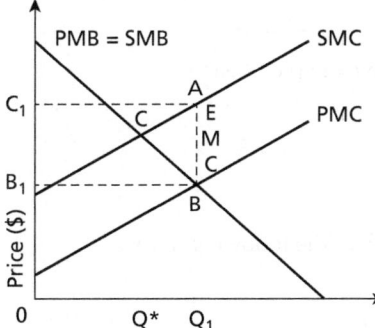

Figure 11.6 Market failure caused by a negative externality (demerit good)

Figure 11.6 illustrates the incorrect quantity of alcohol produced at Q_1.

When negative spillover effects from alcohol (EMC) are added to private costs of alcohol (PMC), the SMC of producing output Q_1 is achieved.

Note: Q_1 – suboptimal quantity;

Q^* – the optimal quantity.

At Q_1, the cost to society (C_1) is higher than the value (P_1) buyers place on Q_1 units since the 'correct' equilibrium is Q^*. ABC (deadweight loss) of welfare is lost by producing Q_1; the good is therefore over-produced by Q^*Q_1.

Market failure 5: asymmetric information

Accurate information is necessary to make sound economic decisions. In any transaction, if one person has more information than another, then this is known as **asymmetric information** – e.g. insuring a vehicle. The principal in this transaction is the buyer and the insurer, the agent.

Two common examples of asymmetric information are **moral hazard** and **adverse selection**.

Moral hazard

Moral hazard takes place when the uneven knowledge of agent or principal may cause them to take undue risk because they do not pay for the risk if it occurs. For example, in vehicle insurance the principal has more information than the agent since the agent is unaware of the principal's possible careless attitude towards securing the insured item. The resulting loss leads to inefficiency and a market failure due to asymmetric information.

Adverse selection

People who apply for insurance (the principals) have more information about their health than the insurance company (the agent). Persons with hidden health problems are more likely to purchase insurance than those in good health. The price of insurance is therefore likely to be high to reflect the risk being taken by the agent due to the principal being in less than average good health.

A healthy applicant will not benefit from a reduced insurance premium because he or she is automatically included in the group with hidden health problems.

Adverse selection in banking A loans manager (agent) will hesitate to make a loan to a prospective borrower (principal) because the manager may not have access to information regarding the principal's ability to repay. A new borrower carries a higher risk of defaulting on a loan due to lack of information.

Test Your Knowledge

1. Define each of the following and give an example of each.
   (a) Asymmetric information;
   (b) Moral hazard;
   (c) Adverse selection.

2. (a) Explain and give an example of each of the following terms:
      (i) Public goods;
      (ii) Externalities;
      (iii) Asymmetric information.
   (b) Explain how each of the concepts listed in (a) causes a market to fail.

MULTIPLE CHOICE QUESTIONS

1. Market failure is a failure to achieve:
   (a) Constant returns to scale;
   (b) Economic efficiency;
   (c) Equilibrium output;
   (d) 50% of output demanded.

2. Which of the following is NOT a cause of market failure?
   (a) Taxation;
   (b) Public goods;
   (c) Externalities;
   (d) Monopoly.

3. When people enjoy benefits without paying for them this is known as:
   (a) The non excludable problem;
   (b) The free-rider problem;
   (c) The excludable problem;
   (d) The rider problem.

4. A situation where consuming a unit of a good does not reduce the quantity available to others is called:
   (a) The non-excludable problem;
   (b) The non-rivalrous problem;
   (c) The marginal cost problem;
   (d) The private benefit problem.

5. Which of the following is maximized when SMB = SMC:
   (a) Profit;
   (b) Total revenue;
   (c) Total welfare to society;
   (d) Market share.

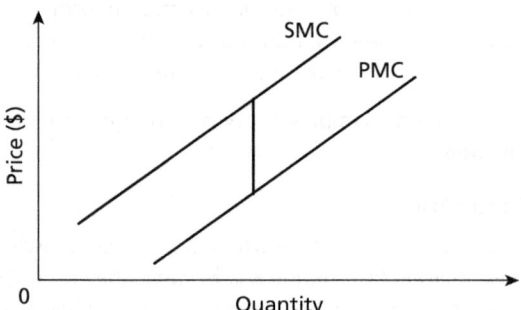

6. In the figure in MCQ5, the vertical distance between PMC and SMC indicates:
   (a) A private marginal benefit;
   (b) Social marginal benefit;
   (c) External marginal cost;
   (d) An indirect tax.

Chapter 12 — Role of Government and Market Failures

Learning Objectives

By the end of this chapter you should be able to:
- Identify and explain state action to correct market failure
- Describe taxation and subsidies
- Explain regulation and anti-trust legislation
- Describe other forms of state ownership – privatization and deregulation
- Explain the limitations of government action
- Identify the pros and cons of government measures used in an attempt to correct market failure

Government intervention

Government may intervene in a free market to correct market failures in the following ways:

- Taxation;
- Subsidies;
- Regulations and deregulation;
- Direct provision;
- Legislation;
- Privatization/nationalization;
- Anti-trust policy;
- Market creation – e.g. tradable permits.

Taxation and regulation of monopolies

- Since monopolies are profit maximizers, their profits may be subjected to a lump sum tax and then redirected to the poor and needy. (Refer to the Figure 9.6 on the effect of lump sum taxes in chapter 9 on monopoly.)
- A government may nationalize a private monopoly and set price where P = MC to achieve allocative efficiency.
- Government may also partially privatize nationalized companies when nationalized companies are productively inefficient.
  Advantages: Promotes efficiency, reduces monopoly excesses, encourages public ownership.
  Disadvantages: Government interference, nepotism, corruption, bureaucracy.

Market failure of public and merit goods

- Governments solve the zero production of public goods – e.g. streetlights – by direct provision free of charge and financed through taxation revenue.
- A government may provide merit goods free of charge to encourage consumption (education and training).
  Advantages: Public empowerment, employment, civil compliance, high literacy levels (education), public safety, reduction in crime (public goods – e.g. streetlights).
  Disadvantages: High maintenance costs, increased taxation, or increased borrowing.

Market failure according to imperfect information

Governments may enact strict laws on product information in different languages, detailed information on product content, expiry dates, storage and instructions for use. They may also undertake the following:

- Impose strict advertising standards to focus on informative advertising;
- Award grants to research institutions – e.g. CARIRI, the Caribbean Industrial Research Institute – to provide information to entrepreneurs;
- Set up the Central Bank and Government Statistic Department to provide accurate information on the economy for better business planning;
- Enact legislation to ensure transparency in government undertakings, such as the Freedom of Information Act.
  Advantages: Public awareness, sound economic planning.
  Disadvantages: Cost of administration.

ROLE OF GOVERNMENT AND MARKET FAILURES

Market failure according to adverse selection and moral hazard

Asymmetric information may be corrected in the following ways:

- Establish the offices of the Bureau of Standards and the Ombudsman related to goods and services traded in the insurance and financial sectors;
- Information programmes to educate the public – e.g. recycling.
  Advantages: Sustainable development, improvement of services to the public.
  Disadvantages: High administrative costs, bureaucracy.

Market failure according to labour immobility

Occupational and geographical immobility are the main causes of the failure of labour markets.

Governments may adopt the following corrective measures:

- Manpower information on job vacancies;
- Retraining of idle labour through government training programmes;
- Regional policy – i.e. industrial zones set up near to high areas of unemployment;
- Legislation enabling the transfer of pension rights to encourage the free movement of labour;
- The Caribbean Single Market and Economy (CSME) which is a Caribbean government agreement for the free movement of labour within a region;
- Government housing policy – i.e. siting housing settlements near to industrial activity;
- Reduction of direct taxes to encourage participation in the labour force.

Market failure according to inequitable distribution of income

One of the primary reasons for market failure is the uneven distribution of income. One remedial measure is the redistribution of wealth from rich to poor via progressive taxation. Other measures include:

Price control

- A price ceiling to protect consumers, especially for necessities such as food (schedule of food prices) and housing (rent control).
  Advantages: Poverty reduction, income redistribution.
  Disadvantages: Distortion of the price mechanism, dependency syndrome.
- For sellers, farmers may receive a guaranteed price for their produce to stabilize their income.
- Workers' incomes are protected against the effects of low wages (below the poverty line) by minimum wage legislation.
- Indirect taxes – e.g. specific taxes on alcohol, tobacco and gambling – are intended to discourage consumption.
  Advantage: Inelastic demand raises revenue for the state.
  Disadvantage: Reduced consumption of demerit goods is not achieved due to addiction.

Other forms of state intervention to correct market failure

Privatization is the sale or transfer of ownership and control of state companies to the private sector. Privatization is also considered to be:

- Sale of housing to tenants;
- Contracting services at state-run organizations – e.g. in hospitals where laundry, cleaning, security and catering services are 'outsourced';
- Creating competition for state-owned companies to make them more profit driven – e.g. DIGICEL competing with Telecommunications Services of Trinidad and Tobago;
- Compulsory competitive tendering by state-run enterprises.

Deregulation is the removal of rules and regulations which constitute barriers to competition between firms – e.g. insurance and other financial institutions to enable competition for deposits and loans.

Deregulation promotes competition with the objective of lowering cost and increasing productive efficiency. The dismantling of tariff barriers also falls into this category.

Tradable permits (market creation) allow a company to pollute up to an acceptable safe level. If the pollution is below a legal level, companies holding a tradable permit are allowed to sell the unused portion of the permit to another company. This system keeps the level of pollution within acceptable levels.

Private sector intervention in the correction of market failures

Private sector measures to regulate and reduce market failures may be summarized as:

- Corporate code conduct – which governs issues such as waste disposal and adherence to health and safety standards;
- Social responsibility – such as ensuring that marketed products are safe, provide multilingual information on safety and storage, and provide expiry date information; the recycling of waste products falls into this category;
- Company voluntary agreements (CVAs) – these are agreements that allow failing companies to renegotiate their debts to prevent insolvency and protect the interest of their clients;
- Corporate ethics – this is related to issues such as insider trading, false advertising, industrial espionage, bribery and money laundering.

Test Your Knowledge

1. Explain and give an example of each of the following terms:
   (i) Public goods;
   (ii) Externalities;
   (iii) Asymmetric information.
   Explain how each of the concepts listed above may cause a market to fail.

2. Define the following terms and explain how asymmetric information causes each to take place:
   (a) Adverse selection;
   (b) Moral hazard.

ROLE OF GOVERNMENT AND MARKET FAILURES

MULTIPLE CHOICE QUESTIONS

1. Productive efficiency in production occurs when:
   (a) All firms are producing where MC = MR;
   (b) There is spare capacity;
   (c) The output of one good can make a person better off but also make another person worse off;
   (d) The economy does not have to depend on imported goods.

2. Which combination BEST describe examples of privatization?
   (a) Deregulation and franchising;
   (b) Contracting out and regulation;
   (c) Deregulation and nationalization;
   (d) Ceiling prices and regulation

3. The concept of 'adverse selection' implies that:
   (a) Persons who have insurance may tend to be less careful and thus increase risks;
   (b) Persons who take out insurance are those with the highest risk;
   (c) Those who sell insurance policies are less well-informed than those who buy them;
   (d) Those who choose insurance policies are often those who do not really need them.

4. Market failure is indicated when:
   (a) SMC > SMB;
   (b) P = MC;
   (c) MC = ATC;
   (d) MC < AFC.

5. Deadweight loss is 0 when:
   (a) Total welfare is maximized;
   (b) Total revenue is 0;
   (c) Total cost is 0;
   (d) P = MC.

Chapter 13 Theory of Income Distribution

THEORY OF INCOME DISTRIBUTION

Wages, interest, rent and profit are the payments to the factors of production. Wages are paid to labour, interest to capital, rent to land and profit to enterprise.

Derived demand

The demand for a factor of production is a **derived demand** because demand is derived from what the factor can produce. For example, the demand for teachers is derived from the demand for education.

Traditional economic theory of wages

Marginal revenue productivity (MRP) theory states that a factor of production will be hired as long it can contribute as much to revenue as it does to the cost of the factor.

The assumptions of this theory for labour are that:

- The factor output is sold in a perfect product market (by workers);
- It is hired in a perfect factor market (by firms);
- The firm is a profit maximize;
- Production takes place in the short-run period.

Each assumption is explained as follows:

- The factor's output (goods and services) is sold in a perfect product market, meaning that there is one ruling price.
- The factor is hired in a perfect labour market as follows:
  - Each unit is equally efficient as any other and has the same quality (homogeneous);
  - Each firm is a wage taker;
  - Perfect mobility of the factor;
  - Perfect knowledge exists.

There are no barriers to entry or exit for any factor.

MRP theory states that a profit maximizing firm would hire an additional factor up to the point where marginal factor contributes as much to the revenue of the firm as the cost of the factor. For example, if the cost of labour or capital is $100 and the value of labour's output is sold for $100 or more, then the factor would be hired. The theory is based on two simple factors:

- the marginal physical product;
- the marginal revenue product.

Marginal revenue productivity and the demand for labour

The marginal physical product

Figure 13.1 shows the short-run product curve, the marginal physical product of labour (MPPL) which is the contribution of each additional worker.

Learning Objectives

By the end of the chapter you should be able to:

- Explain the rewards to the factors of production
- Explain the concept of derived demand
- Outline marginal revenue productivity theory
- Apply marginal productivity theory to the demand for land capital and labour
- Analyse the factors affecting the supply of land, capital and labour
- Analyse the factors determining rent, interest and wages
- Distinguish between transfer earnings and economic rent

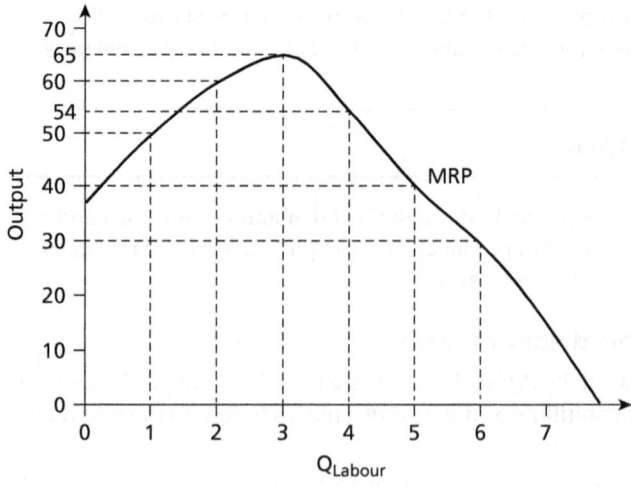

Figure 13.1 The marginal physical product of labour

Table 13.1 Calculating VMP and MRP

No. of workers 1	TPP 2	MPP 3	Price per unit ($) 4	VMP (MPP x AR) 5	MRP (MPP x MR) 6	Wage rate ($) 7
0	0	0		3 x 4	3 x 4 (P = MR)	30.00
1	16	16	2.00	32	32	30.00
2	35	19	2.00	38	38	30.00
3	60	25	2.00	50	50	30.00
4	84	24	2.00	48	48	30.00
5	105	21	2.00	42	42	30.00
6	120	15	2.00	30	30	30.00
7	128	8	2.00	16	16	30.00
8	130	2	2.00	4	4	30.00

> **Exam tip**
>
> Popular with CAPE examiners.

Converting MPP to VMP and MRP

Table 13.1 shows that the value of the marginal product is calculated by multiplying the marginal product of the worker by the price of the output – i.e. (MPP) x P = Value of marginal product (VMP).

MRP is determined by multiplying MPP × the marginal revenue (MR). Since in a perfect market P and MR are the same, then the VMP and marginal revenue product are the same for a perfect labour market.

Note the following in Table 13.1:

- The price of the product is $2.00.
- The wage rate is $30 for all workers.
- MPP is rising and falling due to increasing and diminishing returns to the variable factor. Note that the rise and fall of MPP in Table 13.1 and that MRP (see Figure 13.2) is also following the same shape.
- VMP (MPP × P) and marginal revenue productivity (MPP × MR) are the same in a perfect market since P = MR.
- From workers 1 to 5, the MRP= VMP is higher than the wage of $30 (marginal input factor cost).
- Worker 6 is adding as much to cost as he does to revenue.

Since the firm is a profit maximizer, it will hire where the marginal input cost of labour (wage rate) is equal to MRP; 6 workers will therefore be hired at wage rate of $30.

THEORY OF INCOME DISTRIBUTION

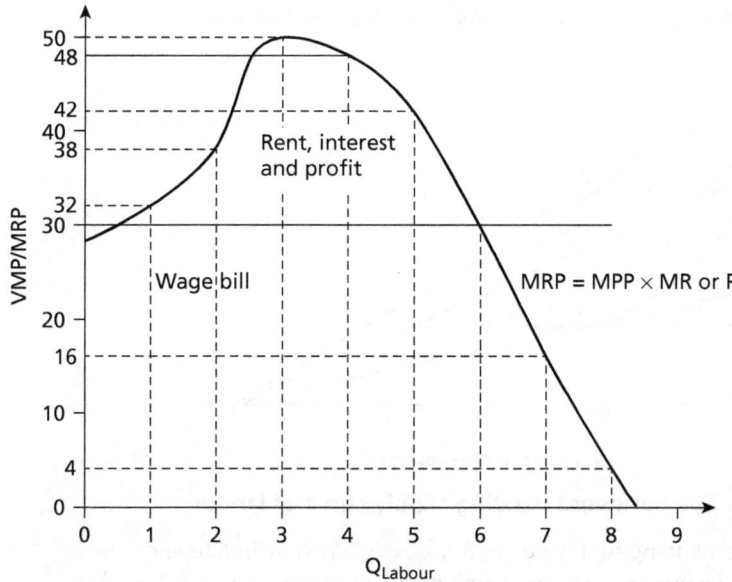

Figure 13.2 The surplus rents that accrue to an entrepreneur

In Figure 13.3, the individual supply curve shows the number of hours that an individual is willing to supply to a firm at a given wage per time period – e.g. $10 per hour per 12-hour day. The curve would slope upward from left to right.

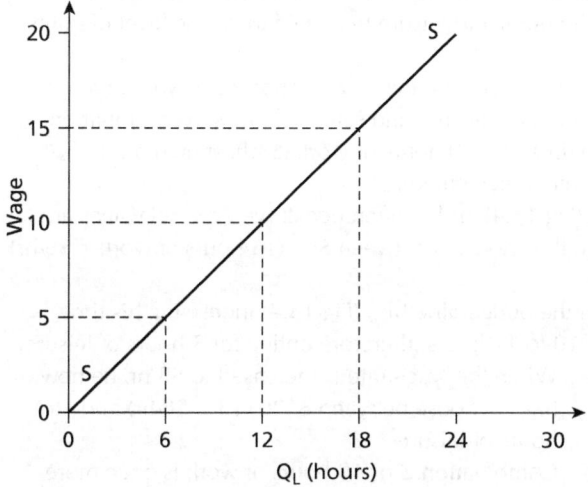

Figure 13.3 Individual supply curve

More hours are supplied at a higher wage because work involves a sacrifice of leisure; working more hours therefore requires compensation of higher wages. When wages rise, a rational worker is encouraged to work more, substituting work for leisure hours. This is called the **substitution effect of wages**. Working more hours has an income effect of increased purchasing power. These combined effects explain the upward sloping curve.

Backward bending supply curve: indifference curve analysis

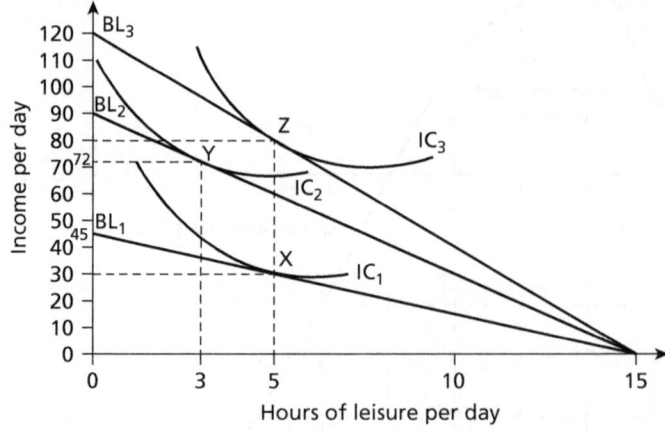

Figure 13.4 The backward bending supply curve of labour

The backward bending supply curve may be explained by indifference curve analysis as in Figure 13.4. The assumptions of this theory are:

- An individual allocates 9 hours of sleep and 15 hours of work and leisure in a 24-hour day.
- If a worker reserves 9 hours for sleep and chooses 5 hours of leisure out of the remaining 15 hours, then he will choose to work 10 hours.

His choices can be illustrated on an indifference curve which shows different combinations of work (income) and leisure that yield the same level of utility. Note the following:

- At a wage of $3 per hour, a sugar cane worker chooses between $45 (15 × $3/hr) and 15 hours of leisure and selects point X, a combination of 5 hours of leisure time and 10 hours of work ($30), shown on BL_1 (Fig 13.4) and the indifference curve IC_1.
- On budget line BL_2 (Fig 13.4) and indifference curve 2, when wages are raised to $6 an hour, the choice is between $90 (15 hours of work × $6/hr) or 15 hours of leisure.
- Point Y is chosen on the budget line BL_2, (Fig 13.4) increasing his time spent working from 10 to 12 hours, therefore opting for 3 hours of leisure.
- When the wage rate is increased to $8/hr, he now has to choose between $120 (15 × $8/hr) and 15 hours of leisure.
- Combination Z or 10 hours of work is once more equal to $80. Since an increase in income caused him to work fewer hours, the income effect of this increase is negative. Working more (12 hours) at $6/hr is called the **substitution effect**.

Figure 13.5 shows a backward bending supply curve because the downward negative income effect is stronger than the upward substitution effect of the curve from wage rate $6/hr to $8/hr.

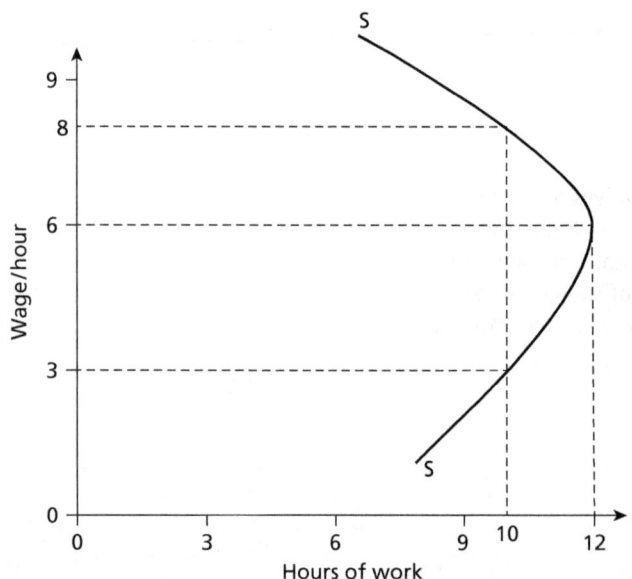

Figure 13.5 The backward bending supply curve of labour

THEORY OF INCOME DISTRIBUTION

The supply curve of labour to an industry

This supply curve will be upward sloping because high wages will attract more hours of labour. Factors affecting the supply of labour are:

- The skill and experience of the worker;
- Job satisfaction/dissatisfaction;
- The conditions of the working environment;
- Non-salaried benefits – e.g. 'perks', (such as medical insurance);
- The elasticity of supply to a particular occupation.
  The two main factors that affect the price elasticity of supply are occupational and geographical mobility.
  - **Occupational mobility** is the ease with which a person can move from one job to another.
  - **Geographical mobility** is the ease with which someone can move to another job in another location or region;
- The length of the working week and number of holidays available to the labour force;
- The activity rate or the labour force participation rate – which is the percentage of the population in the labour force;
- The rate of income tax – which has a discouraging effect on low-income workers;
- The likelihood of unemployment.

The rate of interest

According to conventional economic theory, the rate of interest is the price of capital.

The interest rate is determined when the demand and supply for loanable funds are equal to each other.

The supply of loanable funds

Loanable funds consist of money not spent but saved. The reward for this sacrifice is the rate of interest paid by the bank.

The supply curve of loanable funds is therefore left to right and upward sloping to reflect that increasing amounts of deposits – and, hence, sacrifices – require equally higher compensations for giving up consumption.

The demand for loanable funds

Note:

- The demand for loanable funds focuses on a firm's demand for capital goods.
- The MRP of capital is downward sloping due to diminishing returns to capital.
- These returns or output when sold in a perfect market will give the MRP of each machine and is derived when the firm estimates the net profit of each machine expressed as an annual percentage rate of return.
- These percentage returns are falling due to diminishing returns to capital.
- This percentage yield is called the marginal efficiency of capital and represents the demand for capital. See Figure 13.6.

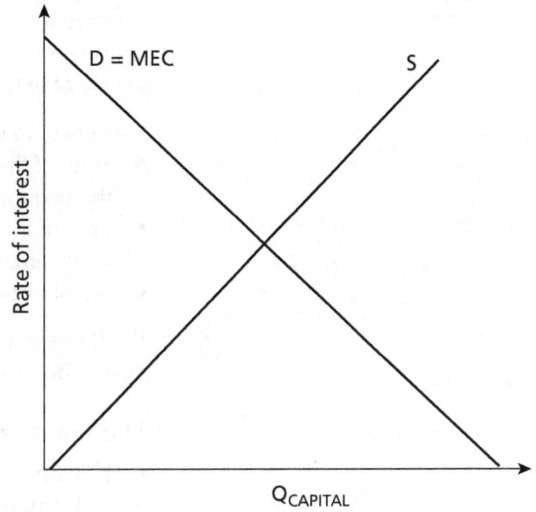

Figure 13.6 The rate of interest

The intersection of the demand and supply curves determines the interest rate according to traditional economics.

A movement of the MEC curve is achieved if:

- The productivity of capital is increased;
- There is an increase in the price of the output created;
- Business optimism is very positive and firms' spending on capital goods increases.

Land

Rent is a factor payment to the landowner for the use of land.

MRP theory holds that rent is determined by the supply and demand for land. The demand for land is derived from the demand for food, housing, or recreation; or commercial, or industrial needs.

The demand curve for land is derived from the MPP of land multiplied by MR and is downward sloping since land is subject to the law of diminishing returns.

The supply of land is assumed to be fixed in supply.

Profit

The reward to the factor of production enterprise is profit which is the reward for taking risks.

The greater the degree of risk, the greater the level of profits – e.g. oil exploration. Profit is determined after output is sold. Many factors other than risk may affect the level of profits. These may be:

- The ability to set price;
- Barriers to entry;
- The demand elasticity of the product or service;
- Monopoly power and the level of competition at home and abroad;
- The state of the economy;
- The level of taxation;
- The cost of production;
- The existence of economies of scale.

Profit is determined by the supply and demand for entrepreneurs. The supply of entrepreneurs is taken to mean the number of firms in an industry. The supply of firms or entrepreneurs is mainly related to risk. Other factors which affect the supply of entrepreneurs are:

- Access to start-up capital – i.e. the rate of interest;
- State of the economy – more entrepreneurs are attracted into business when the economy is growing;
- Rate of taxation on profits;
- Government support for business enterprises – e.g. small business development;
- Number of individuals trained in business education.

The demand for entrepreneurs is a derived demand and is linked to the demand for a good or service.

The limitations of MRP theory

- It is difficult to calculate marginal product when factors operate jointly – e.g. jack hammer and operator.
- It is also difficult to calculate the MPP of a service worker such as a barber because his output is not measureable in a physical sense.
- The assumption of wage determination – i.e. MRP = wage – is based on profit maximization. Many firms are not profit maximizers but may have other objectives, such as survival, or growth and expansion.

THEORY OF INCOME DISTRIBUTION

Transfer earnings and economic rent

The **transfer earnings** of a factor of production are the minimum payments necessary to keep that factor in its current employment. For example, a taxi driver will operate his taxi and expects to earn a minimum amount of $100 a day. This is his transfer earnings. If he makes $250 then he earns an additional $150, which is called **economic rent**. Economic rent is any surplus over a factor's transfer earnings.

Diagrammatically, transfer earnings are identified as the area to the right and under the supply curve. The area to the left of the supply curve and under the price line is known as economic rent. See Figure 13.7.

In the labour market, 1 hour of work may be supplied for $2 by a worker, but the market wage is $12. The transfer earnings are $2 and economic rent is $10. Totalled together, the vertically shaded triangle TE is transfer earnings and ER is economic rent.

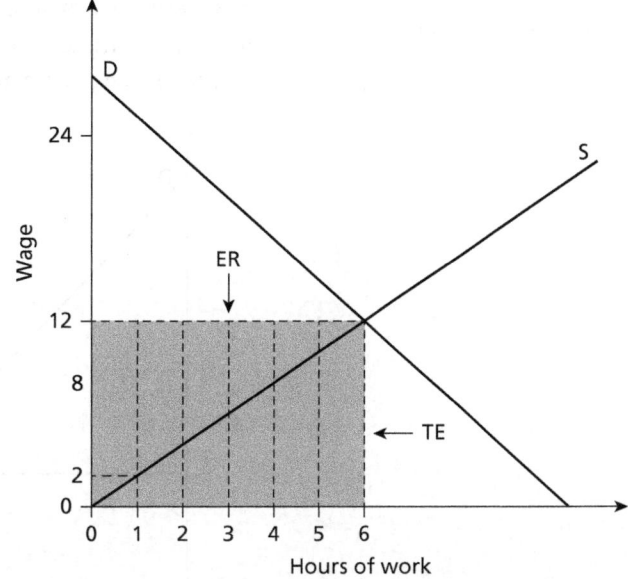

Figure 13.7 Economic rent and transfer earnings

Transfer earnings, economic rent and elasticity of supply

Transfer earnings and economic rent vary with elasticity of supply in any market. See Figures 13.8 and 13.9.

> **Exam tip**
>
> Regularly tested by CAPE.

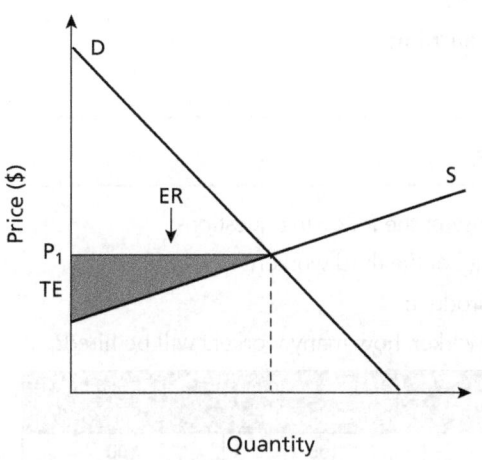

Figure 13.8 Economic rent decreases

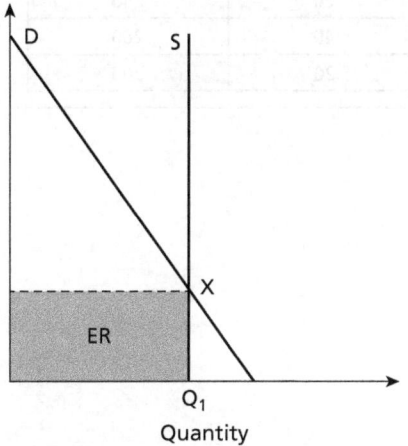

Figure 13.9 When PES = 0 economic rent is maximized (TE = 0)

Note that elastic supply will cause economic rent to be reduced but, when price elasticity of supply = 0, economic rent is maximized.

Price elasticity of supply

In Figure 13.10, when price elasticity of supply is infinite (perfectly elastic) transfer earnings are maximized by the area P_1X_1Q.

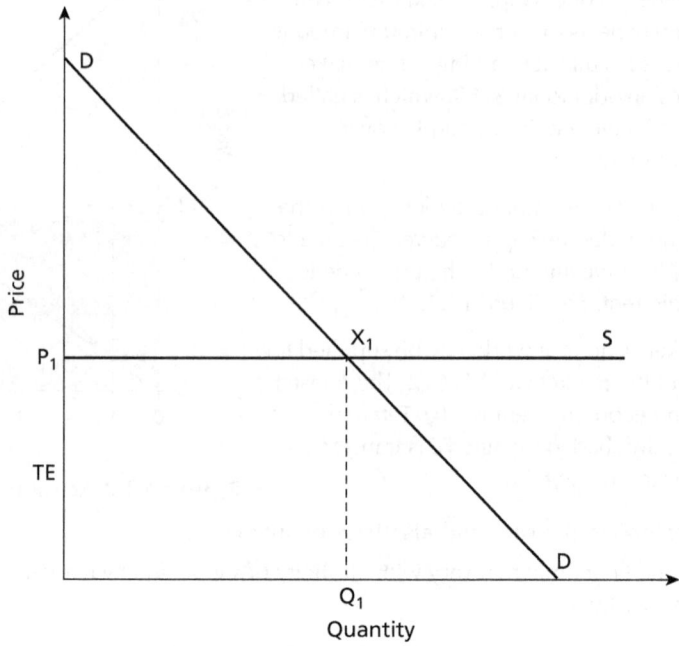

Figure 13.10 Maximum transfer earning

Test Your Knowledge

1. Examine the table below and answer the following questions:
   (a) What is the marginal product of the third worker?
   (b) Calculate the price of the product;
   (c) If the wage rate is $20 per worker, how many workers will be hired?

Number of workers	Output (units)	Marginal revenue product ($)	Total revenue ($)
1	10	100	100
2	18	80	180
3	24	60	240
4	28	40	280
5	30	20	300

THEORY OF INCOME DISTRIBUTION

MULTIPLE CHOICE QUESTIONS

1. The principle of marginal productivity is used to explain how much of a factor of production a profit maximizing firm will:
   (a) Demand, given the price of the input;
   (b) Supply, given the price of the input;
   (c) Produce in the market period;
   (d) Give away in the short run.

2. The marginal revenue product and the value of the marginal product is the same for which labour market?
   (a) Monopsony;
   (b) Perfect market;
   (c) Unionized labour;
   (d) Non-unionized labour.

3. The curve representing the supply of labour may be backward bending due to:
   (a) A negative income effect;
   (b) A positive substitution effect;
   (c) The sacrifice of leisure;
   (d) Increased hours of work.

4. Transfer earnings are:
   (a) A travelling allowance;
   (b) The minimum supply price of a factor of production;
   (c) The same as producer surplus;
   (d) Equal to consumer surplus.

5. Economic rent is:
   (a) Payments to a factor input below transfer earnings;
   (b) The cost of renting a building;
   (c) Payments above transfer earnings;
   (d) The interest paid on a loan.

6. If the supply curve for a perfect labour market changes to become perfectly inelastic, as in Figure (b), then:
   (a) Transfer earnings are maximized;
   (b) Economic rent is maximized;
   (c) Economic rent is equal to zero;
   (d) Transfer earnings is less than economic rent.

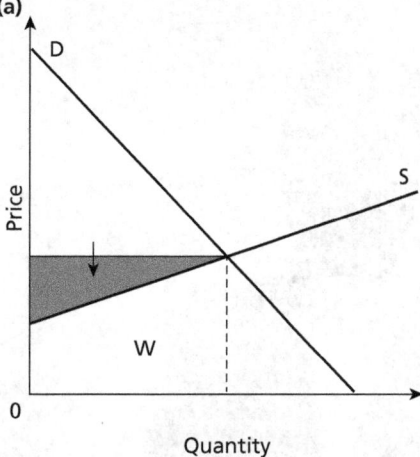

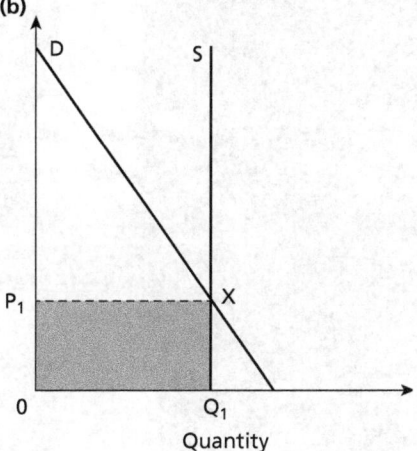

Chapter 14 Wage Differentials

Wage differentials

Wage differentials exist when workers in an industry earn different wages. This may be caused by:

- Imperfect labour markets;
- Separation of labour markets by barriers;
- Different demand and supply conditions;
- Different elasticity of demand and supply that exist in different markets;
- Compensating wage differentials

Learning Objectives

By the end of the chapter you should be able to:
- Explain the concept of wage differentials
- Analyse imperfections in the labour market
- Analyse the effect of labour immobility on wages
- Explain the concept of compensating wage differentials
- Explain the role of government, trade unions and employer associations in the pricing of labour

Wage differentials – the supply factors

Workers are unable to enter another industry due to barriers to entry. These barriers are:

- Ethnic and gender discrimination, which result in lower than average wages for females in the work place performing the same tasks as their male colleagues;
- Very high qualifications for a job;
- Membership associations which require membership enlistment;
- Long internships and apprenticeships for doctors and lawyers;
- The length of time it takes to train or qualify for a profession;
- Occupational and geographical barriers.

Occupational mobility is the ease with which a worker can transfer from one industry to another.

Geographic immobility is the ease of ability to move from one region to another.

- Different workers have different skills, talents and abilities which cause their supply to be very restricted – e.g. Usain Bolt.

Wage differentials – the demand factors

According to economic theory, one of the main factors which determines the demand for labour is the productivity of the worker, which is influenced by the following:

- The level of training, skill and ability of the worker;
- The quality of tools and equipment used;
- Conditions of work;
- Work incentives;
- Job satisfaction;
- Worker morale;
- Security of tenure.

The demand curve for labour is the MRP curve, which is influenced by the following:

- The demand for the product – if there is strong demand for the good, a high price will cause the demand curve to shift to the right;
- The market structure in which the firm operates – if the firm has market power, as in a monopoly, the price is also likely to be high.

The third factor that influences the demand curve for labour is the price of capital capable of replacing labour. If the price of technology is low the demand for labour is likely to fall, since it is likely to be replaced.

REVISION GUIDE TO ECONOMICS

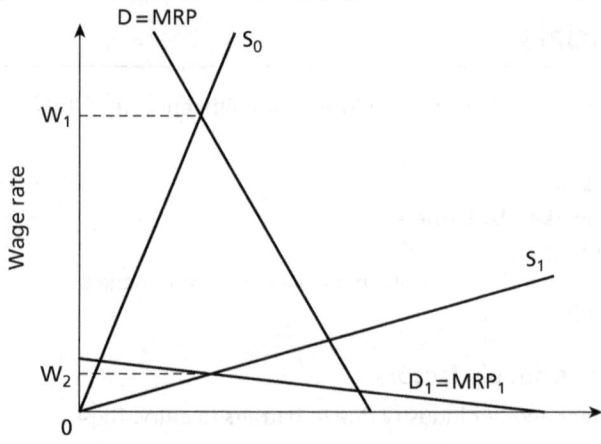

Figure 14.1 Difference in wages due to elasticity of demand and supply for labour

Figure 14.1 shows how differences in the elasticity of demand and supply can lead to different wages.

Note:

- A brain surgeon is likely to earn a wage of W_1 because his supply and demand curves are very inelastic.
- His demand curve is inelastic because he is highly skilled and his productivity is also very high.
- He also offers a critical service and there are not very good substitutes for his service.
- His supply is inelastic and to the left because there are fewer brain surgeons than other specialists.
- The duration of the training period is very long and costly, requires high intelligence, and needs years of experience to practice successfully.
- In comparison, a garbage collector's demand and supply curves are elastic because his productivity level is not high, he needs minimum training and qualification, there are very many at his skill level, and his services are not an absolute necessity since people could dispose of their own garbage.
- These factors affect his productivity and price. He therefore earns a wage of W_2.

Wages in a perfectly competitive industry

> **Exam tip**
>
> Regularly tested by CAPE.

As Figure 14.2 illustrates, Q_{L1} of labour is demanded at a wage of W_1. In this perfectly competitive market, all firms are wage takers. The equilibrium wage rate is W_1 and the number of workers employed is QL_1 of workers.

The demand curve (the MRP) will shift to the right depending on:

- Productivity increases;
- A rise in the product's price;
- A rise in the price of capital requiring substitution of labour.

The supply curve will shift to the right, indicating an increase in supply as follows:

- There is an increase in the size of the population.
- Conditions in other industries worsen causing occupational movement of labour to the market above.
- There is the existence of perks or job satisfaction in this industry compared with others.

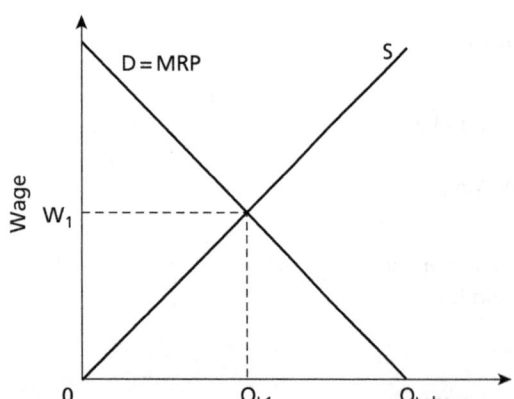

Figure 14.2 The equilibrium wage rate in a perfectly competitive labour market

WAGE DIFFERENTIALS

The manner in which wages are determined in a competitive firm has been analysed in Figure 14.2. Wages determination in an imperfect labour market is illustrated in Figure 14.3.

Wages in an imperfect labour market

In an imperfect labour market, a sole buyer of labour is called a **monopsonist** – e.g. Caribbean Airlines Ltd is the main purchaser of pilot services in the Caribbean.

Notes on Figure 14.3:

- The demand curve for labour is the familiar MRP curve.
- The supply curve of labour is an upward sloping supply curve equal to the average wage (AW).
- The MC of labour is higher than the AC of labour because, to attract a new worker to the firm, a higher wage must be paid and the workforce must also be similarly paid.
- The change in the wage bill is not only for the extra worker but the other workers' increases as well.
- The profit maximizing firm will hire labour according to MRP = MC at point X, resulting in QL_1 of labour being hired.
- The workers are all then paid the average wage W_1 (connect QL_1 to the AW = S curve to obtain W_1).
- Note that if this firm were operating in a perfectly competitive labour market, the equilibrium wage would be W_2 and the quantity of labour Q_{L2}.

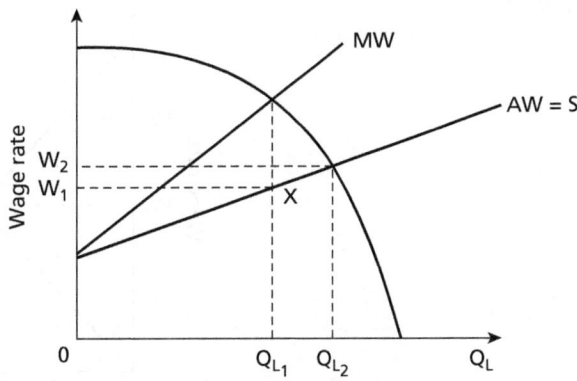

Figure 14.3 Wage determination in an imperfect labour market (monopsony)

The introduction of a union in a perfect labour market or the effect of a legal minimum wage rate

Labour unions bargain for higher wages. In Figures 14.4 and 14.5, the introduction of a union in a perfect labour market is analysed. Note the following:

- Before the introduction of a union, the equilibrium quantity of labour and wage rate were QL_1 and W_1, respectively.
- Figure 14.5 shows the union's wage demand at the newly negotiated wage rate of W_2, causing demand for labour to fall

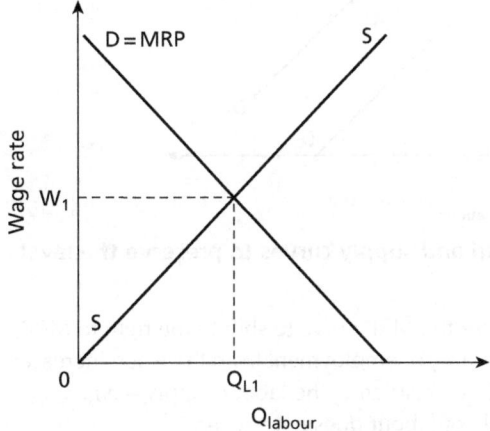

Figure 14.4 Before union negotiated wage rate or legal minimum wage

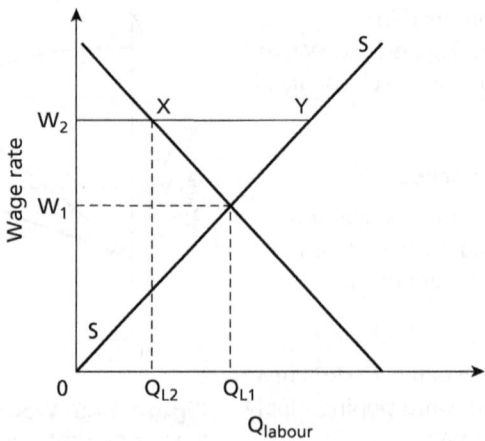

Figure 14.5 After union negotiated wage or legal minimum wage

- Since, because of the minimum wage, no labour will be hired under wage rate W_2, then W_2XYS is, in effect, the new supply curve of labour. There is excess labour at wage rate W_2 equal to XY.
- If the union has total control over XY of surplus labour, then the wage rate will be W_2.
- It is possible to leave employment unaffected if the demand curve could shift to the right or the supply curve to the left, thereby preserving the equilibrium quantity of W_1. Refer to Figure 14.6

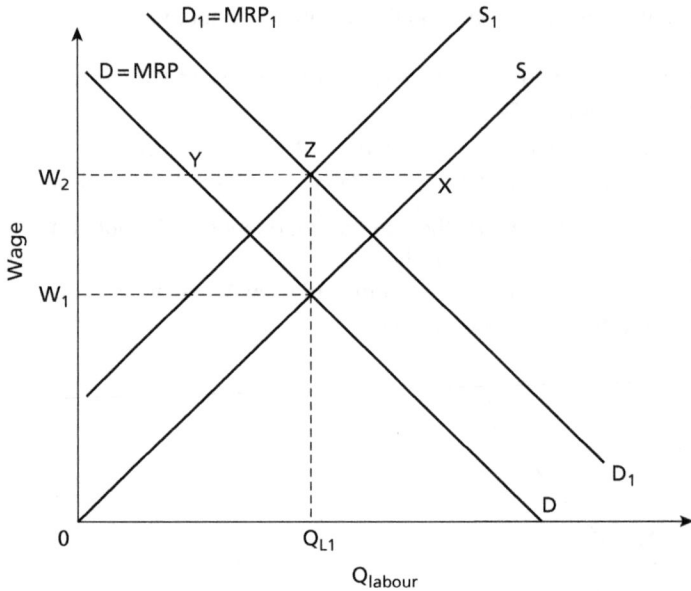

Figure 14.6 Shifts of the demand and supply curves to preserve the level of unemployment

- Increased productivity could cause the MRP curve to shift to the right to MRP_1 intersecting W_2XS at Z, protecting Q_{L1} of employment from the wage increase;
- Shifting the supply curve left to S_1 by restricting the labour supply – e.g. apprenticeships so that the supply of labour does not exceed S_1.

Unions and an imperfect labour market

A union negotiated higher wage rate with a monopsonistic buyer of labour increases both wage and employment in the firm. Refer to Figures 14.7 and 14.8.

WAGE DIFFERENTIALS

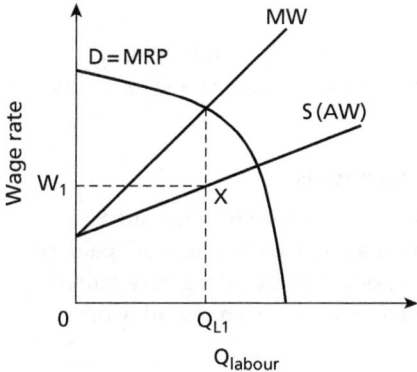

Figure 14.7 Before union intervention

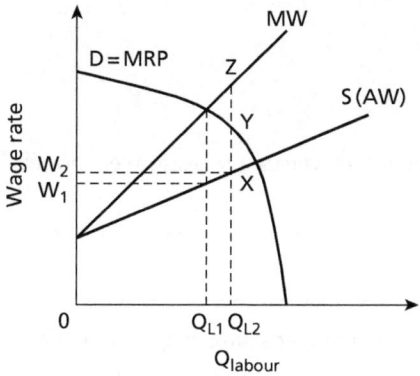

Figure 14.8 Post union intervention

Figure 14.7 represents the familiar monopsonist wage of W_1.

Note:

- When the minimum wage (MW) is equated with MRP, QL_1 of labour is paid the average wage of W_1.
- With the entry of a union or legal minimum wage, a wage of W_2 is negotiated above the non-union wage of W_1, in effect making W_2XS the new supply (AW) curve (Figure 14.8).
- Note that the upward MW curve is drawn to reflect the AW curve (it is higher).
- To construct an MW curve related to XS would result in the MW curve ZMW.

In fact, the MW curve related to W_2XS consists of two portions: W_2X and ZMW.

- The dotted line connecting these two gives an odd shaped MW curve W_2XZ (MW) resulting in a profit maximizing QL_2 of labour.
- All workers are then paid W_2 (connect QL_2 to the AW curve). Note that profit maximizing equilibrium point is Y, where MW = MRP.

The conclusion is simply an increase in wages from W_1 to W_2, whether by a union or the government legal minimum wage, in fact increases both wages and employment from QL_1 to QL_2. The minimum wage in this case alleviates poverty. However, the ability of unions to achieve an increase in wages may also be determined by:

- Public support;
- The extent of a strike fund;
- The elasticity of demand for the product and labour producing it;
- Solidarity with other unions;
- The state of the economy;
- The strength or power of the union itself;
- Government industrial relations law;
- The role of employer's associations.

Employer's associations

Employer's associations unite in their bid to negotiate wages with unions. They meet for the purpose of having consensus on the wage rate that is in their collective interest.

Compensating or equalizing wage differentials

Compensating or equalizing wage differentials are wages which reward a worker for the negative impacts or sacrifices of a job. Higher wages are paid for dangerous jobs – e.g. miners, oil well drillers, or persons working in isolation or overtime. These differences in wages are referred to as **compensating** or **equalizing differentials**.

Wages may also differ in the same profession due to:

- Security;
- Gender;
- Qualification and experience;
- Flat rate versus piece rate of pay;
- Private versus public sectors;
- Rural versus urban workers and boom economy versus a recession. economy.

Test Your Knowledge

1. Distinguish between wage differentials and compensating wage differentials.

2. State four causes of wage differentials.

3. Using two of the causes identified in Q2, explain why wages differ.

4. Explain why a legal minimum wage will alleviate poverty in a monopolistic labour market.

5. Distinguish between wage differentials and compensating wage differentials.

6. State four causes of wage differentials.

7. Using two of the causes identified in Q2, explain why wages differ.

8. Explain why a legal minimum wage will alleviate poverty in a monopolistic labour market but not in a perfect labour market.

MULTIPLE CHOICE QUESTIONS

1. Wages differ among workers due to:
   (a) Labour markets that are not perfect;
   (b) Seniority;
   (c) Different level of skill;
   (d) All of the above.

2. Figure (a) represents:
   (a) A perfect labour market;
   (b) A perfect labour market that is unionized;
   (c) A monopsonistic labour market;
   (d) A monopsonistic labour market that is unionized.

3. Figure (b) represents:
   (a) A monopsonistic labour market;
   (b) A monopsonistic labour market that is unionized;
   (c) A perfect labour market;
   (d) A perfect labour market that is unionized.

4. In Figure (b), the marginal wage is higher than the average wage:
   (a) Because it costs more to hire an additional worker;
   (b) The union is very powerful;
   (c) Workers sacrifice leisure;
   (d) Workers are given an incentive to work harder.

5. In Figures (a) and (b), the supply curve of labour is upward sloping due to:
   (a) A negative income effect;
   (b) A negative substitution effect;
   (c) The sacrifice of leisure time;
   (d) Increasing costs of training.

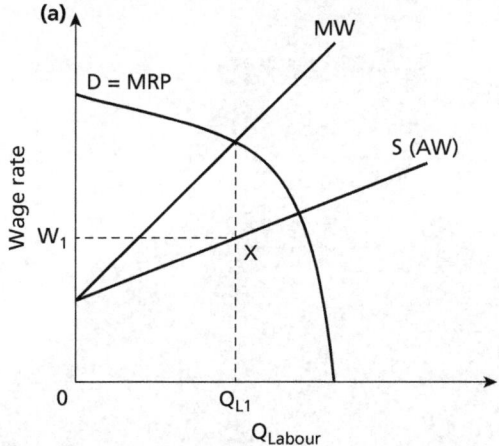

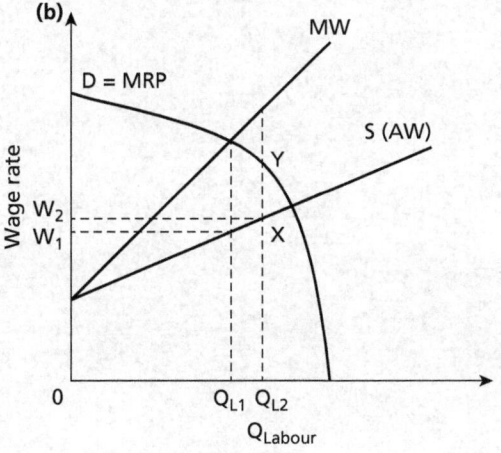

Chapter 15
Income Inequality, Poverty and Poverty Alleviation

INCOME INEQUALITY, POVERTY AND POVERTY ALLEVIATION

Functional distribution of income

- The functional distribution of income analyses how income is distributed among the factors of production. Wages, interest, rent and profit are paid to labour, capital, land and the entrepreneur.
- The size distribution of income measures how the total income of a country is distributed among the different income groups in the population.

Income inequality

Income inequality refers to the uneven distribution of income among the population.

Measures of income inequality

Two common ways to measure income equality are: the Lorenz curve and the Gini coefficient.

Lorenz curve

Refer to Figure 15.1.

Figure 15.1 represents a Lorenz curve which measures the equality in the size distribution of income.

Note:

- The horizontal axis measures the cumulative percentage of the population starting from the poorest to the richest.
- The vertical axis gives the percentage share of the total income. For example, the first 20% of the population measures the poorest 20% of the population on the vertical axis.
- The 45° line illustrates a perfectly even distribution of income – e.g. the poorest 20% of the country on the horizontal axis is receiving 20% of the total income on the vertical axis.

Learning Objectives

By the end of this chapter you should be able to:
- Differentiate between size and functional distribution of income
- Explain income inequality
- Explain measures of income inequality
- Explain measures to reduce income inequality
- Distinguish between absolute and relative poverty
- Outline factors that cause poverty
- Explain why certain categories of people are prone to poverty
- Evaluate the different ways to measure poverty
- Outline government strategies to alleviate poverty
- Analyse the economic costs of poverty
- Assess the economic benefits of government intervention to alleviate poverty

Exam tip

Regularly tested by CAPE.

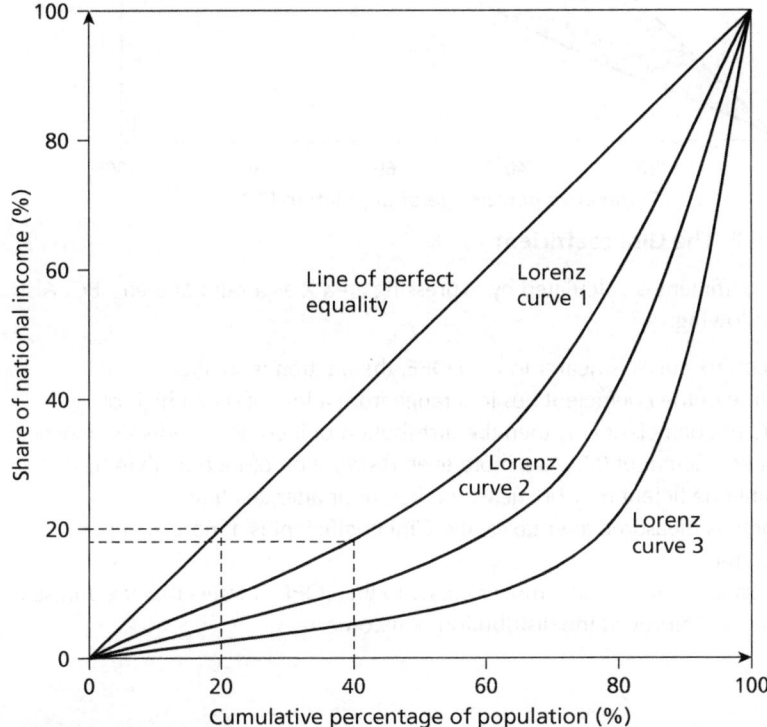

Figure 15.1 The Lorenz curve

The 45% line therefore, is called the **line of perfect equality** (LOPE). In reality, the Lorenz curve is likely to be a curved line.

In Figure 15.1, it is assumed that the Lorenz curve is measured prior to the imposition of taxes.

Note:

- For Lorenz curve #1, 40% of the population is only earning 18% of the total income.
- Lorenz curves #2 and #3 show increasing inequalities in the distribution of income.
- The further to the right that the Lorenz curve moves, the greater will be the inequality of distribution.
- The nearer to the LOPE, the distribution of incomes will be more even.

Gini coefficient

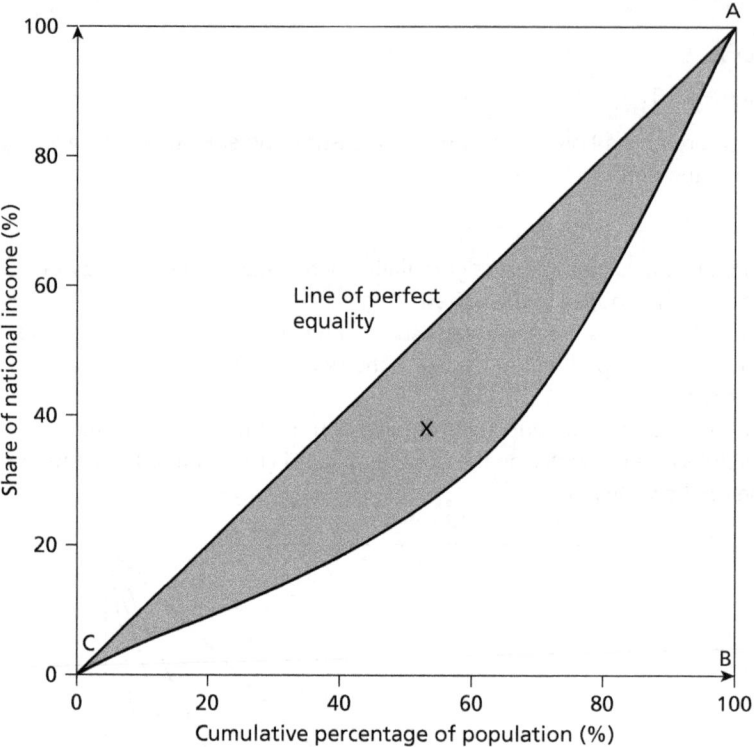

Figure 15.2 The Gini coefficient

The Gini coefficient is calculated by expressing area X as a ratio of area ABC. Also note the following:

- If the Lorenz curve is nearer to the LOPE, the fraction is smaller
- The value of the coefficient lies in a range from a low of 0 to a high of 1.
- If the Gini coefficient is 1, then the distribution of income is perfectly uneven.
- A Gini coefficient of 0.25 is a more even distribution of income than 0.45.
- The Gini coefficient may be measured before or after taxation.
- If income is measured after taxes, the Gini coefficient is a more accurate measurement.
- As a post-tax Lorenz curve moves closer to the LOPE, it infers that tax adjusted income has improved the distribution of income.

INCOME INEQUALITY, POVERTY AND POVERTY ALLEVIATION

Factors that cause income inequality

The factors which cause income inequality in the size distribution of income are:

Human capital and education Higher incomes are earned by skilled workers who are trained.

Household size Where there are large families, the income per person will be low if there is a sole earner.

Marital status A single parent earns less than a gainfully employed married couple. Also, if individuals are divorced with dependents, the income per dependent is reduced.

Age and seniority The older one becomes, the greater will be earnings through promotion and seniority. Older persons tend to be in more positions of management than younger persons.

Geographical location Workers in urban areas tend to have higher incomes than those in rural areas because the demand for skilled labour in commercial districts attracts high wages – e.g. a medical practitioner practicing in a town rather than in a rural setting.

Ability Highly skilled individuals with high demand for their skills earn high incomes and salaries – e.g. gifted athletes, underwater welders.

Inheritance Persons inheriting wealth use their inheritance to enlarge their income and wealth.

Work intensity Men tend to earn higher wages than women based on a combination of gender discrimination and duration of service. They are given more training and work in high value industries such as banking and petrochemicals. Semi-skilled women tend to work in secretarial services or flower shops, or as waitresses.

Discrimination Minorities tend to earn less in multicultural societies due to ethnic and religious discrimination.

Measures designed to reduce income inequality

Benefits in cash and kind

The government may correct the unequal distribution of income in the following ways.

- Progressive taxation based on horizontal equity – i.e. persons with the same circumstances having the same liability;
- Price ceilings – maximum prices that may be charged by law for basic necessities to life – e.g. rent control for housing and basic food items;
- Price floors – minimum prices to protect producers with fluctuating incomes – e.g. farmers;
- Subsidies which reduce prices of selected goods – e.g. food and gasoline;
- Subsidies for basic medicines;
- Government scholarships for education and professional training – e.g. teachers;
- Direct provision of merit goods – education, libraries, museum, sporting facilities, health facilities;
- Transfer payment – monetary or non-monetary payment intended to reduce income inequality; such as:
  - Assistance to vulnerable groups – e.g. single parents, the disabled;
  - Old age assistance;
  - Care for unwed mothers;
  - 'Smart card' voucher for the purchase of basic amenities;
  - Bus transport – for pensioners and school children;
  - School meals;
  - Self-help and other state-funded training.

Absolute poverty and relative poverty

Absolute poverty arises when an individual has limited access to food, water, clothing and transport.

Relative poverty is experienced if someone is living below an average standard of living. For example, in some countries a basic standard of living may be ownership of a house, car or refrigerator.

Factors that contribute to poverty

Social and physical environment

The socially displaced may not have reliable access to water, electricity, good roads, transport or social amenities such as schools, hospitals, community centres, recreational facilities and places of worship.

Discrimination

Discrimination such as unfair treatment due to ethnicity, gender, religion, or income status may deny someone employment opportunities and services in the public domain.

Restrictions from certain economic activities

A lack of training and education may limit opportunities to obtain a rewarding job and to engage in professions such as the law and medicine.

Non-ownership of resources

This involves having very limited legal access to land and property, savings and ownership of capital.

Persons most susceptible to poverty

Persons most at risk with respect to poverty are found in the following categories:

- **Physically challenged** People with physical or mental disabilities encounter difficulty in finding employment due to insufficient training or discrimination.
- **The elderly** Elderly persons do not have the capacity to work and earn a living, and live on private or state pensions that are insufficient for their needs.
- **Young individuals** Most young persons have limited earning power since they are at the entry point of their careers.
- **Indigenous people** Indigenous people are discriminated against and are also prone to poverty since they practice traditional methods of subsistence farming and craft for a limited market.

Poverty may be measured in the following ways:

- **Basic needs** The basic needs measurement identifies the minimum requirements necessary to sustain life, such as food, water, shelter clothing and transport.
- **The poverty line** The poverty line refers to the minimum level of income necessary to meet one's basic needs. This is called the basic needs poverty line.
- A related concept is the **relative poverty line** which identifies the minimum income necessary to live an average standard of living as determined for a region such as the Caribbean.
- **Head count** The head count index of poverty measures the percentage of the population that lives below the poverty line.
- **Human Development Index** The Human Development Index (HDI) is a measure of poverty and is linked to three indicators: life expectancy, literacy levels (which includes school enrolment at all levels) and per capita GDP.

INCOME INEQUALITY, POVERTY AND POVERTY ALLEVIATION

The costs of poverty

The **costs of poverty** include the following:

- The loss of output arising out of unemployed human resources who are ill-trained due to their lack of education and skill.
- The diverting of government expenditure from developing infrastructure and public and merit goods to provide poverty alleviation.
- Social decline – crime, drug addiction, marriage breakdown related to low levels of literacy and suicide rates are all the by-products of poverty.
- Environmental costs – poverty leads to squatter settlements in which slash and burn subsistence causes erosion of land and flooding.
- The existence of slum communities in urban centres gives rise to the dumping of garbage, sewerage effluent and polluted waterways, all with harmful effects on the environment.

Economic benefits of poverty alleviating measures

The **economic benefits of poverty alleviating measures** may be summarized as follows:

- The provision of health and education leads to improvements in literacy levels and has a positive impact on productivity.
- There is also an increase in the standard of living over time.
- The distribution of income becomes more equitable over time.

Linkages are developed between sectors – e.g. agriculture and processing, banking and transport, craft and tourism. Measures to reduce poverty also fall into two basic categories:

- Benefits in cash;
- Benefits in kind.

Benefits: some limitations

Not all who are entitled to these benefits receive them because of lack of information – e.g. failure to disclose personal information, ignorance, illiteracy and pride. Vulnerable groups such as the physically and mentally challenged are not necessarily included in the social safety net.

The inequality of the distribution of income and wealth and poverty invariably focus on social welfare. **Social welfare** must be seen as the best distribution of resources.

The benefits of any social welfare programme funded by the state may be for reasons of:

- Welfare equity;
- Beneficial externality.

Welfare equity is the creation of a fair society.

Beneficial externality is the provision of education and health, the benefits of which go beyond the direct benefit to the recipient to promote productivity.

- Welfare programmes have been criticized by economists and other commentators for creating a dependency syndrome.
- Social welfare involves the most efficient allocation of resources and the best distribution of those resources.
- Poverty may be absolute if a person's income cannot purchase the basic necessities of life.
- The poverty line is calculated under the assumption that an individual spends one third of their income on food. That number is multiplied by 3 and adjusted for family size.

- Social welfare programmes are designed by the government to alleviate poverty and reduce inequalities.
- Equity and equality are not the same. Equality means 'same quantity' while equity means 'fairness'. While equality is based on fact, fairness is based on judgement that varies according to society's expectations and standard of living.
- The objectives of government welfare programmes may be based on equity, poverty reduction, beneficial externality, paternalism and votechasing.
- Apart from the poverty line, the HDI and the measure of economic welfare (MEW) are other measures of welfare or standard of living.

Test Your Knowledge

1. (a) Give two cases of the high levels of poverty in the Caribbean;
   (b) The Gini coefficient in Dominica changed from 0.34 to 0.46 between 1998 and 2000. Explain what this change implies about the dynamics of poverty in Dominica during that period;
   (c) Suggest one policy measure that may be useful in reducing poverty in the Caribbean.

2. Critically assess the role government should play with respect to each of the following:
   (a) The housing market;
   (b) National security;
   (c) Environmental degradation.

3. Explain each of the following:
   (a) How can regulation be used to remove the effects of monopoly power?
   (b) How can taxes or subsidies be used to remove the effects of externalities?
   (c) How can governments intervene to ensure optimal production of public goods?

4. Explain the meaning of each of the following terms:
   (a) Functional distribution of income;
   (b) Inequality;
   (c) Gini coefficient;
   (d) Lorenz curve;
   (e) What is the range of values of the Gini coefficient?
   (f) What do the values of the Gini coefficient indicate about the unequal distribution of income?

5. (a) List three measures that government can take to achieve an equal distribution of income.
   (b) Explain how each of the measures listed in (5a) is used to achieve the goal of income equity.

6. Define the term poverty.

INCOME INEQUALITY, POVERTY AND POVERTY ALLEVIATION

MULTIPLE CHOICE QUESTIONS

1. ABC Co. paid rent in the amount of $10,000, interest $6000, and wages of $20,000; and realized a profit of $25,000.

   For the factor of production capital, how much did ABC Co. pay?
   (a) $10,000;
   (b) $6000;
   (c) $20,000;
   (d) $25,000.

2. For the factor of production entrepreneurship, how much did the ABC company pay?
   (a) 10,000;
   (b) $6000;
   (c) $20,000;
   (d) $25,000.

3. In the figure below, which of the of the Lorenz curves indicates the poorest distribution of income?
   (a) Lorenz curve 1;
   (b) Lorenz curve 2;
   (c) Lorenz curve 3;
   (d) The 45° line.

4. In the figure above, which of the of the Lorenz curves indicates a perfectly even distribution of income?
   (a) Lorenz curve 1;
   (b) Lorenz curve 2;
   (c) Lorenz curve 3;
   (d) The 45° line.

5. In the figure below, the Gini coefficient is calculated as:
   (a) Area X/AC;
   (b) Area BC/X;
   (c) Area X/ABC;
   (d) Area X/AB.

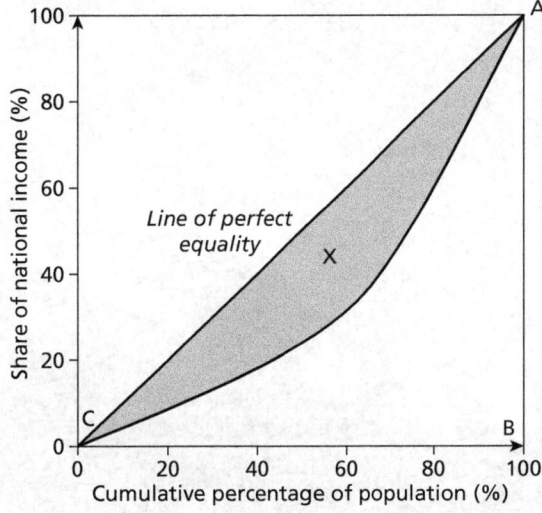

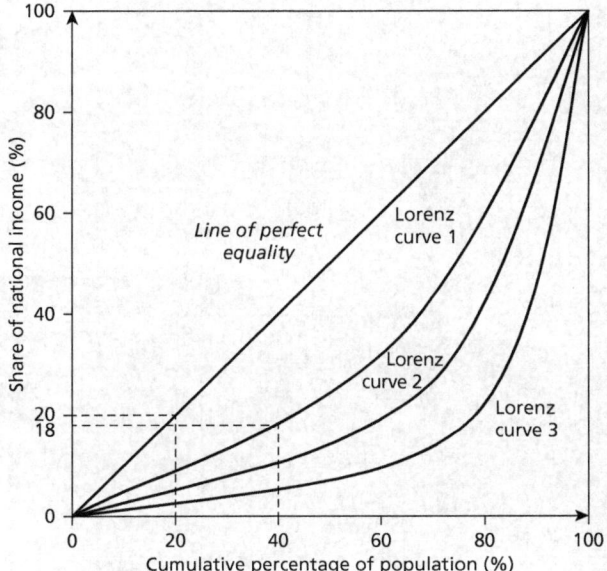

Chapter 16: National Income Accounting

NATIONAL INCOME ACCOUNTING

The circular flow of income

The circular flow of income diagram was briefly introduced to explain factor rewards and the functional distribution of income. Figure 16.1 presents this model and shows how the income earned by factor inputs is used to purchase the output of firms.

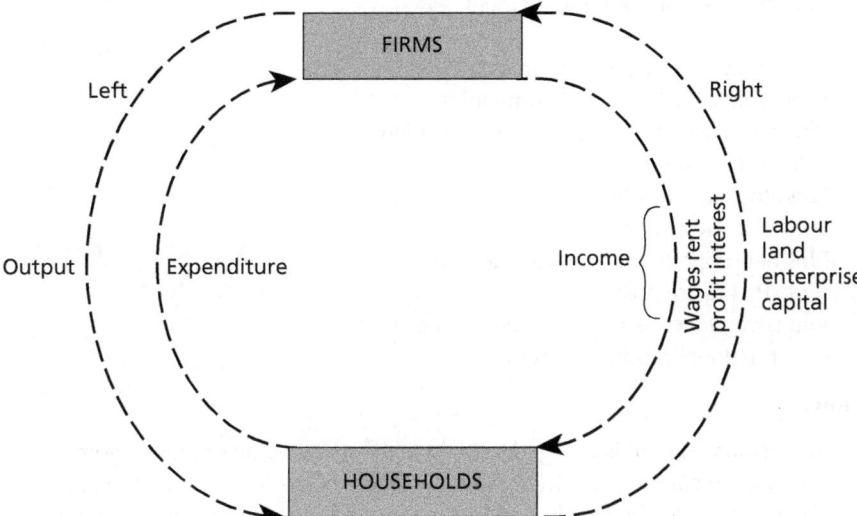

Figure 16.1 The circular flow in a two-sector circular flow diagram

Figure 16.1 shows:

- A simplified exchange of money for output in a two-sector economy consisting of producers and consumers. It is called a closed economy – without government and the foreign sector.
- Producers pay factors incomes – such as wages, interest, rent and profit – in return for labour, capital, land and enterprise supplied by households.
- Producers use these factor inputs to create planned output, which is purchased by consumers under planned spending. It is assumed that households do not save and therefore spend all incomes earned.
- Two more sectors could be added to this flow of income: the government – who contribute spending but take out taxes to the circular flow, and the foreign sector – who contribute export earnings and take out import spending.

All activities in the model in figure 16.1 contribute to gross domestic product (GDP), gross national product (GNP) and net national product (NNP).

Gross domestic product (GDP) is the monetary value of the flow of output produced within the land and maritime boundaries of a country over a 12-month period.

Gross national product (GNP) measures the value of output of factors of production of the home country at home or abroad. GNP = GDP + net property income from abroad.

Net national product (NNP) = GNP – depreciation.

Depreciation takes place when capital assets depreciate over the 12-month period, or become out-dated and are replaced. NNP = GNP – depreciation = NNP or national income.

There are three ways to measure the national income of a country. These are: the income method, the expenditure method; and the output method.

Learning Objectives

By the end of the chapter you should be able to:

- Explain the circular flow of income
- Explain the concept of national income accounting
- Explain the different ways of deriving national income accounts
- Interpret national income statistics
- Use national income accounts to analyse the performance on an economy as a whole
- Derive real GDP from nominal GDP
- Explain the limitations of GDP

Exam tip

Often tested at CAPE.

Exam tip

Often tested at CAPE.

Exam tip

Often tested at CAPE.

Exam tip

Often tested at CAPE.

The income method

The income method of calculating national income is related to the wages, interest, profit and rent that the factor inputs earn when they are sold to producers.

The income method runs as follows:

> Income from employment
> Plus income from self-employment
> Plus rent
> Plus profits of private companies
> Plus profit of nationalized companies
> Plus estimated charge for occupied residence
> = Total domestic income
> Less stock appreciation
> = GDP at factor cost
> Plus net property income from abroad
> = GNP at factor cost
> minus capital consumption (depreciation)
> = Net national product at factor cost

Note:

- An 'estimated rent' is charged to include the rental value of private homes.
- Stock appreciation is the increase in the value of stock caused by inflation.
- Factor cost is achieved when indirect taxes and subsidies are adjusted to GDP figures. (Indirect taxes increase prices and subsidies lower prices, so taxes are taken away and subsidies are added on.)
- Net property income represents the difference between outflows and inflows of interest, profits or dividends.
- Transfer payments are incomes received from non-economic activity and are not included in the income method – e.g. retirement pension paid by the government.

The expenditure method

The expenditure method of measuring national output is calculated by adding up the expenditure of the four main purchasers of the national output – i.e. consumers, firms, the government and the foreign sector. It is possible to derive a simple formula for this method. C (consumer spending) + I (investment spending) + G (government expenditure) + X (exports) – i.e. the formula $C + I + G + (X - M) = Y$ (national income) represents a concise way of measuring the value of a country's output using the expenditure method, which runs as follows:

> Consumer expenditure
> Plus general government final consumption
> Plus gross fixed investment
> Plus exports of goods and services
> = Total final expenditure at market prices
> Less import of goods and services
> = GDP at market prices
> Less indirect taxes
> Plus subsidies
> = GDP at factor cost
> Plus net property income from abroad
> = GNP at factor cost
> Less depreciation
> = Net national product at factor cost (national income)

Notes on the expenditure method

- The value of physical increases in stock and work-in-progress is part of the flow of output produced and must therefore be counted, even if it is not sold.

- GDP at market prices means GDP that has not been adjusted for the effects of subsidies and indirect taxes.

The output method

The output method totals the output of the different sectors of an economy – e.g. agriculture, forestry, fishing, manufacturing, construction, distribution and transportation.

The value of the final output of all the different sectors is added up and adjusted for double counting. For example, the value of intermediate goods (e.g. lumber) contributes to the value of final goods (furniture) and could be counted twice. This is avoided by only counting the added value.

The uses of national income statistics

National income data may be used in the following ways:

- To analyse the allocation of resources;
- To calculate standard of living in a country by dividing the real national income by the population – this is called per capita income;
- To measure short-term economic growth;
- To compare standards of living between countries;
- To guide economic planning since it will reveal which sectors are growing and which are in decline.

The limitations of national income statistics

National income data fails to give a realistic reflection of the factors that do determine the standard of living. Factors that affect the standard of living in a country that are not represented by per capita are:

- The distribution of income as measured by the Lorenz curve or Gini coefficient;
- The extent of the illegal economy;
- Output created by 'do-it-yourself' projects undertaken by homeowners;
- The level of pollution;
- Life expectancy, infant mortality and literacy rates;
- The length of the working week and conditions of employment;
- The level of criminal activity;
- Respect for human rights.

> **Exam tip**
>
> Often tested at CAPE.

International comparisons

GDP and per capita income statistics that are used to measure the standard of living between countries may be misleading on the following grounds:

- Countries may have similar GDP but differ with respect to distribution of income.
- There is a need for a standard method of measurement if two countries' standard of living are to be compared, since different methods of calculation may be employed.
- Defence or military output may not affect a country's standard of living but will add high value to national accounts.
- The quality of goods and services and the working conditions of individuals in different countries may differ widely.
- Citizens residing in the temperate countries spend more money to cope with climate changes than residents in the tropical zone.

Alternative measures of standard of living

Other measures of standard of living are the Human Development Index (HDI) developed by the United Nations. This is an index of literacy levels, life expectancy and real per capita income.

Another measure is the Measure of Economic Welfare (MEW) developed by Nordhaus and Tobin. This adjusts GDP for positive and negative externalities.

An example of positive externalities is recreation; an example of a negative externality is criminal activity.

Nominal and real GDP

Nominal national income is calculated as price × quantity – e.g. in Table 16.1 it is $50 million.

> **Exam tip**
>
> Often tested at CAPE.

Real GDP is nominal GDP in a given year adjusted for price increases in a selected base year.

For example, in Table 16.1 if the base year is 2013, then nominal GDP is calculated as price × quantity, which is equal to $50 million:

(5 m × $4) + (6 m × $5)

Table 16.1 Nominal GDP in Year 1 at year 1 (2013) prices

Year	Goods	Quantity (m)	Unit Price ($)	Nominal GDP ($m)
2013	Oranges	5	4	20
2013	Bananas	6	5	30
				50

In the year 2014 (Table 16.2), nominal GDP for 2014 is $70 million.

Table 16.2 Nominal GDP in Year 2 (2014) at year 2 prices

Year	Goods	Quantity (m)	Unit Price ($)	Nominal GDP ($m)
2014	Oranges	8	5	40
2014	Bananas	5	6	30
				70

Real GDP in year 2014 at base year prices (2013) is calculated by multiplying the 2014 quantity of oranges by the base year price of oranges:

= 8 m × $4

= $32 m + 2014 quantity of bananas 5 m × at base year prices of bananas $5

= $25 m.

Real GDP for year 2014 = $57 m ($32 + $25) m as at Table 16.3.

Real GDP for 2013 is calculated in Table 16.1 – e.g.:

Quantity (oranges) 5 m × base year price $4   = $20 m
Added to quantity (bananas) 6 m × $5   = $30 m
Real GDP for 2013   = $50 m

In Table 16.3, year 2014 output at base year (2013) prices is $57 m.

Table 16.3 Real GDP in Year (2014) at base year prices (2013)

Year	Goods	Quantity (m)	Unit Price ($)	Nominal GDP ($m)
1	Oranges	8	4	32
1	Bananas	5	5	25
				57

The GDP deflator for any year is calculated according to the formula: nominal GDP/real GDP.

So, the GDP deflator year 2014 is: nominal GDP for 2014 = $70 divided by real GDP for 2014 = $57.

= $70 m/$57 m × 100 = 122.8

GDP deflator for year 2 = 122.8

NATIONAL INCOME ACCOUNTING

Test Your Knowledge

1. Explain the difference between gross domestic product (GDP) and gross national product (GNP).

2. Explain why each of the following is NOT counted in GDP calculations:
   (a) Purely financial transactions;
   (b) Second-hand sales.

3. Briefly describe how each of the following is calculated:
   (a) Net domestic product;
   (b) National income;
   (c) Disposable income.

4. Define the following:
   (a) GDP deflator;
   (b) The consumer price index.

MULTIPLE CHOICE QUESTIONS

1. The difference between gross domestic product (GDP) and gross national product (GNP) is:
   (a) Factor cost;
   (b) Depreciation;
   (c) Net property income;
   (d) The GDP deflator.

2. GDP is defined as:
   (a) The value of output of foreign investment;
   (b) The annual value of total output produced within the land and maritime boundaries of a country;
   (c) The value of output produced by national factors of production;
   (d) The value of output produced by domestic factors of production in foreign countries.

3. Calculate the GNP at factor costs in the table below:
   (a) $253 m;
   (b) $267 m;
   (c) $268 m;
   (d) $275 m.

Item	$ (m)
Exports and net property income from abroad	80
Imports and property income paid abroad	65
Taxes	25
Subsidies	18
Total domestic expenditure at market prices	260

4. Which of the following is NOT counted in GDP calculations?
   (a) Purely financial transactions;
   (b) Building a new house;
   (c) Building a new bridge;
   (d) Salesman commissions on a used car.

5. National income is calculated as:
   (a) GNP minus depreciation;
   (b) GDP minus net property income;
   (c) GNP minus net property income;
   (d) GNP plus factor costs.

Chapter 17: Classical Models of the Macro-Economy

CLASSICAL MODELS OF THE MACRO-ECONOMY

Introduction

Classic economics is based on the following main ideas:

- All markets are self-regulating because the price mechanism is able to eliminate any temporary disequilibrium in all markets.
- The economy would tend towards full employment in the long run as a result of flexibility in wage rates in labour markets.
- Equilibrium in the capital markets would be achieved through flexibility in the interest rate.
- Equilibrium in international trade would be achieved by exchange rate flexibility.

Classic theory also asserts that:

- The aggregate demand curve is left to right and downward sloping.
- The aggregate supply curve is vertical at long-run full employment.
- The economy is driven by the forces of the aggregate supply side and not by aggregate demand.
- The role of the government is to keep a stable stock of money to finance aggregate demand so that output can be absorbed.

The assumptions of classic theory are:

- A closed economy without interaction with the foreign sector;
- The supply of factors of production except capital is elastic in the short term;
- The goods and factor markets are responsive to price changes;
- There is equilibrium in all markets in the short run and the long run;
- All factors are identical in perfect markets.

The classic aggregate demand (AD) and aggregate supply (AS) model of the economy

Figure 17.1 represents a classic AS/AD model of the economy.

Note:

- The vertical axis represents the average price level that exists in the economy.
- The horizontal axis represents real GDP output.
- Figure 17.1 illustrates how the entire economy can reach equilibrium, where AD = AS.
- A downward sloping aggregate demand curve infers that an increased quantity in real GDP is demanded at lower price levels in the economy.

Learning Objectives

By the end of the chapter you should be able to:

- Outline the main classic and Keynesian ideas
- Explain the factors that influence aggregate demand and aggregate supply
- Explain shifts in aggregate demand and aggregate supply
- Interpret the long run supply curve
- Explain the flexibility of wages and prices
- Explain the role of wage price and interest rate flexibility
- Explain how full employment is restored in the classic model

Exam tip

Often tested at CAPE.

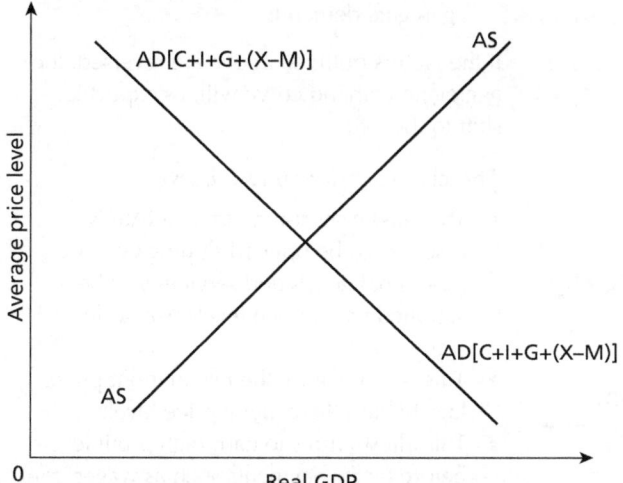

Figure 17.1 The AS/AD model

Consumption

- As the price level falls, consumers are able to purchase more goods and services with their income, which now has greater purchasing power.
- Rising price levels decrease purchasing power, and a reduced quantity of goods and services will be demanded.
- Rising prices lead to increased demand for money to meet typical everyday transactions, causing the interest rate to rise and causing mortgage rates to increase.
- As a result, consumers are unable to demand other goods and services.

Investment

- Lower price levels lower the interest rate, enabling firms to undertake investments that previously were not profitable.
- Lower interest rates also lower the cost of borrowing for raw materials.
- Firms' demand for capital increases at lower price levels.

Exports and imports

- Lower price levels enable cheaper domestic goods to be competitive in export markets.
- Foreign demand for domestic goods is likely to fall if domestic rates of inflation are higher than those of trading partners.

There is therefore greater aggregate demand (C + I + GX + M) for real output at lower price levels than at higher price levels.

Shifts in the AD curve

If the price level is unchanged, the following will shift the aggregate demand curve to the right:

- Positive economic growth;
- Increased consumer confidence, which will increase consumption expenditure;
- An increase in government spending will inject money into the economy, increasing the demand for output at the existing price levels;
- A positive business climate is optimistic;
- Growth in both the economy and government spending will impact favourably on employment;
- The increase in income will increase aggregate demand;
- An expansionary fiscal policy;
- An even distribution of wealth;
- Technologies that maximize credit purchases also have a favourable impact on aggregate demand.

If the factors outlined above are reversed, the aggregate demand curve will, as expected, shift to the left.

The classic short-run AS curve

- The classic short-run curve (SRAS) is assumed to be upward sloping because more final goods and services will be supplied when price levels rise, as in Figure 17.3.
- This is so because the rise in input prices lags behind the general price level.
- This allows firms to earn high profit levels before factor payments such as wages, rent and interest are renegotiated.

> **Exam tip**
> Often tested at CAPE.

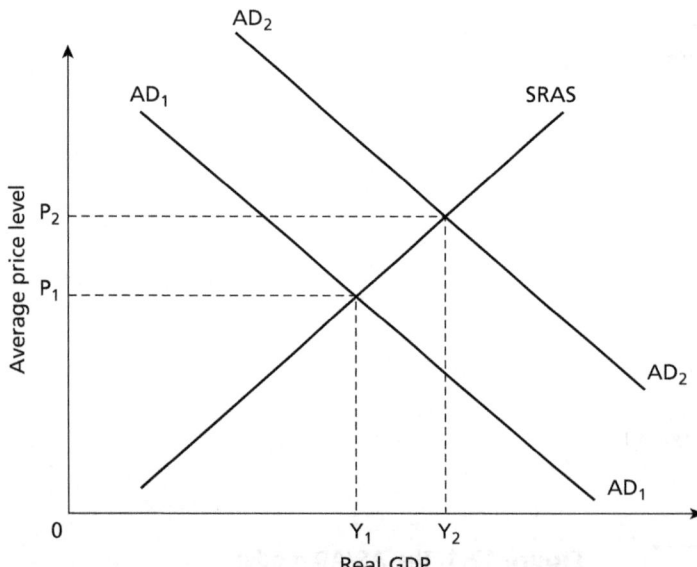

Figure 17.2 Shifts in the aggregate demand curve: classical model

CLASSICAL MODELS OF THE MACRO-ECONOMY

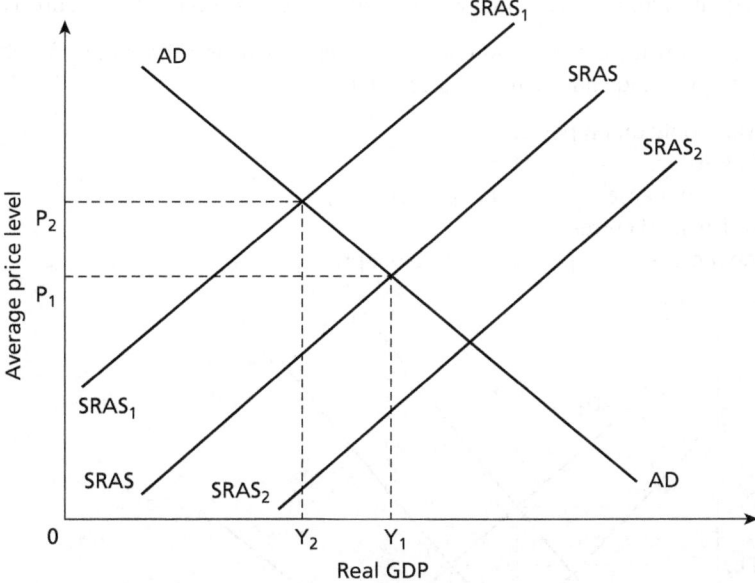

Figure 17.3 Shifts in the short-run aggregate supply curve: classical model

In Figure 17.3, a shift of the AS curve to the right (SRAS$_2$) is caused by factors other than the price level, such as:

- A government subsidy for certain types of goods and services;
- An increase in raw material prices will shift the AS curve to the left (SRAS$_1$) at the prevailing price level, as will an increase in wage rates;
- Indirect taxes, such as VAT, on almost all goods and services;
- If a country's exchange rate were to devalue, or the costs of imported goods were to rise, all of these factors would be likely to shift the AS curve to the left;
- The AS curve will shift to the left due to: (1) indirect taxes, (2) high raw material prices, or (3) failing labour productivity – all of which will cause reduced output and cause the economy to recede from Y$_1$ to Y$_2$.

The long-run AS curve

The classic long-run AS curve

See Figure 17.4

- Classical economists believed the long-run AS curve (LRAS) to be vertical at the level of full employment.
- The LRAS is influenced by factor prices such as wages, interest, rent, productivity, a trained labour force, technology and innovation.
- If the economy is operating at full capacity in the long run (Y$_{FE}$), increases in aggregate demand caused by lower taxes, low interest rates or increased government spending would cause the AD curve to move up the vertical AS curve, resulting in a rising price level from PL$_1$ to PL$_2$.

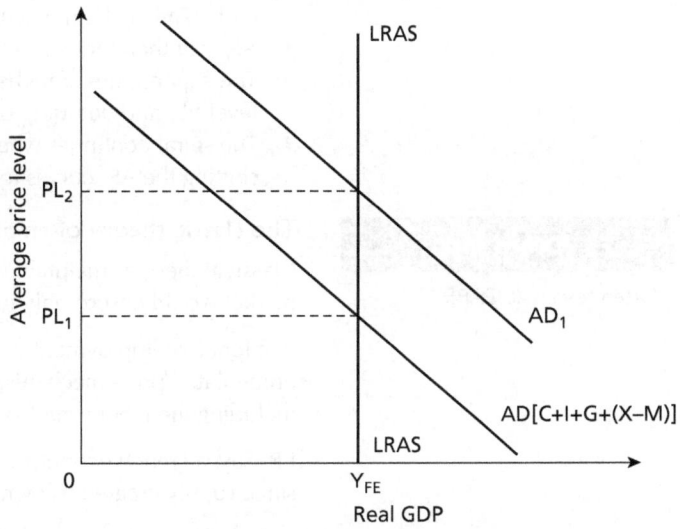

Figure 17.4 Rising price level in the long run at full employment

The equilibrium level of output is achieved where AD equals AS in Figure 17.5.

The following factors may cause the AS curves initially to shift to the left, initiating a price spiral and causing real output to fall.

- Monopoly union power;
- Indirect taxes – e.g. VAT;
- Wage increases unrelated to productivity;
- A devalued currency;
- An increase in imported raw material prices.

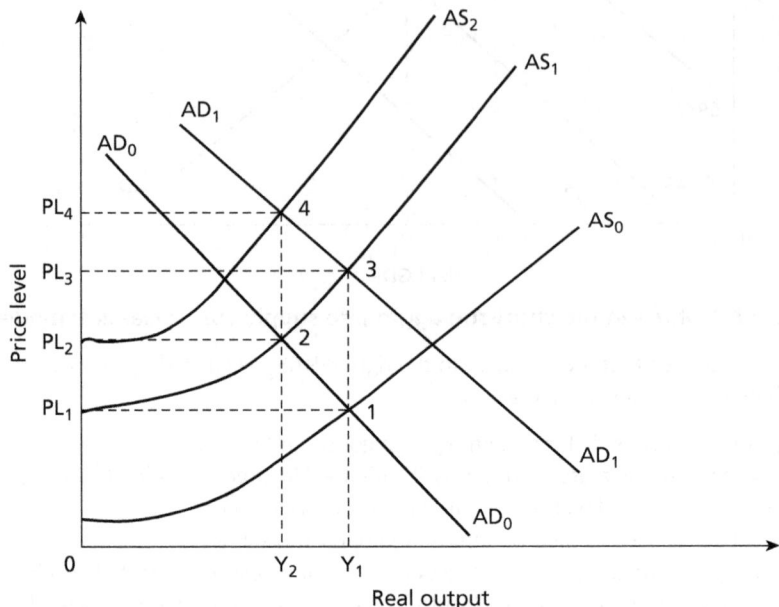

Figure 17.5 Interaction of AD and AS curves

Figure 17.5 illustrates how the movement of both curves can lead to a rise in the price level.

Note:

- Equilibrium is at output Y_1 and price level of PL_1.
- Wages paid as a result of new wage agreements increase costs of production and create a chain reaction.
- AS_0 will therefore shift to AS_1 and a new price level of PL_2 and output Y_2.
- The expenditure of higher wages paid will cause AD_0 to shift to AD_1 to price level PL_3 and output Y_1 once more.
- The spiral continues when PL_3 leads to fresh demand for increased wages, shifting the AS_1 curves to AS_2 and so on according to the wage price spiral.

The classic theory of employment

Classical theories maintained that the unregulated price mechanism in the labour market would ensure only frictional (voluntary) unemployment in the long run.

Frictional unemployment would be the only consequence based on: (1) the unregulated price mechanism bringing all markets into long-run equilibrium, including the labour market; and (2) Say's law of markets.

J.B. Say, a French economist, claimed that unemployment should never exist, since supply created its own demand.

Exam tip

Often tested at CAPE.

He claimed that:

- The payment of wages, interest, profit and rent provided income to purchase the output created by firms in a two-sector economy.
- The act of supplying goods and services would cause factors of production to be hired.
- These factor rewards enable the purchase of the output of the firms.
- Aggregate demand should then always be equal to aggregate supply.

The short-run equilibrium: how free market forces bring the labour market into equilibrium

- Classical theorists claim that if unemployment existed, then the supply of labour would be greater than the demand for labour.

In Figure 17.6, the vertical axis shows real wages.

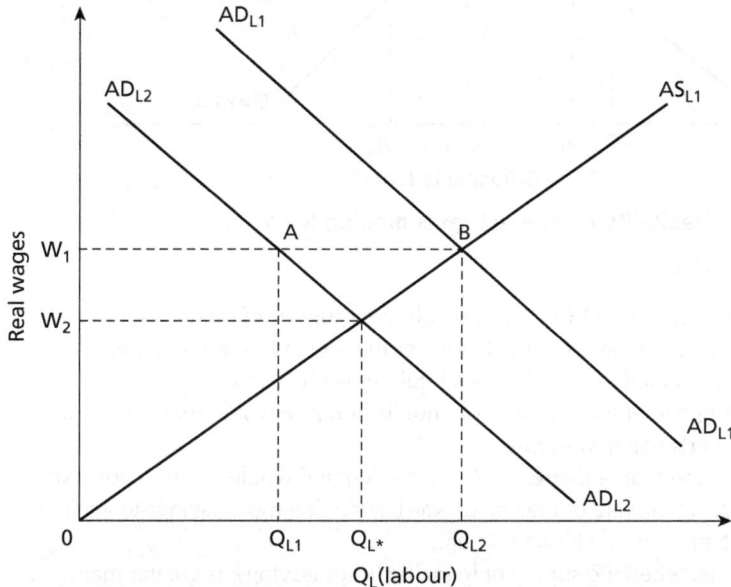

Figure 17.6 The flexibility of wage rates to eliminate unemployment

The sequence is as follows:

1. The supply of labour is greater than demand at AB.
2. Wage levels are pushed down as a result.
3. Firms, seeing that labour costs are low, will demand more cheap labour to make a profit.
4. Surplus labour is therefore employed.

Classic theory also advanced the notion that money and capital markets would tend to equilibrium-making savings equal to investment, which is explained as follows:

- Loanable funds are depositors' funds that banks lend to firms.
- In Figure 17.7, the demand for loanable funds is assumed to come from firms who wish to invest.
- Classic theory assumes that the demand for capital is represented by the marginal efficiency of capital (MEC) curve.
- The supply curve represents depositors who would deposit more into banks as the rate of interest increases.
- The rate of interest is the market price for loanable funds.

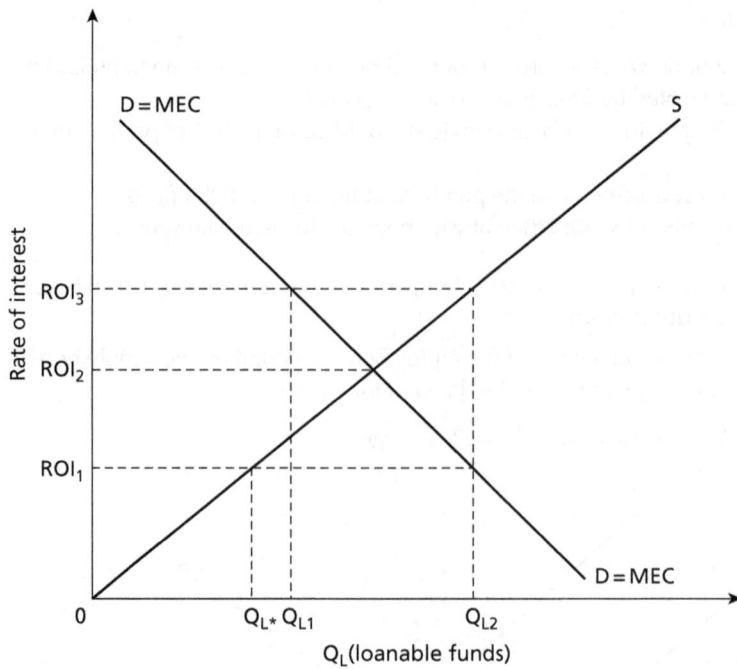

Figure 17.7 Flexibility of interest rates making S = 1

Note the following:

- If the rate of interest is ROI_3, there would be a surplus of funds of QL_1QL_2.
- Banks would therefore be forced to lower the rate of interest to attract borrowers. A situation called **excess liquidity** is said to exist.
- The clearing rate of interest ROI_2 or **equilibrium rate** would make demand for loanable funds equal to supply.
- Similarly, if the rate of interest is ROI_1, the demand would, in this case, exceed supply forcing the rate of interest upward, attracting more savings to achieve eventual equilibrium with investment.
- To conclude, when the supply of loanable funds (savings) is greater than demand (investment), the rate of interest will fall, making savings equal to investment. If investment demand is greater than savings, the opposite will result.

External market equilibrium

The external market is also self-regulating and is explained as follows:

- When import spending is greater than export earnings, the resulting deficit would cause a fall in a country's exchange rate (provided it is flexible) and make exports competitive once again.
- Both prices and wages would fall as a result, making domestic production cheaper.
- This would provide a stimulus to exports and a disincentive to imports.

Important point

The flexibility of prices in the labour market, loanable funds and external trade markets would ensure that there would be equilibrium in the final analysis. There is, therefore, a built-in tendency towards full employment equilibrium in the long run, according to classic economic thinking.

TEST YOUR KNOWLEDGE
MULTIPLE CHOICE QUESTIONS

1. Classic economics is based mainly on:
   (a) A major role for the government;
   (b) Free market forces to achieve macroeconomic market equilibrium;
   (c) Stimulating aggregate demand as a main policy;
   (d) Taxation as a main policy.

2. Classical economists claim that there will be long-run full employment due to:
   (a) A flexible wage rate which will clear any disequilibrium with frictional unemployment;
   (b) The supporting role of unions;
   (c) The government providing employment for all workers;
   (d) Employment from foreign direct investment (FDI).

3. According to classical economists, the capital market will always be in equilibrium because:
   (a) The government will borrow any excess capital;
   (b) The government will supply any shortage of capital;
   (c) A flexible interest rate will always ensure savings equal to investment;
   (d) Foreign lending agencies will ensure equilibrium.

4. The classical aggregate demand (AD) curve is:
   (a) Vertical;
   (b) Horizontal;
   (c) Upward sloping;
   (d) Left to right and downward sloping.

5. The long-run classic aggregate supply (AS) curve is:
   (a) Horizontal;
   (b) Vertical at long-run full employment;
   (c) Part horizontal and part vertical;
   (d) Left to right and upward sloping.

Chapter 18
The Keynesian Model of the Macro-Economy

The role of consumption and savings on economic activity

Consumption is expenditure by consumers on goods and services that satisfy wants.

Consumption consists of two parts:

- fixed or autonomous consumption
- induced consumption which J.M. Keynes expressed in the equation:
  C = a + bYd
  where C = consumption
  a = fixed or autonomous consumption
  b = the fraction of every additional dollar earned that is consumed called the **marginal propensity to consume** (MPC)
  Yd = disposable income.

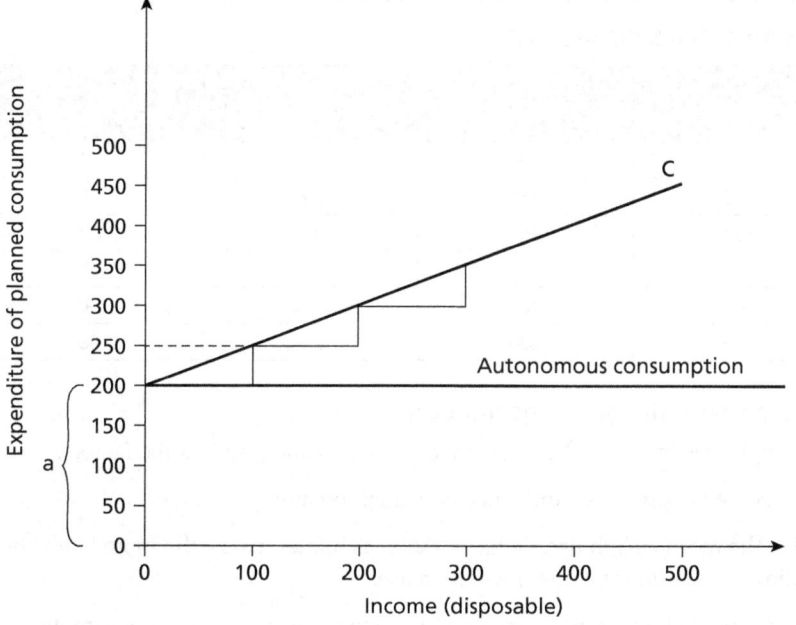

Figure 18.1 A consumption function

In Figure 18.1, note:

- At 0 income, consumption is $200.
- At 0 income, consumption is financed from past savings.
- At 0 income or any other level of income, the level of autonomous consumption is fixed.
- The letter 'b' in the equation above represents the fraction of every additional dollar earned that goes to consumption – the MPC.

If income increases from $300 to $400 and the change in consumption is $50, then $50 out of an additional $100 is equal to 0.5. The letter 'b' therefore represents this fraction of every additional dollar earned given to consumption or the MPC.

In Figure 18.1, 50/100 or 0.5 may be calculated as $\Delta C/\Delta Y$. Rewriting the consumption function with these values, C = a + bY becomes C = 200 + 0.5Y.

A related concept is the **average propensity to consume** or APC, which is represented by the formula $\frac{C}{Y}$. In Figure 18.2 at a consumption level of 200, it is 200/200 = 1Y.

Learning Objectives

By the end of this chapter you should be able to:

- Explain the consumption function
- Explain the relationship between saving and consumption
- Calculate the simple multiplier
- Explain the effect of changes in investment on national income
- Explain the effect of government spending on national income
- Describe the effect of withdrawals and injections on national income
- Explain the relationship between net exports and national income
- Determine the equilibrium level of national income
- Explain inflationary and deflationary gaps

Exam tip

Tested at CAPE.

Exam tip

Tested at CAPE.

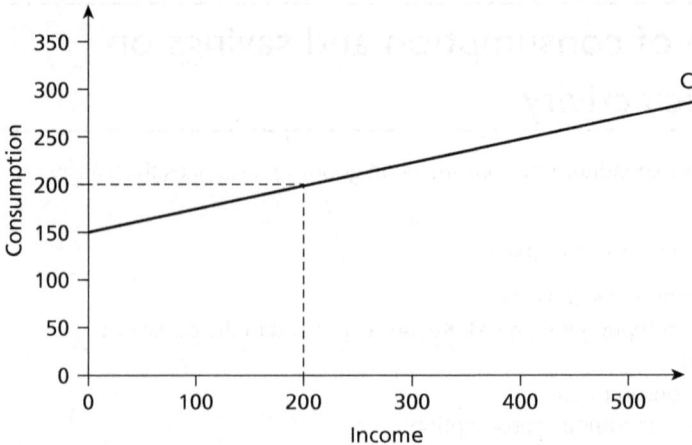

Figure 18.2 Average propensity to consume (APC)

When the consumption function is a straight line, the MPC is constant, while the APC is declining in value throughout. See Table 18.1.

> **Exam tip**
>
> Tested at CAPE – MCQ.

Table 18.1 The MPC and APC

Income	Consumption	MPC $\left(\dfrac{\Delta C}{\Delta Y}\right)$	APC $\left(\dfrac{C}{Y}\right)$
0	80	0.8	0
100	160	0.8	1.6
200	240	0.8	1.2
300	320	0.8	1.06
400	400	0.8	1.00
500	480	0.8	0.96

Factors that influence consumption

Consumption is influenced by both income factors and non-income factors.

Non-income factors which influence consumption are:

Wealth The more wealth people have – such as homes, cars – the more likely the spending out of current income will increase.

Interest rates Falling interest rates provide financing for increased consumption.

Access to easy borrowing Automatic teller devices cause consumer spending to rise.

Rates of taxation High levels of taxation reduce disposable income and reduce spending.

Expectations of inflation If consumers anticipate future inflation, they may increase spending in the present when money has more purchasing power.

Composition of households Young income earners spend more than middle- and upper-income earners.

Tastes If people have expensive tastes, they will increase expenditure on expensive items.

THE KEYNESIAN MODEL OF THE MACRO-ECONOMY

Important points

Determinants of consumption are:

- Income; and
- Non-income factors – such as wealth, distribution of income, rate of taxation, expectations of inflation in the future, and cost availability of credit.

A change in disposable income is likely to cause a movement along the consumption function, while a change in any of the non-income factors may cause a shift of the entire consumption function to the right or left.

> **Exam tip**
>
> Tested at CAPE – MCQ.

Savings

- Savings may be defined as income not spent out of disposable income and expressed as $S = -a + syd$ where: $s = 1-b$
  (Note: Capital S = savings; lower case s = the fraction of every extra dollar that is saved.)
- $-a$ = negative savings (money withdrawn to finance autonomous consumption).
- s = the fraction of every extra dollar that is saved, called the **marginal propensity to save** (MPS) and expressed as $1/(1-b)$ where b is the MPC.
- If the MPC is 0.5, then the MPS is 0.5 because MPC + MPS = 1.
  Yd = disposable income.
- Figure 18.3 shows the relationship between savings and changes in national income.
  (Note: Savings is induced by increasing income.)
- The marginal propensity to save (MPS) is the fraction of every additional dollar that goes to savings and is expressed in formula as ΔS, so that if $S = -a + 0.5y$, the MPS is 50 cents out of every additional dollar: ΔY
- The **average propensity to save** (APS) is the average level of savings and it is expressed as S/Y.

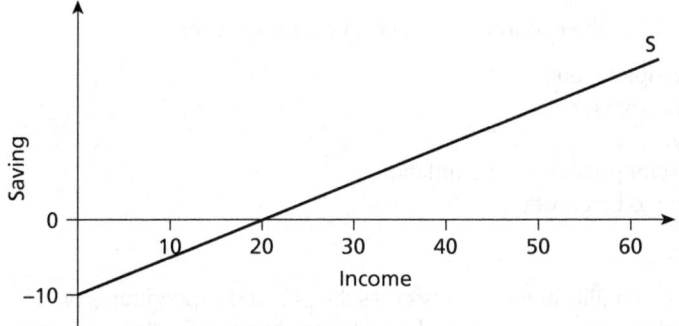

Figure 18.3 The savings function

The diagrammatic relationship between the consumption and saving function

The relationship between consumption and savings is expressed as $S = Y - C$.

Therefore, $C = Y - S$.

Figure 18.4 shows the relationship between consumption and savings where area A indicates negative savings.

Beyond income level $300m, savings are positive. Factors which influence savings are income and non-income factors.

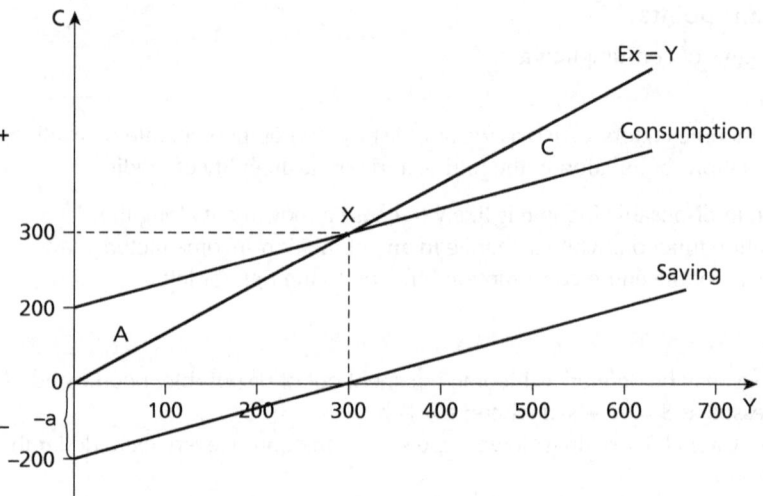

Figure 18.4 Relationship between consumption and savings

The main determinant of savings is the level of disposable income. Other factors are:

- The rate of interest, since at higher rates of interest savers increase their savings;
- A high rate of inflation discourages savings because inflation reduces the value of savings;
- Attitudes towards thrift;
- Confidence in finance institutions;
- Competition among financial institutions for savings deposits;
- Government tax concessions – e.g. on insurance products.

National income equilibrium

The Keynesian model of the economy assumes an economy with:

- Less than full employment;
- A given level of stocks;
- Spare capacity;
- Output at constant prices – i.e. no inflation;
- Wages assumed to be constant.

Note the following:

- National income equilibrium is expressed as the planned expenditures of households and firms (C + I equal to planned income or output (Y), or C + I = Y).
- Planned injections (J) are equal to planned withdrawals or leakages (W).
- An injection (J) is any expenditure on the domestic output of a country except for domestic consumer spending.
- In a four-sector model, injections are investment, government spending, and exports – summarized as I + G + X.
- Injections are assumed to be autonomously determined and not influenced by changes in national income.
- A **withdrawal** or **leakage** is any income earned in the circular flow (wages, interest, rent, and profit) not returned to firms in the year of production.
- In a four-sector model, withdrawals are savings, imports, and taxes – summarized as S + M + T

Exam tip

Tested at CAPE – MCQ.

Exam tip

Tested at CAPE – MCQ.

THE KEYNESIAN MODEL OF THE MACRO-ECONOMY

Figure 18.5 represents a Keynesian cross model of a two-sector economy without government.

Note:

Figure 18.5 illustrates the C + I = Y approach to national income. Figure 18.6 represents the injection/leakages approach. In Figure 18.5, an autonomous increase in investment of $20m added to Consumption = $C + I_1$ = $40m. If a further $20m of investment is added ($C + I_2$), the new equilibrium will be at output Y_2.

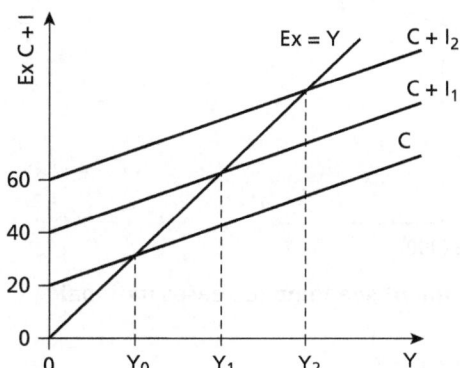

Figure 18.5 Keynesian analysis of national income

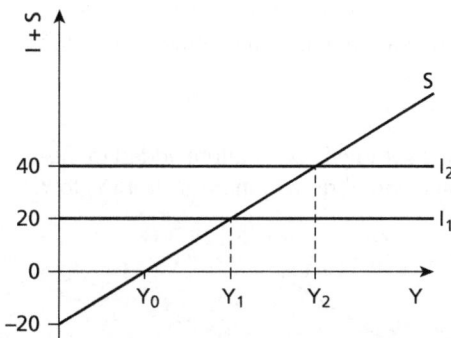

Figure 18.6 Injections and leakage approach to national income

The autonomous upward shift of the investment function from I_1 to I_2 in Figure 18.6 increases national income from Y_1 to Y_2. Both models illustrate the economy in two different ways with the same result of a change in national income.

Exam tip

Both tested at CAPE.

A 3-sector Keynesian cross model of equilibrium

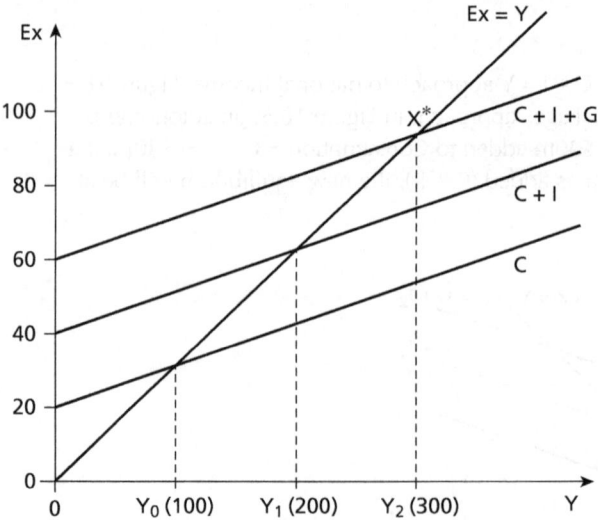

Figure 18.7 Keynesian cross-government spending increases national income

Figure 18.7 illustrates a three-sector model.

Note:

- Autonomous government expenditure of $20m moves the C + I function upward and parallel to C + I and an increase in national income from Y_2 to Y_3 at point X*.
- This function is now C + I + G.

Figure 18.8 similarly shows autonomous government expenditure added to the investment also causes the national income equilibrium to increase from Y_1 to Y_2 at point X*.

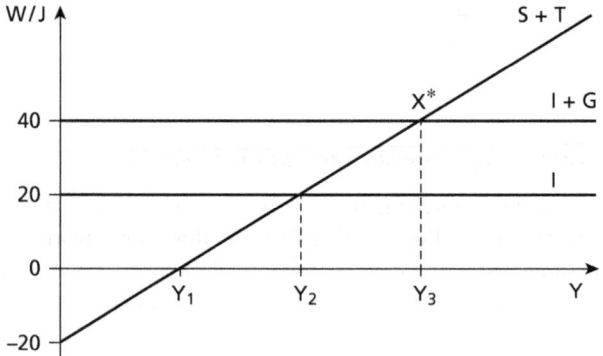

Figure 18.8 Injections and leakages approach – government spending increases national income

Exam tip

Tested at CAPE – Papers 1 and 2.

The multiplier

The multiplier (K) is a number which links the change in national income to the change in autonomous spending which causes it. From this definition, we may view the value of multiplier as:

$$K = \frac{\Delta Y}{\Delta G}$$

THE KEYNESIAN MODEL OF THE MACRO-ECONOMY

where Δ in Y is the change in national income (Y) of $100m and ΔG means a change in government spending of $20m. In Figure 18.8, K is the result of a change in Y_1 to Y_2 ($100m). The multiplier is therefore:

$$K = \frac{\Delta Y}{\Delta G} = \frac{100}{20} \quad \therefore K = 5$$

An injection of $100m of government spending can cause a change in national income greater than the original $100m. The multiplier process is shown in Table 18.1, where the MPC is 0.5. Therefore, MPS = 0.5 (MPC + MPS = 1).

Table 18.2 The multiplier process

Spending	Income	Consumption	Savings	Income created
1	100	50.00	50.00	100.00
2	50	25.00	25.00	150.00
3	25	12.50	12.50	175.00
4	12.5	6.25	6.25	187.5
5	6.25	3.12	3.12	193.75

If the spending rounds continue until income reaches 0 in column 2, then $100m of government spending could create an additional $100m (column 5) in national income, assuming the MPC and MPS of all income recipients are 0.5.

In this case, the value of the multiplier would then be:

$$\frac{\Delta Y}{\Delta G} = \frac{200}{100} = 2$$

The more approved method of calculating the multiplier in any instance is:

$$\frac{1}{\text{Withdrawals}}$$

For a four-sector economy, it would = 1/MPS + MPT + MPM.

Other multipliers in a four-sector economy are related to autonomous consumption, investment, government and exports (C + I + G + X).

The value of the multiplier may be determined in the following way:

- Consumption spending = Change in Y ÷ change in C.
- Investment spending = Change in Y ÷ change in I.
- Exports spending = Change in Y ÷ change in X.

The multipliers explained above all cause positive changes in national income as long as total injections (I + G + X) are greater than total withdrawals (S + M + T).

> **Exam tip**
>
> Tested at CAPE – Paper 2.

The algebraic model of the economy

The national income equilibrium may also be expressed in simple algebra.

If $C = 40m + 0.5y$, investment = 60m, government spending = 100m, export expenditure = 60 and imports = 40 the equation should then be:
$C + I + G + (X - M)$:

$40 + 0.5y + 60 + 100 + 60 - 40 = Y$

Solving:

$40 + 60 + 100 + 60 - 40 \quad = Y - 0.5Y$

$220 \quad\quad\quad\quad\quad\quad = 1/2Y$

$Y \quad\quad\quad\quad\quad\quad\quad = 440$

> **Exam tip**
>
> Regularly tested at CAPE – Papers 1 and 2.

Deflationary and inflationary and gaps

Note the following:

- The full employment level of national income represents maximum attainable output from resources of the economy represented as Y_{FE} in Figure 18.9.
- If the equilibrium national income Y_1 is less than the full employment (Y_{FE}) level, this leads to a **deflationary gap** or **recessionary gap** XY.
- The gap XY represents the amount by which aggregate expenditure must be increased in order to achieve the full employment level Y_{FE}.

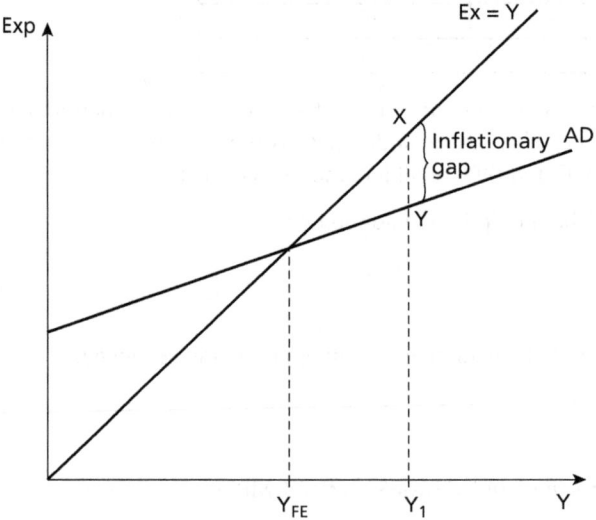

Figure 18.9 The inflationary Gap XY

Deflationary gaps are associated with the following:

- Recession and high rates of unemployment;
- Aggregate demand less than aggregate output;
- Low consumer and business confidence;
- Reduced external trade.

A deflationary gap may be closed in the following ways:

- Increased government spending and reduced interest rates to stimulate consumption and investment;
- The reduction of savings, taxes and imports.

If the equilibrium national income exceeds the full employment level (Y_{FE}), an inflationary gap will result.

THE KEYNESIAN MODEL OF THE MACRO-ECONOMY

Note:

- This is caused when government spending creates an excess demand for goods and services that cannot be produced because all resources are already fully employed.
- This leads to a rise in the general price level.
- The inflationary gap is the distance XY, which identifies the reduction in expenditure that is required to bring the economy back to the full employment level of national income Y_{FE}.

> **Exam tip**
>
> Regularly tested at CAPE – Papers 1 and 2.

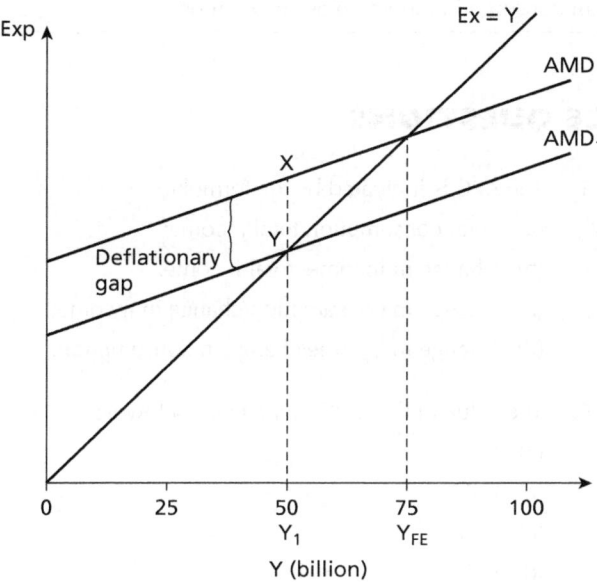

Figure 18.10 The deflationary gap

In Figure 18.10, the vertical distance XY is called the **inflationary gap**.

The short and long term in macroeconomics

In macroeconomics, there are two types of equilibria: short-run and long-run. The microeconomic short run is the period in which:

- Wages and prices do not respond to changes in economic conditions such as aggregate demand and aggregate supply.
- As economic conditions change, prices (including wages) may not adjust quickly enough to maintain equilibrium in markets in the economy.
- Inflexible prices are slow to achieve equilibrium level, creating prolonged periods of shortage or surplus.
- Wage and price stickiness inhibit the economy from achieving its natural level of employment and its potential output.
- The long run in macroeconomic analysis is a period in which wage and price are flexible, allowing employment to move to its natural level – represented by the vertical long-run AS curve and real GDP to move to potential GDP after full market adjustment has been achieved.
- The long run also allows time for disequilibrium between different sectors within the economy to be in equilibrium as well as the external economy. Changes in the different rates of interest, wages, and exchange rates eventually lead to equilibrium.

Test Your Knowledge

1. Distinguish between consumption, saving and investment.
2. What is meant by induced consumption?
3. Distinguish between the average and marginal propensities to consume and save.
4. Express the Keynesian consumption function as an equation.

MULTIPLE CHOICE QUESTIONS

1. Keynesian economics emphasize a very significant role for:
   (a) The monetary authorities;
   (b) Government spending and taxation;
   (c) Consumers;
   (d) Producers.

2. Consumption is represented by the equation:
   (a) $C = byd + y$;
   (b) $C = a + byd$;
   (c) $C = a + yd$;
   (d) $C = S - byd$.

3. The letter 'b' in the consumption function represents:
   (a) Total consumption;
   (b) Average consumption;
   (c) The marginal propensity to consume (MPC);
   (d) The average propensity to consume (APC).

4. The MPC is indicated by the formula:
   (a) Total consumption/total income;
   (b) Change in income/ total income;
   (c) Change in consumption/change in income;
   (d) Change in income/change in consumption.

5. The APC is indicated by the formula:
   (a) Total consumption/total income;
   (b) Change in income/ total income;
   (c) Change in consumption/change in income;
   (d) Change in income/change in consumption.

6. The value of the MPC in the table below is:
   (a) 0.36;
   (b) 0.77;
   (c) 0.80;
   (d) 0.94.

Income	Consumption
0	60
100	140
200	220
300	300
400	380

Chapter 19　Investment

Learning Objectives

By the end of this chapter you should be able to:

- Explain the nature of investment
- Differentiate between the investment demand curve, the MEC and the MEI
- Explain the determinants of investment
- Outline the factors that account for the volatility of investment
- Explain the accelerator theory

Investment is defined as a flow of expenditure on capital goods which adds to a nation's stock of capital in a given year, creating wealth and capacity enhancement in the future.

Expenditure on buildings and machinery are examples of investment in capital.

Important terms

Gross investment Gross investment refers to the total output of capital goods produced in a given year. It includes the addition of new capital to its existing stock and the replacement of worn out or outdated capital.

Depreciation Depreciation is a measure of the value of worn out capital. Obsolescence refers to the value of replacing outdated capital – e.g. replacing a typewriter with a computer and printer.

Net investment Net investment is a flow of expenditure on new additions to the capital stock but excludes replacement capital. It maintains the size of existing stock and the country's productive capacity.

Physical capital This represents expenditure on new plant and machinery.

Autonomous investment This type of investment is independent of national income.

Induced investment This represents investment expenditure in response to changes in national income – i.e. a change in the growth of sales or national income as a whole.

Planned investment This represents the expenditure on capital that firms plan to make in a given year.

Unplanned investment This explains additions to stock when aggregate supply is greater than aggregate demand.

Unplanned disinvestment This explains subtractions from stock by firms when aggregate demand is greater than aggregate supply.

Categories of investment

Since investment is undertaken for many different reasons, it may be necessary to classify them.

Note that:

- Additions to stock – e.g. finished goods and raw materials – are regarded as investment, since they represent current output.
- Construction is also considered an addition to the stock of capital.
- Construction of residential and commercial buildings are considered investment, since they add to the productive capacity of a country.
- Work-in-progress and semi-finished goods also have productive capacity and are regarded as investment.
- Public investment refers to state expenditure on infrastructure which adds to productive capacity – e.g. roads, ports.

The marginal efficiency of capital (MEC)

- The marginal efficiency of capital represents the demand for investment as a function of estimated future returns and is, in theory, regarded as the demand curve for capital.
- The price of capital is the rate of interest of borrowed funds for the purchase of capital.
- Future returns is the sale of capital's output during the life of the investment.

The estimated future returns on investment may be expressed in monetary or percentage terms in the same way as a loan instalment may be expressed in percentage rather than monetary terms. If the estimated future returns on investment (MEC) is equal to or greater than the cost of the investment (rate of interest) the investment is deemed profitable.

For the economy as a whole, the investment schedule called the **marginal efficiency of investment** (MEI) can be calculated and expressed according to the prevailing rate of interest. Planned investment may be expressed as a function of the interest rate. Refer to Table 19.1, which shows a marginal efficiency schedule for the economy as a whole.

Table 19.1 The marginal efficiency of investment

Rate of interest	Planned investment (billions per year)
30	5
20	10
10	15
5	20

A planned investment function or curve may be derived from the data in Table 19.1.

Note:

- There is an inverse relationship between the rate of interest and the marginal efficiency of investment.
- At a rate of return of 30%, only $5bn of investment is profitable.
- In contrast, when the marginal efficiency of capital is 5%, $20bn of investment is now possible because the cost of borrowing (5%) is low, allowing a previously unattainable investment to take place; at 30%, this cost of borrowing may be difficult to cover in terms of returns.
- The MEI would shift to the right if the conditions of investment change.

Factors that shift the MEI curve

The planned investment schedule may shift to the left or right in the manner of most demand curves under certain conditions.

These conditions are:

Expectations of the economy If investment planners have a pessimistic view of the economy, they will anticipate a fall in the future rates of return and reduce investment spending as a result.

Cost of capital If the cost of capital goods rises, the rate of return will fall and so will the level of planned investment.

Technological change This will increase the productivity of capital and, hence, the rate of return. Planned investment will rise at all levels of interest rates.

Government incentives If the government provides incentives for depreciation via reduced corporation taxes, this will reduce costs and increase the rate of return on investment. Planned investment will accordingly rise.

Level of profit A firm's rising level of profits may stimulate the demand for capital. This will shift the planned investment schedule to the right, as illustrated in Figure 19.1.

The initial cost of the project and other related operational costs. If these costs increase, then the estimated future returns may be revised downward and the MEI would shift to the left.

Criticisms of MEC and interest determined investment

- The rate of interest is a determining factor for investment but it ignores the fact that firms may finance a project from retained profit. However, a firm may obtain a higher rate of return if retained profit is saved than if it is invested at high interest rates.
- Firms' planned investment takes into account small changes in interest rates in their yearly business planning.
- Much of a firm's financing is undertaken through trade credit and not wholly dependent on the rate of interest.
- Interest rates may be written off as an expense to firms when calculating net profit.
- Even when interest rates are low, assuming that the demand for capital is high the supply of capital may be inelastic.

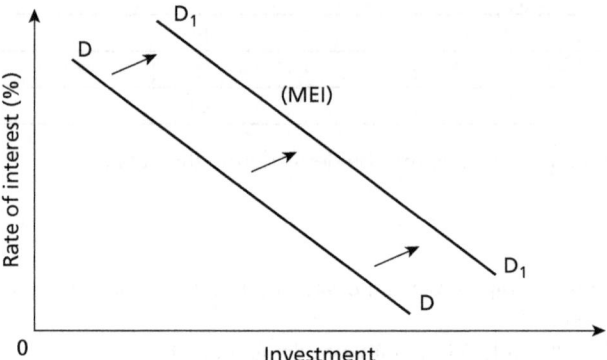

Figure 19.1 Increased demand for capital shifts investment schedule (D to D_1)

The MEI will shift to the right as a result of the following:

- An increase in business confidence;
- An increase in capital productivity;
- An increase in the price of capital's output.

The accelerator principle of investment

- The accelerator principle theorizes that investment spending is induced by the rate and magnitude of a change in national income or output over time.
- If the rate of increase in national income or national sales is maintained, the level of investment will not change.
- Planned investment will be 'accelerated' by the rate of change of output and income/sales from the previous year.
- Firms are assumed to keep a fixed capital to output ratio. For example, if a firm requires $4 of capital to produce $1 of output, the capital output ratio is 4:1, or simply 4. This is known as the accelerator coefficient.

For example, assuming no replacement capital and a capital output ratio of 4, a change in demand for cement from $100m to $110m will require a change in investment of $40m of capital.

When the rate of national income increases at an increasing rate, the rate of change in investment increases by a percentage greater than the change in national income, as explained in the summary below.

INVESTMENT

Table 19.2 The accelerator

Year (t)	NI (m)	Net investment (m) (I_n)
2000	100	–
2001	110	40 (10 x 4)
2002	130	80 (20 x 4) = 100% increase
2003	180	200 (50 x 4) = 150% increase
2004	200	80 (20 x 4) = 60% decrease

Summary

- Assume there is no replacement investment.
- An increase in investment from $110m to $130m (18%) induces investment from $40m to $80m (100%).
- An increase in investment from $130m to $180m (38%) induces investment from $80m to $200m (150%).
- An increase in investment from $180m to $200m (11%) induces a significant fall in investment by 60%.

NB It is not the increase in national income that induces an accelerated rate of investment but, rather, the rate and magnitude. A simplified formula for the accelerator principle is:

$I_n = a (\Delta NI)$

where I_n = net investment, a = capital output ratio and ΔNI is the change in national income.

If the rate of change in national income falls, the change in investment falls significantly by a greater percentage than the change in national income.

Limitations of the accelerator theory

- The theory assumes that firms have no spare capacity to accommodate an increase in demand in the short run.
- It also assumes that firms will respond to increases in demand by investing in new machinery.
  But firms may determine that increase in demand is temporary and may use the factors of production more intensively – e.g. working 24-hour shifts.
- Even if demand is permanent, the supply of capital in the short term may be inelastic in supply.
- Capital output ratios are not constant and may vary to a greater degree in the short term when excess capacity exists in a recession, rather than in a boom when the firm's capital is fully employed.
- There are time lags which are associated with changes in investment and changes in national income

The volatility of investment

The unstable nature of investment may be attributed to the following:

- Business expectations are strongly influenced by the confidence and optimism of the business sector. In computing the MEC, there is much guesswork and forecasting.
- Changes in taste and fashion, changes in government policy, the pressures of globalization, shocks to the economic global environment and natural disasters are some of the factors which affect future demand.
- The accelerator principle also provides reasons for volatility of investment, since a change in the rate of income or sales can induce large fluctuations in investment.
- If capital is long-lasting, then this durability will slow the rate of replacement.
- Innovation plays a crucial role in the modernizing of capital goods and processes, therefore the rate of innovation will influence the rate of investment.
- Variability of profit levels will have a negative influence on investment decisions.

Exam tip

Tested at CAPE – Paper 2.

Test Your Knowledge

1. (a) What do economists mean by 'investment'?
   (b) What are the main determinants of investment in your country?
   (c) Why is investment considered important?

2. (a) Distinguish between autonomous and induced investment.
   (b) State four reasons why investment is considered volatile.
   (c) Explain and comment on the measures that the government of a selected Caribbean economy has taken to increase investment.

MULTIPLE CHOICE QUESTIONS

1. The basic assumption underlying the accelerator principle is that:
   (a) Investment is sensitive to the rate of interest;
   (b) Investment depends on the willingness of banks to make advances;
   (c) Firms maintain a fixed ratio between capital employed and borrowed funds;
   (d) There is a target relationship between the rate of change in national income and net investment in capital stock.

2. What would cause the value of the accelerator to increase?
   (a) A reduction in tax rates;
   (b) An increase in the capital-output ratio;
   (c) An increase in the saving ratio;
   (d) An increase in the marginal propensity to consume.

3. Which of the following is LEAST likely to cause volatility of investment?
   (a) Variability of profit;
   (b) Rate of innovation;
   (c) The accelerator principle;
   (d) The rate of interest.

4. All of the following are limitations of the accelerator principle except:
   (a) Firms may have spare capacity;
   (b) The supply of capital goods may be inelastic in demand;
   (c) There are investment time lags;
   (d) Capital output ratios are always constant in practice.

5. The MEC curve for investment is:
   (a) Sloped left to right and downward sloping;
   (b) Perfectly elastic;
   (c) Perfectly inelastic;
   (d) Backward bending.

Chapter 20
Unemployment and Inflation

Learning Objectives

By the end of this chapter you should be able to:
- Explain what is meant by the labour force
- Explain the unemployment rate
- Distinguish between unemployment and underemployment
- Evaluate the costs of unemployment
- Explain the causes of unemployment
- Evaluate the policies used to reduce unemployment
- Explain the causes of inflation
- Distinguish between real and nominal variables
- Explain how inflation is measured
- Evaluate the effects of inflation
- Evaluate the policies used to combat inflation
- Explain the relationship between the unemployment rate and inflation

Exam tip

Tested at CAPE – MCQ and Paper 2.

The labour force and unemployment

The **labour force** is defined as the number of persons over the age of 15 years who are employed and also who are willing to be employed and are actively seeking employment.

Unemployment refers to the percentage of the labour force comprising the unemployed. It is expressed in formula as:

$$\frac{\text{Number of persons unemployed}}{\text{Labour force}} \times 100$$

Unemployment is a key objective of all governments because it is linked to poverty and the standard of living. Solving unemployment is, therefore, a means to reduce poverty and raise the standard of living.

Employment refers to persons who are employed full time in a job for which they are qualified.

Underemployment refers to persons who are employed in a job beneath their qualifications and experience, or who may also work part time, especially during a slowdown in economic activity.

Costs of unemployment

The costs of unemployment are summarized as:

Economic costs:

- Loss of tax revenue to the government – e.g. PAYE and VAT;
- High levels of unemployment make labour an idle resource and an opportunity cost of production sacrificed;
- High rates of unemployment increase the level of government spending – e.g. unemployment relief schemes.

Social costs:

- Loss of personal income;
- Resort to dissaving and borrowing;
- Loss of status;
- Alienation;
- Social fallout – such as crime, alcoholism and domestic violence, all of which require government intervention.

The causes and types of unemployment

- Disequilibrium in the labour market is the main reason for unemployment.
- Figure 20.1 shows the macroeconomic equilibrium of the labour market with QL_1 of labour and a wage rate of W_1. If the wage rate becomes W_2, there is an excess supply of labour equal to $Q_{L2} - Q_{L3}$.
- Although the supply of labour exceeds the demand for labour, there is no downward pressure on wages as unions are unyielding.

Trade union power or minimum wages may also lead to disequilibrium.

A deflationary gap gives rise to unemployed labour resources, since aggregate demand is insufficient to absorb aggregate supply.

When aggregate supply exceeds aggregate demand at the full employment level of national income, a recession will be caused and *can lead to another form of disequilibrium unemployment.*

UNEMPLOYMENT AND INFLATION

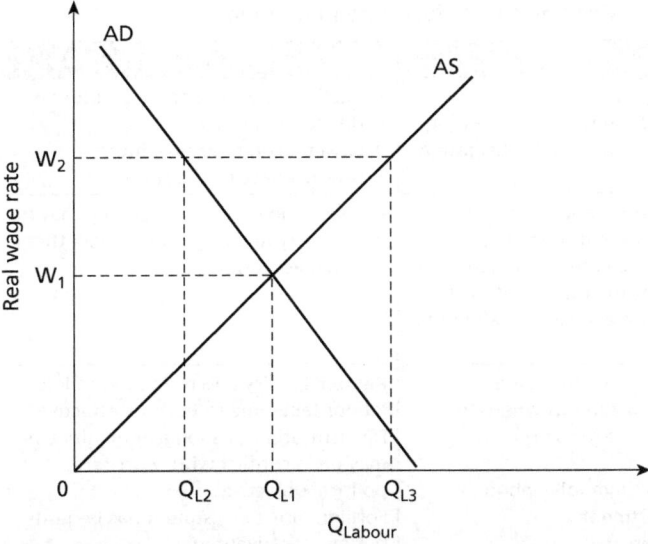

Figure 20.1 Labour market disequilibrium unemployment

Structural unemployment
Structural unemployment arises when there is a fall in the demand for labour related to a decline in an industry. For example, when the Windward Islands banana plantations are ravaged by hurricanes, structural unemployment in these territories rises.

Technological unemployment
Technological unemployment is caused by a fall in demand for labour due to the introduction of technology – e.g. combined harvesters replacing manual harvesting.

International unemployment
International unemployment is related to the negative impact on labour due to a fall in demand for goods and services due to international competition – e.g. low-priced imported beet sugar replacing domestically produced sugar.

Frictional/transitional unemployment
Frictional unemployment occurs when people are temporarily unemployed while seeking a better paying job. It is caused by occupational and geographic immobility of labour.

Seasonal/casual unemployment
The entertainment industry in the Caribbean experiences unemployment after the Trinidad Carnival, Barbados 'crop over' celebration or 'Vincy Mas' festivities.

Search unemployment
Search unemployment occurs when the unemployed do not take the first available job but 'search' until the best job is found. This is usually found in economies enjoying boom conditions.

Policies to reduce unemployment
Policies to reduce specific types of unemployment are presented in Table 20.1 but, generally, most focus on: (1) fiscal policy, (2) monetary policy, (3) wage subsidies, (4) retraining programmes, (5) Investment Tax credit, (6) Employment Tax credits, and (7) government employment programmes and the reduction of market imperfections.

> **Exam tip**
>
> Tested at CAPE – MCQ Paper 2.

REVISION GUIDE TO ECONOMICS

Table 20.1 A summary and an evaluation of policies designed to reduce unemployment

Type of unemployment	Policy	Disadvantages
Classical disequilibrium	Supply side – e.g. eliminating unemployment benefits and decreasing income taxes to encourage participation.	1. Cutting government expenditure is difficult to achieve; 2. Lower income taxes reduce the revenue base of the state.
Keynesian cyclical or demand deficient unemployment	1. Expansionary fiscal and monetary policies which raise government expenditure, decrease taxes (demand side) and lower the rate of interest. 2. Supply side policies – e.g. retraining of idle labour.	Increased government spending may be inflationary and negatively affect the external accounts.
Structural/regional	A regional policy – i.e. providing employment opportunities where there is unemployment – e.g. using housing initiatives. • Retraining of immobile labour; • Foreign investment; • Diversification.	Regional policy and retraining of idle labour take time to become effective. Diversification as a long-term initiative may be in conflict with short-term political objectives. Foreign direct investment has benefits but also disadvantages.
Frictional or search	Supply side – e.g. improving job information services and withdrawal of unemployment benefits.	The time lag delays the impact of this measure. Supply side measures are long-term. Withdrawing benefits may be politically undesirable.
Technological	Supply side – e.g. retraining of idle labour together with diversification initiatives. Indigenous economic activity – e.g. micro enterprises linked to agriculture.	Much formalized planning and mobilization of resources are needed. The time lag is a factor.
International unemployment	Monetary, fiscal and exchange rate policies are necessary in the short run. • In the long run, supply side and diversification initiatives may increase competitiveness. • Import protection and declining industries.	Lack of competitiveness may be due to inflation. Deflationary fiscal and monetary policies may lead to negative growth. Raising taxes and interest rates has negative effects. Import protection may encourage complacency.
Seasonal	Diversification of the economy. Retraining of labour. Entertainers and musicians may be used to export tourism sector with training.	Difficulties associated with immobility of labour may weigh against policy measures – e.g. unemployed unskilled workers may be functionally illiterate.

Inflation

Inflation is defined as a persistent increase in the average level of prices over time which results in a fall in purchasing power of a domestic currency.

Inflation is classified according to core and headline rates:

- Core inflation measures the price increases of all items excluding food;
- Headline inflation measures increases in food prices.

Causes of inflation

Inflation may be caused in the following ways:

- Demand pull inflation, caused by aggregate demand factors;
- Wage or cost push inflation, caused by aggregate supply factors;
- Increases in the money supply (monetarist theory).

Demand pull inflation

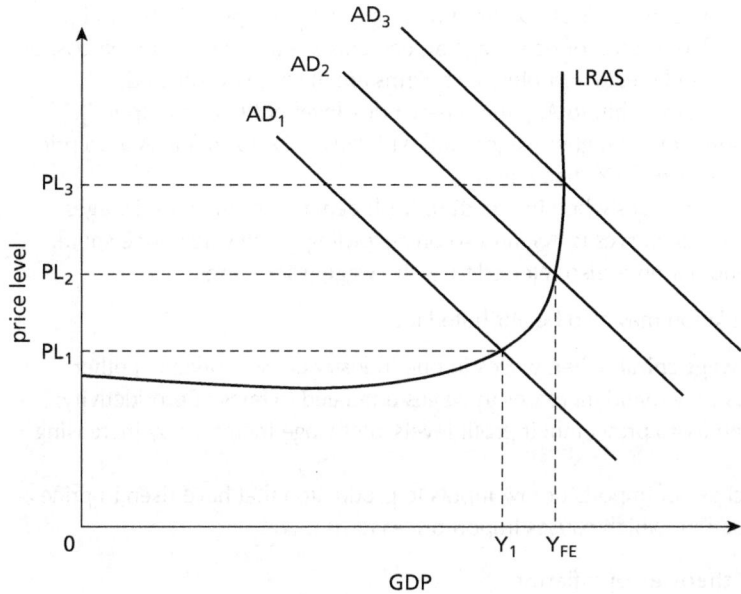

Figure 20.2 Demand pull inflation

Figure 20.2 illustrates a simple model of demand pull inflation as follows:

- Starting at an equilibrium level of income Y_1, an increase in government spending or reduced interest rates causes aggregate demand to shift to the right along the LRAS curve from AD_1 to AD_2.
- The increase in GDP from Y_1 to Y_{FE} is achieved with a PL_1 to PL_2 rise in the price level and the achievement of full employment equilibrium.
- When the AD curve shifts from AD_2 to AD_3 the full employment level (Y_{FE}) is exceeded with no change in real GDP but with a rise in the price level from PL_1 to PL_2.
- If any injection is greater than a leakage, or a combination of all three injections is greater than a combination of withdrawals, the resulting multiplier effect may cause AD to exceed AS at the full employment level

Cost push inflation

Cost push inflation is caused in a similar way to demand pull inflation as the AS and AD curves shift. Independent increases in costs of production unrelated to demand push up prices, leading to cost push inflation.

The following factors may also, either by themselves or collectively, cause the AS curves to shift initially to the left, initiating a price spiral and causing real output to fall:

- Monopoly union power;
- Indirect taxes – e.g. VAT;
- Wage increases unrelated to productivity;
- A devalued currency;
- An increase in imported raw material prices.

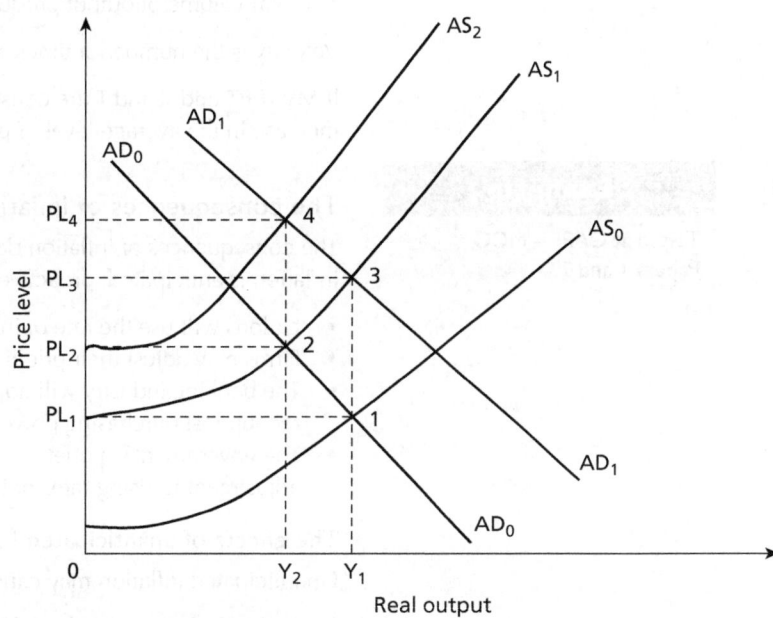

Figure 20.3 Cost push inflation

Figure 20.3 illustrates the cost push phenomenon as follows:

- Initially, the economy is at equilibrium at output Y_1 and price level of PL_1.
- Wages paid as a result of new wage agreements are an increase in the cost of production and create a ripple effect. Firms are likely to be affected.
- AS_0 will therefore shift to AS_1 and a new price level of PL_2 and output Y_2.
- The spending of the higher wages paid will cause AD_0 to shift to AD_1 to price level PL_3 and output Y_1 once more.
- The spiral continues when PL_3 leads to fresh demand for increased wages shifting the AS_1 curves to AS_2 and so on according to the wage price spiral. This phenomenon is also referred to as the **wage price spiral**.

Cost push inflation may also be attributed to:

- A **wage/wage spiral**, when wages in one industry cause workers in other industries to demand increases in wages unrelated to rates of productivity;
- Firms who try to protect their profit levels after wage increases by increasing prices;
- The purchase of imports or raw inputs to production that have risen in prices;
- A devaluation, which causes import prices to rise.

Monetarist theories of inflation

Monetarist economic theorists argue that a rise in the price level results in an increase in the money supply to facilitate it, a phenomenon called **monetary validation**.

Monetarists claim that there is a direct and proportional relationship between changes in the money supply and corresponding changes in the price level. This is called the quantity theory. The quantity theory is represented in a simple equation $MV = PT$ where:

M = the money supply;

V = the income velocity of money – i.e. the number of times money changes hands to purchase the final output of a country;

P = the average price level – i.e. total value of output divided by the total number of final transactions;

T = total volume of output produced;

Velocity is the number of times money changes hands;

If $MV = PT$ and V and T are constant, an increase in M would cause an equivalent increase in the average level of prices.

The consequences of inflation

The consequences of inflation depend on whether it has been anticipated. If inflation is anticipated, proactive action may be taken as follows:

- Unions will use the rate of inflation to argue their claims.
- Firms may adjust their pricing to include the rising price level.
- The banking industry will adjust interest rates with an 'inflation cover' to recoup lost purchasing power from the issue of loans.
- The government's monetary, fiscal or exchange rate policy will also reflect an adjustment to rising rates of inflation.

The effects of unanticipated inflation

Unanticipated inflation may cause the following internal effects:

Internal income is redistributed from one source to another. For example, borrowers in the financial markets gain at the expense of lenders because the rate of inflation rises faster than the rate of interest.

> **Exam tip**
>
> Tested at CAPE – MCQ Papers 1 and 2.

- Workers in less aggressive labour unions benefit from the aggressive negotiations of strong unions.
- The government will receive more tax revenue during periods of inflation as prices, profits and incomes rise. This form of redistribution is from firms and individuals to government. Inflation benefits the government with respect to the national debt as the real debt burden will fall as more taxes collected make payment easy. The redistributive effect in this instance is from the holders of government debt to the government.
- High prices domestically increase demand for lower-priced foreign import substitutes, redistributing revenue from domestic to foreign firms.

Apart from redistributive effects, other effects of inflation are:

- The investment climate will be less optimistic for weak firms. Investment levels will decline.
- Well-established firms may enjoy soaring profits during inflationary times, since most of their costs are contract-based and fixed.
- Fiscal drag takes place during inflationary periods when rising incomes place income recipients in a higher tax bracket.
- Inflation will cause consumers to suffer from money illusion – i.e. confusing nominal income with real income.
- During periods of inflation, the expectation of rising prices causes consumers and firms to purchase in advance to avoid higher future prices.
- House owners benefit during periods of inflation when property prices rise by more than the rate of inflation.

External effects

High rates of domestic prices will increase the demand for cheaper imported substitutes. Import spending is likely to exceed export earnings. The three external effects are:

- A balance of trade deficit;
- A balance of payments deficit;
- A falling exchange rate that is floating freely.

Governments tend to raise interest rates to curb demand inflation, encouraging inflows of foreign capital to boost the external accounts.

Lesser developed countries (LDCs) experience capital flight into relatively stable reserve currencies.

Immediate measures to control inflation

Before the root causes of inflation can be determined, immediate measures may be employed to combat inflation. These measures are:

- Indexation, which simply involves an index that determines the increase in inflation and makes the necessary adjustments to prevent loss of purchasing power.
- Floating exchange rates may reduce the effects of inflation by depreciation but make exports more competitive.
- An immediate limit may be placed on wage increases through an incomes policy.
- If inflation has been caused by excess demand, the government may reduce aggregate demand by using deflationary monetary and fiscal policies.

Deflationary fiscal policy

A deflationary fiscal policy – such as a cut in government spending together with an increase in direct taxes and budget surplus – will achieve the desired deflationary effect necessary to control demand inflation.

Immediate measures to combat cost push inflation

Immediate measures to curb cost push inflation are:

- A freeze on prices and incomes to prevent wage/price, inflationary spirals;
- Reducing indirect taxes – such as VAT and import duty – to reduce cost inflation;
- Subsidizing the production of goods during inflationary periods;
- Reducing the cost of imported raw materials to domestic producers.

Measuring inflation

Inflation measures the general price level over time. The statistical procedure to calculate the change in the general price level is as follows:

- An expenditure survey of a typical basket of goods of 1000 purchased items is taken of these randomly selected households.
- A weight is assigned to each good, representing a percentage of the budget. For example, if $600 out of $1000 is spent on transport, the weight out of 100 would be 60.
- The next step is to select a base year with which to compare price levels changes in other years.
- Every good or service measured is given a value of 100 in the base year. For example, if transport prices rose by 10% in 2014, then the base year index should be equal to 100 in the year 2011 and the index for 2014 = 110, showing that transport prices rose by 10%. Refer to Table 20.2.

Table 20.2 The Retail Price Index (RPI)

A good	B (2000) base year index	C (2008) index	Weight	(C x D) weighted index
W	100	110	10	1,100
X	100	120	20	2,400
Y	100	100	30	3,000
Z	100	90	40	3,600
			100	10,100

Step:

1. Multiply 2008 index by the weights for goods WXY and Z.
2. Add up total weighted index = 10,100.
3. Divide this total by the total of weights (100).

Therefore, $\frac{10,100}{100}$ = 101 – i.e. average level of prices in 2008 is 1% higher than the base year 2005

If the average price level rises by 105 in year 2009, then the change in the average price level between 2008 and 2009 is calculated as 105 – 101/101 = 4/101 x 100 = 3.9%

Limitations of the weighted Retail Price Index

- The index may fail to include new goods and services entering the market place – e.g. video games and personal computers.
- Weights may differ between families with different incomes because low-income groups tend to spend a higher proportion of their monthly earnings than high-income groups.
- It is difficult to choose an average basket of items due to different spending patterns.
- Changes in the economy may affect consumer expenditure patterns – such as a decrease in a recession rather than in a boom.

- Information provided to researchers may not be true or accurate.
- The types of outlets used by consumers must be carefully monitored – e.g. large retail supermarkets where prices are cheaper.
- Consumption patterns change over time – e.g. people are living healthy lifestyles, so that expenditure on tobacco or meat products is giving way to expenditure on exercise equipment and healthy eating.
- The RPI ignores changes in quality of goods and services over time.

Other measures of the price level

The Tax and Price Index measures the average household purchasing power and how changes in direct taxes affect purchasing power.

The Producer Price Index measures changes in material and product prices.

The Pensioners' Retail Price Index measures price changes of goods and services purchased by pensioners.

Figure 20.4 Illustrates the concept of the Phillips curve

Exam tip

Tested at CAPE – MCQ Paper 1.

The Phillips curve and stagflation

Research done by economist William Phillips in 1958 provided evidence to suggest that:

- Between the years 1861 and 1957, high rates of inflation (represented by percentage changes in money wages) coexisted with low rates of unemployment, as shown in Figure 20.4;
- When unemployment was low, workers were in a stronger position to bargain for higher wages but, when the rate of unemployment was high, there was competition for jobs and the supply of labour was greater than demand – wages were stabilized at a low rate;
- Governments can choose a combination of inflation and unemployment, or simply a trade-off.

Test Your Knowledge

1. Define the term inflation.
2. Explain the difference between cost push and demand pull inflation.
3. What are the effects of inflation?
4. What measures should the government take to control inflation in your country?

MULTIPLE CHOICE QUESTIONS

1. The relationship between price levels and inflation is embodied in which of the following notions:
   (a) The higher the rate of increase in the price level, the higher the rate of inflation;
   (b) The higher the rate of increase in the price level, the lower the rate of inflation;
   (c) The higher the rate of interest, the higher the rate of inflation;
   (d) The higher the rate of interest, the lower the rate of inflation.

2. The term 'price index' is BEST defined as:
   (a) A continuous increase in the average price level;
   (b) Decrease in the average price level of all goods produced in a country;
   (c) Measurement showing the cost of goods at a particular point in time;
   (d) Measurement showing how the average price of a basket of goods changes over time.

3. Which of the following CANNOT be used to measure inflation?
   (a) GDP deflator;
   (b) Expenditure method;
   (c) Producer price index;
   (d) Consumer price index.

4. When aggregate demand exceeds aggregate output at the full employment level, this leads to:
   (a) Demand pull inflation;
   (b) Cost push inflation;
   (c) Monetary inflation;
   (d) Unemployment.

5. Unemployment is associated with:
   (a) An inflationary gap;
   (b) Recessionary gap;
   (c) Economic growth;
   (d) Increased government spending.

6. High rates of inflation with low rates of unemployment are best explained by:
   (a) The Phillips curve;
   (b) The liquidity preference schedule;
   (c) The multiplier;
   (d) The accelerator.

Chapter 21: Monetary Theory and Policy

Learning Objectives

By the end of this chapter you should be able to:

- Explain the meaning of money
- Identify the characteristics of money
- Identify different types of money
- Explain the functions of money
- Explain liquidity preference theory
- Identify the motives for holding money
- Identify the items of money supply
- Explain monetary policy (expansionary and contractionary)
- Explain the role of the Central Bank in money creation
- Identify and explain the instruments of monetary control
- Explain credit creation and the money multiplier
- Explain money substitution and hoarding
- Outline the quantity theory
- Explain how monetary policy affects national income
- Identify the limitations of monetary policy

Exam tip
Tested at CAPE – MCQ.

Exam tip
Tested at CAPE – MCQ.

Money is anything acceptable as a payment for a financial transaction and which satisfies the functions of money.

The introduction of money replaced the ancient system of barter for the following reasons:

- **Double coincidence:** Barter failed to solve the problems of wants because traders' needs did not coincide with wants, which remained unsatisfied. Money can be used at any time.
- **Indivisibility:** Bartering items could only be traded wholly, rather than in parts – e.g. one could only trade a whole goat rather than a part. Money is divisible – e.g. different value bank notes.
- **Rate of exchange:** There were disagreements on the value of traded goods. Money was a rating mechanism – e.g. a 10-dollar pen is five times the value of a 2-dollar pencil.
- **Store of value:** Traded goods failed to keep their quality as time passed and lost their value. Money holds its value, except when price levels are rising.

The functions of money

Money must fulfil functions as a:

- **Medium of exchange** Money facilitates the purchase of goods, even if wants do not coincide.
- **Measure of value** Money allows goods to be 'rated' against other goods – e.g. if 1 pen costs $5.00 and 1 fish costs $20.00, then 1 fish is worth 4 pens.
- **Store of value** Except during periods of inflation, money holds its value into the future.
- **Standard for future payment** Money allows an exact calculation of future credit instalment payment and therefore enables the satisfaction of wants now and payment in the future.

The characteristics of money

Money must possess the following characteristics:

- Acceptability;
- Durability;
- Divisibility;
- Scarcity;
- Stability in value;
- Uniformity;
- Portability;
- Difficulty of replication.

The different types of money circulating in an economy

Many assets can act as money.

- **Commodity money** Assets that have value function as commodity money because they can carry out the functions of money.
  Gold, silver, and other scarce metals are examples of commodity money.
- **Convertible bank notes** These are bank notes that, in the recent past, were backed by gold to the extent that it was possible to 'convert' these notes into gold.
- **Fiat money** also referred to as **token money** is money in circulation. It consists of notes and coins, and functions as units of money according to government law. It is also called **legal tender**.

The demand for money

The demand for money is based on the quantity of money firms and individuals wish to hold to carry out the functions of money.

MONETARY THEORY AND POLICY

One such function is the purchase of assets as a store of wealth.

- **The Keynesian view of money demand** – liquidity preference theory J.M. Keynes asserted that money was demanded to carry out transactions, precautionary and speculative needs.
- **The transaction demand** The transaction demand for money is the use of money as a medium of exchange because we are paid money at one time and spend it at different times. See Figure 21.1.
  Factors which determine our transactions demand are: the level of income, the frequency of pay, and spending patterns which are fixed over time. The demand curve is therefore vertical.
- **The level of income** As incomes rise so will expenditure (the upward sloping consumption function). The more individuals and firms spend, the more money is needed to complete transactions.
- **The frequency of pay** Changing the frequency of pay days will increase the demand for money even if the income itself does not change.

> **Exam tip**
> Tested at CAPE – MCQ.

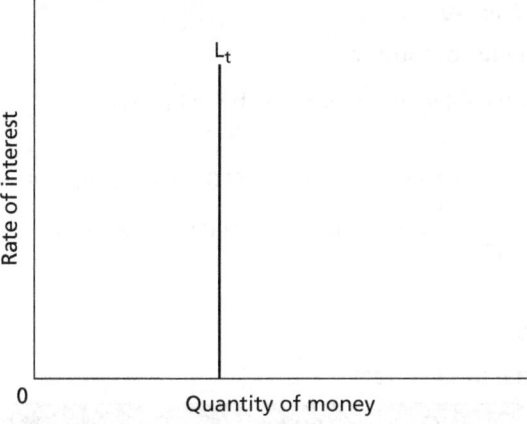

Figure 21.1 Transactions demand for money

- **Spending patterns** Purchases are made in the period between pay days and money is therefore demanded to finance these purchases. If our spending patterns vary, so will our transactions demands.
- **The precautionary demand for money** The precautionary demand for money is caused by the unplanned events of firms and individuals – e.g. illness.

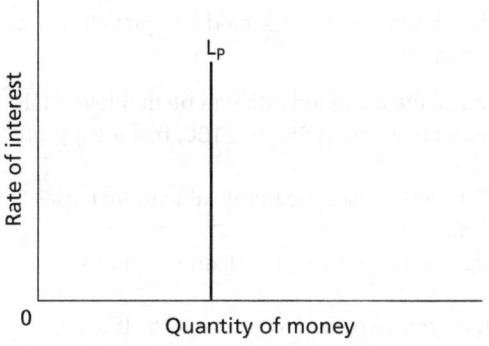

Figure 21.2 Precautionary demand for money

A factor affecting this motive is the level of income. The curve is vertical because these factors are also fixed in the short run.

The speculative motive – liquidity preference theory

The speculative motive for money is the theoretical demand for it as a store of wealth – e.g. money or bonds – and is focused on whether to hold money or

> **Exam tip**
> Tested at CAPE – MCQ.

bonds. Holding bonds involves risk because, when the rate of interest rises, the value of the bond falls. If bond prices are expected to rise, it will be preferred to money as will be explained.

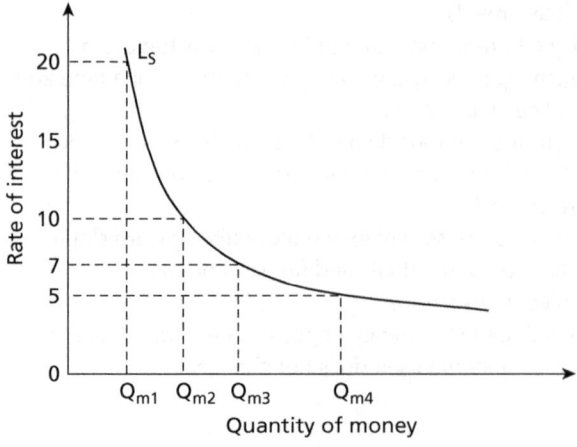

Figure 21.3 Speculative demand for money

Figure 21.3 and Table 21.1 show the relationship between bond prices and interest rates.

If the bond has a fixed return of $10 and a market price of $50, then the current market rate of interest will be $\dfrac{\$10 \times 100}{50} = 20\%$ and, at a bond price of $200, the market rate of interest = 5%

These rates are summarized below.

Table 21.1 Bond prices and the interest rate

Bond price ($)	Market rate of interest (%)	Fixed yield ($)
50	20	10
100	10	10
200	5	10

From Table 21.1, note that bond prices move in opposite directions to the market rate of interest.

The decision to hold money or bonds is based on the expected and prevailing rate of interest. In Table 21.1 note, the following:

- If the prevailing rate is a high of 20%, the expected rate will be that it will fall to 10%; the value of the bond will increase from $50 to $100, making a profit of $50.
- A further fall in the rate from 10% to 5% causes the bond value to increase from $100 to $200, a profit of $100.
  Conclusion: If interest rates are high, they are likely to fall and it will be prudent to prefer bonds to money.
- At a low rate of 5%, the rate of interest is expected to rise to 20%. It will be prudent to sell bonds and hold money because bond values will fall from $200 to $50.
  Conclusion: At low interest rates hold money not bonds.
- The speculative motive is drawn left to right and downward sloping, as shown in Figure 21.3. At a rate of 20%, bonds are preferred to money as the rate of interest is expected to fall, so only Q_{m1} of money is demanded. At a rate of interest of 5%, money is preferred to bonds to avoid a loss, so a significant Q_{m3} of money is demanded.

MONETARY THEORY AND POLICY

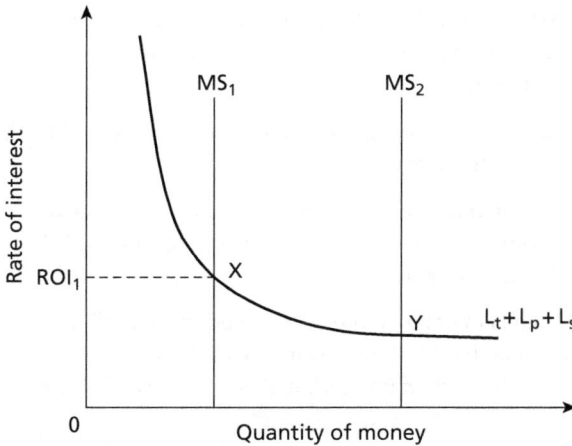

Figure 21.4 The liquidity preference schedule

The liquidity preference schedule in Figure 21.4 shows that the prevailing rate of interest is determined by the demand ($L_t + L_p + L_s$) and supply for loanable funds

How demand responds to changes in the rate of interest

See Figure 21.4.

In liquidity preference theory, the money supply is assumed to be fixed by the Central Bank and therefore vertical. If the rate of interest is ROI, the demand for money will exceed supply by XY. In order to meet this extra demand for money, firms and individuals will observe bond prices moving downward and, at the same time, forcing the rate of interest to go up.

The money supply refers to the quantity of money circulating in the economy and consists of the following:

- Narrow money (very liquid) – M_0 comprises notes, coins in public circulation plus banks' till money. $M_1 = M_0$ + current account deposits;
- $M_2 = M_0 + M_1$ + savings accounts deposits + time deposits + foreign earned deposits;
- Current account deposits are accounts from which cheques are issued;
- Time deposits are fixed deposits which yield interest for a specific period.

Monetary policy

Monetary policy consists of monetary instruments designed to regulate aggregate demand by influencing the money supply and the level of interest and exchange rates to achieve the five macroeconomic objectives of: full employment, sustained economic growth, a low rate of inflation, equilibrium in the balance of payments, and a stable exchange rate.

Instruments of monetary policy

The seven main instruments of monetary policy are:

- Moral suasion;
- Open market operations;
- Special deposits;
- The repo rate;
- The reserve ratio;
- Selective credit controls;
- Discount rate.

Moral suasion is an open declaration of the Central Bank's plans and objectives, which acts as a signal to commercial banks to encourage compliance with government's monetary policy.

> **Exam tip**
>
> Tested at CAPE – Papers 1 and 2.

Open market operations (OMO) This is the sale of government short-term securities and bills to the public sector, payments for which cause a reduction of banks' liquid assets and a rise in interest rates.

Buying securities from the public and banking sector increases commercial banks' liquid assets and reduces the rate of interest.

Special deposits The Central Bank may require commercial banks to lodge a portion of their liquid assets with the Central Bank, which reduces the banks' liquid assets and increases the rate of interest.

Repo rate policy The 'repo' rate is the rate of interest charged for providing overnight financing to commercial banks. If increasing the repo rate to commercial banks will increase the rate of borrowing, this will cause the level of interest rates to rise.

Reserve ratio The liquidity reserve ratio reflects the reserves that banks cannot lend. It is set aside a percentage of their bank deposits and influences their ability to lend; it has an impact on the rate of interest.

Selective controls These are the upper limits on the volume of bank lending imposed on commercial banks by the Central Banks and have an impact on the rate of interest.

The Central Bank may also issue directives to commercial banks with respect to the type of borrower they engage – e.g. consumers or firms.

Discount rate The discount rate is the rate of interest that commercial banks pay to the Central Bank for loans. Reducing the discount rate increases commercial banks' borrowing, increases the money supply and lowers the interest rate.

The targets of monetary policy

The primary task of monetary policy focuses on the following targets:

- The level and structure of interest rates;
- The exchange rate – to achieve a balance-of-payments equilibrium;
- Controlling the rate of growth of the money supply by targeting bank deposits and the liquid assets of commercial banks;
- Influencing the volume of spending by regulating the rate of interest;
- The volume of bank credit, which influences the rate of growth of the money supply.

Expansionary monetary policy is achieved by increasing the money supply, causing interest rates to fall and a consequent increase in components of aggregate demand – such as consumption and investment – in order to achieve economic growth and full employment.

Contractionary monetary policy is achieved by reducing the money supply, which raises interest rates and reduces the level of aggregate demand related to consumption and investment, reduces inflation and reduces import spending to achieve a balance–of-payments equilibrium.

How monetary policy works

The instruments of monetary policy impacts on two initial targets before the final objective is achieved, as shown in Table 21.2:

Table 21.2 How monetary policy works

Instrument	First target	Second target	Final objective
(1) Open market operations (buying)	Fall in the level of interest rates	Increase in the volume of bank credit	Full employment
(2) Special deposits increase	Banks liquid assets are reduced	Interest rates increase	Inflation

MONETARY THEORY AND POLICY

Credit creation is the creation of money through the borrowing and lending activities of financial institutions in a country which can cause an expansion of money circulating in an economy.

Assume only one bank in a small economy and that the Central Bank directs that the bank must retain 10% of its bank deposit. This is called the **cash reserve ratio (CRR)** or the **reserve requirement ratio**. A $100 deposit will expand according to the formula:

$$\text{Deposit} \times \frac{1}{\text{Cash ratio}} \quad \text{or} \quad \text{Deposit} \times \frac{1}{10\%}$$

equal to $100 \times \frac{1}{10\%}$

$= \$100 \times 10 = \$1000$

> **Exam tip**
>
> Tested at CAPE – Paper 2.

The money multiplier is a number which links the value of deposits to the eventual increase in total bank deposits. In the above example, a $100 deposit created a further $900 in bank deposits, as illustrated in Table 21.3.

Table 21.3 The money multiplier

	Deposit	CRR 10%	Loaned
1st	100.00	10.00	90.00
2nd	90.00	9.00	81.00
3rd	81.00	8.10	72.90
4th	72.90	7.29	65.61
Etc.			

- Assume, initially, that there is one bank in a system and CRR = 10%.
- Also assume that, when $100 is deposited, the bank retains $10 and makes a loan of $90.
- This $90 eventually returns to the bank, where $9 is retained and $81 is loaned, and so on.
- Eventually, the $100 will be reduced to $0 through successive lending rounds but will have expanded the money in circulation by a further $900.

Since a total of $100 of the $1000 retained by the bank amounts to the 10% CRR, this type of banking is called **fractional reserve banking** and the number 10 is the value of the money multiplier.

Currency substitution and hoarding of money

People invest in foreign currency for the following reasons:

- When there is a threat of inflation, money loses its store of value leading to loss of confidence in a currency;
- When individuals and firms expect their currency to lose value against another foreign currency to which it is tied;
- If the government institutes exchange controls and attempts to ration scarce foreign exchange;
- When there is political instability leading to capital flight;
- When the demand for foreign exchange in cash is high due to illegal activity;
- When expectations in the economy are pessimistic, citizens may purchase foreign currency to avoid financial insecurity;
- When there are high rates of taxation;
- If the interest rate in a foreign country is higher than the domestic rate, foreign currencies will be purchased.

Monetary policy and national income

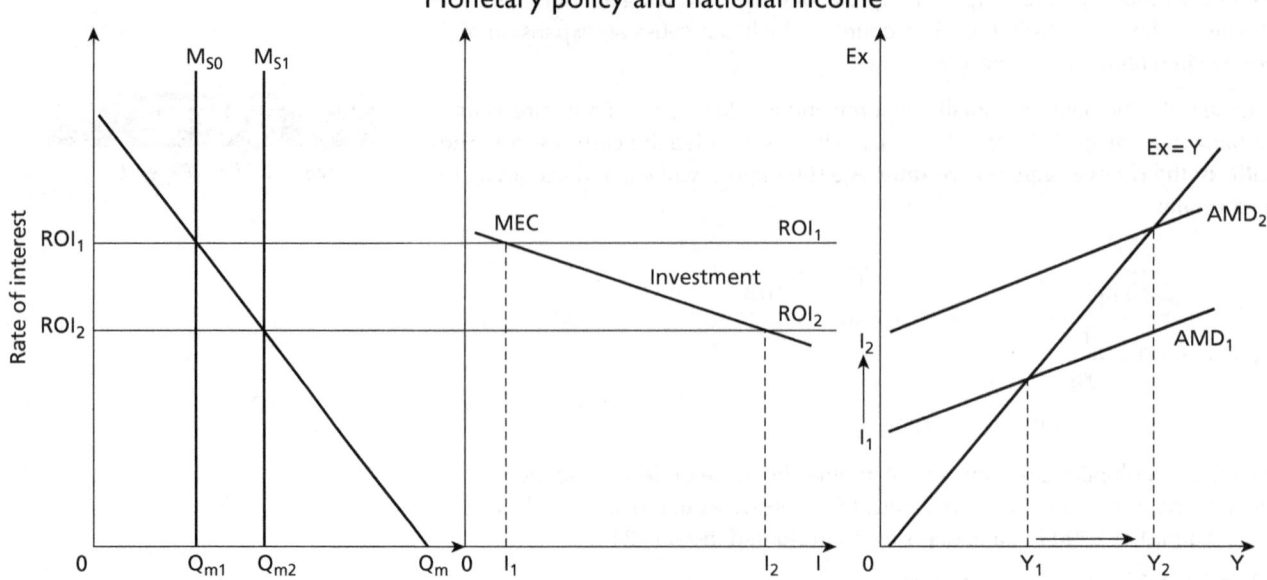

Figure 21.5 Monetary policy increases investment and aggregate demand

Monetary policy may impact on national income in the following ways:

- In Figure 21.5, the money supply increases from MS_0 to MS_1;
- The rate of interest falls from ROI_1 to ROI_2;
- This fall causes investment to increase from I_1 to I_2 and aggregate monetary demand to shift upward and to the right;
- National income increases from Y_1 to Y_2, causing a positive impact on economic growth and employment;
- The fall in the interest rate also has a positive impact on consumption, shifting the aggregate monetary demand curve to the right, resulting in economic growth and employment;
- Falling interest rates also cause an outward flow of capital in favour of higher interest rates, with a negative impact on the balance of payments;
- An increase in consumer and investment spending may cause an inflationary gap, if the economy is at the full employment level.

The limitations of monetary policy

The limitations of monetary policy are summarized as follows:

- It may conflict with fiscal policy.
- The increase of interest rate to combat demand inflation may conflict with the government's borrowing to finance a budget deficit counteracting monetary policy.
- Time lags – reducing interest rates to stimulate consumption and investment to achieve economic growth and full employment takes time.
- Open market operations may be neutralized if commercial banks have a cushion of spare liquid assets over and above their ratio requirements.
- Commercial banks get around the Central Banks' control of their liquidity by arranging loans for their customers from foreign branches.
- Reducing interest in a recession to stimulate investment and economic growth is not likely to succeed when expectation of profit is low.
- Monetary policy is indirect in its impact on government objectives because it only creates the environment to be effective and is not direct and compelling as fiscal policy.

Quantity theory seeks to explain the role of the money supply in the management of the economy, particularly with regard to inflation. Refer to Chapter 20 for an explanation of the quantity theory.

> **Exam tip**
>
> Tested at CAPE – MCQ.

MONETARY THEORY AND POLICY

Test Your Knowledge

1. Describe three types of demand for money.

2. Define each of the following instruments of monetary policy:
   (a) Open market operations;
   (b) Discount rate;
   (c) Reserve requirement.

3. State the quantity theory of money.

4. Explain how monetary policy can have a positive impact on aggregate demand.

MULTIPLE CHOICE QUESTIONS

1. The demand for money is determined by:
   (a) (i) and (ii) only;
   (b) (i) and (iv) only;
   (c) (ii) and (iii) only;
   (d) (iii) and (iv) only.
   - (i) Rate of interest;
   - (ii) Level of income;
   - (iii) Level of subsidies;
   - (iv) Level of savings.

2. The precautionary motive for holding money is based on:
   (a) Doubts about the movement of bond share prices;
   (b) Preparedness for unplanned events;
   (c) The fact that money is needed for purchasing equities and received money is received at different intervals;
   (d) The fact that equity prices have a downward trend.

3. An example of expansionary monetary policy is an increase in the Central Banks':
   (a) Repo rate;
   (b) Open-market sales;
   (c) Reserve ratio;
   (d) Open-market purchases.

4. The velocity of money circulation can be defined as:
   (a) The average time in which households spend their money income;
   (b) The money stock in a given time period divided by the level of prices;
   (c) The total value of transactions in a given time period divided by the average price level;
   (d) The number of times in a given time period that a unit is used to purchase final output.

5. The speculative motive for holding money is based on money's function as a:
   (a) Store of value;
   (b) Unit of account;
   (c) Medium of exchange;
   (d) Means of deferred payment.

Chapter 22: Fiscal Policy

Fiscal policy

Fiscal policy is the deliberate use of government expenditure, taxation, the national debt and transfers, to regulate economic activity and to achieve the government's objectives.

- Government expenditure and taxation influence aggregate demand (consumption, investment, government spending, exports and imports or CIGX and M) to achieve sustained economic growth, full employment, balance of payments equilibrium and a low rate of inflation.
- Budget deficits are used to remove deflationary gaps. Budget surpluses are employed to resolve inflationary gaps targeting aggregate demand.
- Monetarist fiscal policy focuses on the supply side of the economy to shift the LRAS curve to the right.
- Examples of monetarist long-term objectives are regulation of monopolies, privatization, productivity in all factor markets, competition and the promotion of efficiency.
- Observe the shift of the LRAS curve to the right as monetarist supply side measures impact on it.

Figures 22.1 and 22.2 show how Keynesian short-run and Monetarist long-run fiscal policies are intended to achieve their respective objectives.

Learning Objectives

By the end of this chapter you should be able to:
- Explain the concept of fiscal policy
- Outline the goals of fiscal policy
- Explain the nature of the budget
- Explain the balanced budget multiplier
- Outline methods of financing budget deficits
- Outline the limitations of fiscal policy
- Distinguish between discretionary and automatic fiscal policy

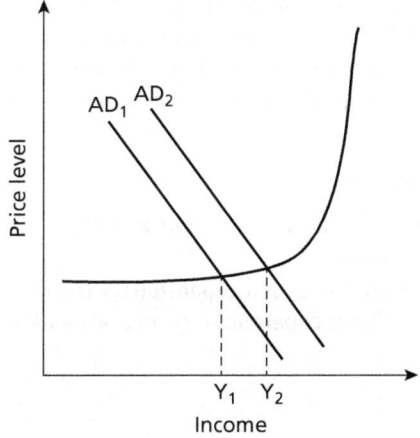

Figure 22.1 Keynesian fiscal policies

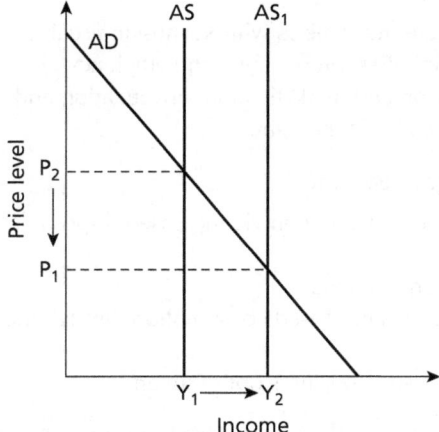

Figure 22.2 Monetarist fiscal policies

Note in Figure 22.1 the movement of the AD curve to the right as Keynesian fiscal measures impact on aggregate demand.

There are two main branches of fiscal policy: **stabilization** or **automatic fiscal policy**, and **discretionary fiscal policy**.

Automatic fiscal policy

- Automatic or stabilization policy employs measures that are implemented to act automatically to prevent large fluctuations in economic activity and to stabilize aggregate demand.
- If the economy is fully employed, rising incomes create inflationary pressure which is automatically reduced by direct taxes that are already in place.
- Income tax as a stabilizer automatically reduces disposable income and, hence, consumer spending.
- Transfer payments – such as unemployment benefits – are automatically reduced during a boom since recipients cannot qualify for assistance.
- The net effect of rising progressive taxes and falling government expenditure stabilizes aggregate demand and economic activity.
- In a recession, the reverse takes place. As incomes fall, reduced taxation on incomes and rising government expenditure (transfer payments and unemployment benefits) together automatically stabilize aggregate demand.

Discretionary fiscal policy

- Discretionary fiscal policy is the deliberate use of taxation, government spending, transfers and the National Debt to regulate economic activity.
- If the government increases expenditure on public works, this will cause the aggregate demand curve to shift to the right and increase national income, as shown in Figure 22.1.

Discretionary fiscal policy of changing taxation

- If income taxes are reduced, disposable incomes will rise, and so will consumption spending and aggregate demand.
- Expenditure increases and/or tax reductions are called **expansionary fiscal policy**. A **contractionary fiscal policy** includes expenditure reductions and/or tax increases.

The aims of fiscal policy

- The aims of **Keynesian fiscal policy** are the achievement of full employment, control of inflation, positive economic growth, and both a stable balance of payments position and exchange rate.
- The aims of **monetarist fiscal policy** are the same as with Keynesian fiscal policy but include regulation of monopolies, productivity and efficiency increases, the promotion of competition and marketization, privatization and resolving externalities to shift the AS curve to the right.

Discretionary fiscal policy and aggregate demand

- A reduction in taxes induces increased consumption via increased disposable incomes.
- Reduced corporation taxes stimulate investment.
- Increased government expenditure targets increased consumption through the multiplier effect.
- The resulting economic growth gives rise to business optimism and investment.

> **Exam tip**
> Tested at CAPE – MCQ and Paper 2.

> **Exam tip**
> Tested at CAPE – Paper 2.

FISCAL POLICY

Discretionary fiscal policy and unemployment

- An expansionary fiscal budget deficit (G > T) is achieved when government expenditure exceeds tax revenues, as illustrated in Figure 22.3.
- The deficit may increase national income from Y_1 to Y_2 when increased government expenditure increases national income through the multiplier effect, achieving economic growth and creating employment.
- A tax cut also has an incentive effect, in that it provides an incentive to work.

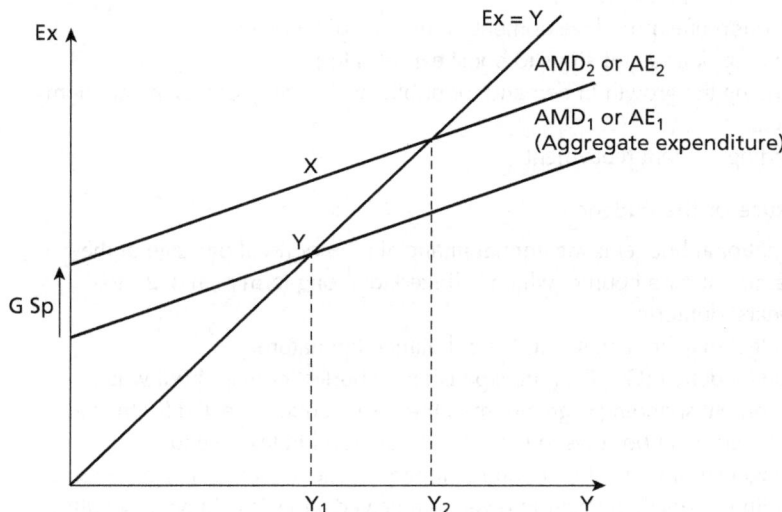

Figure 22.3 Discretionary fiscal policy: a budget deficit

- An inflationary gap is removed by a deflationary fiscal policy (T > G) to reduce demand inflation.
- The removal of the gap may be achieved by a budget surplus which reduces government expenditure and to a reverse multiplier effect and a fall in national income back to the full employment level.

Discretionary fiscal policy and the balance of payments

- The balance of payments is in deficit when external financial outflows exceed inflows.
- Reduced government expenditure via a budget surplus will cause national income to fall and a reduction in import spending, which reduces a balance-of-payments deficit.
- Increased import taxes – such as tariffs – also help to curb import spending and resolve a balance-of-payments deficit.
- The government may also grant subsidies to exporters to stimulate export revenue.
- A reverse strategy may be employed in the event of a balance-of-payments surplus.

Government expenditure

Social reasons for government expenditure

1. The government allocates expenditure to maintain law and order, alleviate poverty, reduce vagrancy, deal with homelessness, and provide health care and a social safety net to ensure a basic standard of living for vulnerable groups in society.
2. The government allocates expenditure on public education and social issues – such as contagious diseases, tobacco and alcoholism. State spending also seeks to promote a fair society – e.g. wealth and income distribution, school meal plans, free medicine and transport.

Economic reasons for government expenditure

1. Management of the economy – e.g. to promote economic growth and development and overall productivity by providing infrastructure to accommodate the private sector – for instance, roads, ports, power, water and communication;
2. Retraining idle labour to encourage occupational mobility;
3. Regional policy – i.e. the development of underdeveloped regions by establishing industrial zones;
4. Promotion of export development in the area of tourism;
5. Financing of trade missions to boost export sales;
6. Financing the growth in demand for public and merit goods as the economy grows;
7. Spending on debt repayment

The nature of the budget

- The national budget is the annual financial plan or fiscal package of the government for a country which is linked to a long-term plan of 25 to 30 years' duration.
- A budget may be deficit, surplus or balanced in nature.
- A budget deficit (G > T) or an expansionary budget comes about when government spending is greater than the tax revenue collected for the year. The government borrows to make up the shortfall in tax revenue.
- A budget surplus (T > G) or contractionary budget occurs when government spending is less than taxation revenue received – this is achieved by cutting expenditure and raising taxes.
- A balanced budget occurs when government spending is equal to taxes received.

Refer to Table 22.1.

Table 22.1 Summary of budget type and objectives

Budget type	Objectives
Deficit	<ul><li>To remove a deflationary gap;</li><li>To stimulate aggregate demand, investment, growth and employment by reducing taxes on incomes and profits;</li><li>To increase spending on public goods, merit goods and infrastructure.</li></ul>
Surplus	<ul><li>To remove an inflationary gap;</li><li>To reduce aggregate demand;</li><li>To curb demand inflation;</li><li>To dampen import spending, by reducing government spending and raising taxes on income and profits.</li></ul> Note: A balance-of-payments equilibrium may be achieved in this way.
Balanced budget	<ul><li>To avoid surpluses which can cause unemployment, or</li><li>To avoid a deficit, which can lead to inflation and a balance-of-payments disequilibrium.</li></ul>

Financing budget deficits

Budgets may be financed in the following ways:

- From domestic finance institutions – such as banks and finance houses;
- Borrowing from foreign sources;
- Borrowing from the non-bank public by the sale of bonds.

The balanced budget multiplier

If the government spends $20 m and imposes taxes equal to $20 m, there is an actual increase in the national income equal to $20 m. The multiplier is equal to 1.

This increase comes about because government spending is subject to a full multiplier increase but taxation does not cause a full decline of $20m.

Therefore, combined injections and leakages of $20m increase the national income by $20m, making the overall multiplier = 1. A simple formula for calculating the balanced budget multiplier is tax multiplier minus MPC/MPS + 1/MPS (government spending multiplier) = 1.

The limitations of discretionary fiscal policy

There are many disadvantages associated with fiscal policy: these are:

- Government spending committed to maintaining new assets is difficult to cut.
- Government spending financed by borrowing raises interest rates to private firms who are financially crowded out.
- Increased government spending on large public works causes the prices of material resources to rise. Private investment is crowding out in terms of resource prices.
- Government spending on resources causes shortages leading to rising prices and cost push inflation.
- Government spending may also have inflationary effects, if the economy is at full employment national income.
- An expansionary fiscal policy may achieve full employment and economic growth but may also cause inflation, trade and balance of payments deficits, and a weakened exchange rate. This is called **policy conflict**.
- Direct taxes may reduce disposable income and lower the standard of living. Taxes are also a disincentive to work, saving and investing.
- Fiscal policy may be affected by time lags which may serve to delay a recovery from a recession when the economy may already be in the upswing phase.

The potency of fiscal policy

The degree to which fiscal policy is effective depends on the following:

- Accurate forecasting in terms of predicting what changes are likely to take place with the components of aggregate demand (C + I + G + X);
- The extent to which a budget deficit or surplus will impact on injections and leakages; some injections may be nullified or dampened by leakages;
- The accurate determination of the size of the multiplier and accelerator effects, since these may change when expectations in the economy change;
- Successful linking of fiscal changes to changes in aggregate demand in order to achieve changes in the desired objectives – e.g. reducing inflation by a successful increase in direct taxation;
- Determining disincentive effects of fiscal policy on the incentive to work, save and invest;
- Solving the time lag problem.

Time lags

Time lags are the delay that takes place before a fiscal measure achieves the planned effect.

There are five time lags associated with fiscal policy. These are:

- Information to recognition lag – the gathering of information confirming the economic problem may take some time for the economic researchers to determine;
- Recognition to decision lag – the government must be certain about its strategy, which may involve economic decision-making with technocrats;
- Decision to mobilization lag – time is required to mobilize resources to implement economic strategy;

> **Exam tip**
>
> Tested at CAPE – MCQ.

- Mobilization to implementation lag – an expansionary fiscal policy may require time to implement;
- Implementation to achievement lag – a tax cut or an increase in government spending may take some time to bring about a desired result – e.g. consumption may respond slowly during a recession.

Test Your Knowledge

1. Define:
   (i) Fiscal policy;
   (ii) Budget surplus;
   (iii) Transfer payments.

2. Explain what is meant by 'automatic stabilizers'. Give two examples of automatic stabilizers.

3. Outline three ways in which fiscal policy can be used in your country to increase the level of employment and output.

4. Outline three limitations of fiscal policy.

MULTIPLE CHOICE QUESTIONS

1. Which of the definitions is TRUE about automatic fiscal policy?
   (a) i and ii only;
   (b) i and iv only;
   (c) ii and iii only;
   (d) iii and iv only.
      (i) They prevent recession from occurring;
      (ii) They reduce the volatility of output and employment levels;
      (iii) They cushion the economy from the full effects of a recession;
      (iv) They cause output and unemployment levels to fluctuate uncontrollably.

2. What type of policy is a government implementing when it places a tax on gasoline?
   (a) Expansionary monetary policy;
   (b) Contractionary monetary policy;
   (c) Expansionary fiscal policy;
   (d) Contractionary fiscal policy.

3. Which of the following is NOT a fiscal stabilizer?
   (a) Old age pensions;
   (b) Social security contributions;
   (c) Value added taxes;
   (d) Unemployment benefits.

4. Which fiscal action should the government take in a recession?
   (a) A budget deficit;
   (b) A budget surplus;
   (c) A reduction in interest rates;
   (d) A budget surplus and an increase in interest rates.

5. Which fiscal action should the government take to control inflation?
   (a) A budget surplus;
   (b) Tax reductions;
   (c) A reduction in interest rates;
   (d) A budget deficit and a decrease in interest rates.

Chapter 23 The Public Debt

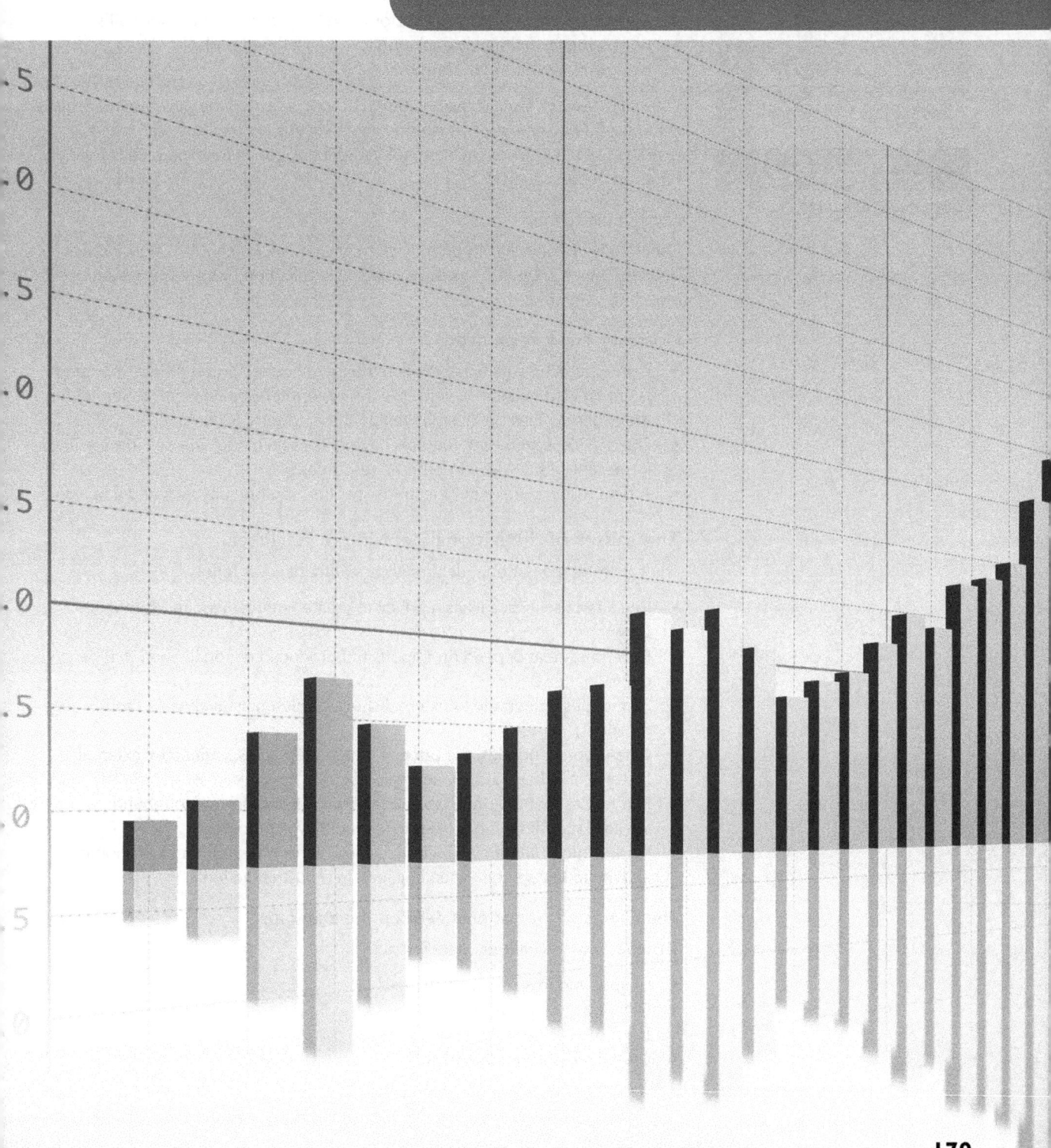

Learning Objectives

By the end of this chapter you should be able to:

- Explain the national debt
- Explain the cause of the national debt
- Evaluate the effects of the national debt
- Explain the burden of the national debt
- Identify and evaluate ways to reduce the debt
- Interpret and calculate the debt service ratio

Exam tip

Tested at CAPE – MCQ.

The national debt

The national debt consists of the internal and external borrowings of the government or its agents. Borrowings to finance a budget deficit is referred to as the **Public Sector Net Cash Requirement** (PSNCR). The summation of several deficits accumulate over a period of time is referred to as the **national debt**.

The PSNCR may be financed by:

- The government printing money;
- Borrowing from the banking sector by selling bonds and treasury bills;
- Borrowing from the non-bank public – e.g. selling bonds;
- Borrowing from foreign sources.

The **Public Sector Debt Repayment** (PSDR) occurs when the government achieves a surplus – i.e. when government revenue exceeds expenditure. The excess revenue is used to repay an accumulated debt. A government surplus is used to repay an accumulated debt.

Fiscal indiscipline

Fiscal indiscipline refers to poor fiscal management which arises from budget deficits. This may be due to poor rates of tax collection or from mismanagement of public expenditure.

Domestic and foreign debt

- Domestic debt – such as between the town council and building contractors – is not viewed negatively since the debt and interest payments remain within the economy and the overall wealth of the country is unaltered.
- External debt, however, requires payments to be made using export earnings. Represents a sacrifice of domestic resources.
- A debt for procurement of technology offers a future payback and a benefit.

The causes of the national debt in the Caribbean

The causes of the national debt may be summarized as follows:

- Repeated fiscal deficits as a policy to create employment and stimulate growth;
- Economies that depend on imports not produced regionally and that become debtor nations;
- Economies vulnerable to external shocks which negatively affect tourism revenues;
- One-crop economies, the price of which crop is determined by external factors – e.g. bananas, oil and gas;
- Economies that are prone to natural disasters and borrow to rebuild;
- Welfare spending that creates a dependency syndrome;
- Trade Union militancy which may cause serious disruption to economic activity to key sectors when engaged in industrial action.

The effects of the national debt on the economy

The effects of the national debt impact:

- Output and investment decisions;
- Exchange rate pressures;
- Inflation;
- Crowding in and crowding out.

THE PUBLIC DEBT

The national debt and output and investment decisions

The impact on output and investment decision is seen in:

- The payment of interest to foreign creditors, which diverts financial resources away from infrastructural development necessary to attract domestic and foreign investment;
- Initiatives in tourism and food security being sacrificed in favour of debt repayment, delaying attempts to diversify the economy.

The effect of the national debt on exchange rates

Repayment of external debt reduces foreign reserves and an inability to finance imports, leading to a balance-of-payments deficit, which can cause the rate of exchange to depreciate.

The effect of the national debt on inflation

The expenditure of borrowings is an injection into the economy and has the potential to create demand inflation.

The national debt and crowding out effects

Government borrowings from the banking sector increase the demand for loans, increasing interest rates which negatively crowd out private sector investment.

Resource crowding out takes place when large state projects lead to material and labour shortages. This raises their prices, which negatively affects private investment.

The burden of the national debt

The burden of the national debt depends on the size of the debt, who benefits from the debt, who pays the debt and who receives the interest payments. A government debt is actually borrowing from lenders from one generation – e.g. government bonds, the future repayment of which is financed by citizens from the same country – and, effectively, is a transfer of wealth from one to another.

In fact, the real burden may be on those who lived 20 years ago when the loan was taken out and for whom resources could have been put to other uses.

Borrowing from overseas residents does, however, incur a loss, since interest payments are made in foreign currency which is earned through the sale of exports and, therefore, a sacrifice of home resources.

If, however, the external debt was incurred to purchase technology or capital resources, the debt may yield future revenue from the investment and is, therefore, not viewed as a burden.

Managing the debt

The most common form of debt management is repayment through taxation revenues. The government is obliged to be efficient in their tax collection and to pursue tax reforms which limit the avoidance of tax payments. Other ways to manage the debt are as follows:

- **Debt refinancing** is converting an existing debt, including arrears and future payments, into a new loan in which the creditor pays off the debtor's debt and starts a new loan arrangement.
- **Debt rescheduling** is a lengthening of the time to repay the debt so that new and long-dated securities are applied to the outstanding balance. In effect, the debtor nation is granted debt relief.

Exam tip

Tested at CAPE – MCQ.

REVISION GUIDE TO ECONOMICS

Exam tip

Tested at CAPE – MCQ.

- **Debt restructuring** is a strategic plan to prevent the debtor from incurring further debts. This may involve closing down state-owned firms that are a drain on the public purse, are heavily indebted or are making huge losses.
- **Debt for equity swap** takes place when a creditor agrees to cancel all or a portion of a debt owed in exchange for a share in a profitable state-owned firm.
- **Debt write off** is when a creditor nation cancels the debt obligations of a debtor nation. In the majority of cases, the debtor nation is usually a poor nation in terms of earning foreign exchange.

The debt ratio

The debt ratio expresses the national debt as a percentage of GDP. The external debt (the 'principal' in the formula below) is expressed as a percentage of export revenue, reflecting the ability to repay the debt.

The formula for calculating the debt ratio is as follows:

$$\frac{\text{Principal} + \text{Interest} \times 100}{\text{GDP}} \quad \text{or} \quad \frac{\text{Principal} + \text{Interest} \times 100}{\text{Valued exports}}$$

Exam tip

Tested at CAPE – MCQ.

The debt trap A debt trap refers to an unusually high debt ratio which persists for many years and which requires the government to commit revenue, usually reserved for management of the economy, to servicing the debt. When infrastructural development is postponed through committing funds to repay debt, growth in the economy is reduced.

TEST YOUR KNOWLEDGE
MULTIPLE CHOICE QUESTIONS

1. The national debt is defined as:
   (a) The domestic debt only;
   (b) The external debt only;
   (c) The accumulated domestic and external debt;
   (d) The yearly domestic debt.

2. The national debt may be repaid through:
   (a) A budget surplus;
   (b) A budget deficit;
   (c) Foreign aid;
   (d) Central Bank purchasing commercial banks.

3. The domestic debt ratio is calculated by:
   (a) Principal divided by GDP;
   (b) Principal + Interest divided by GDP;
   (c) Principal – Interest divided by valued imports;
   (d) Principal divided by valued exports.

4. A high debt ratio debt may NOT be resolved by which of the following?
   (a) Debt refinancing;
   (b) Debt for equity swap;
   (c) Defaulting on the debt;
   (d) Debt rescheduling.

5. A debt trap is:
   (a) A very high and persistent debt ratio over 200%;
   (b) Under 50% debt ratio;
   (c) Under 75% debt ratio;
   (d) Under 100% debt ratio.

Chapter 24: Economic Growth and Sustainable Development

REVISION GUIDE TO ECONOMICS

Learning Objectives

By the end of the chapter you should be able to:

- Distinguish between economic growth and economic development
- Explain the concept of sustainable development
- Outline the factors that determine growth
- Outline the factors that contribute to sustainable development
- Explain the concept of human development
- Analyse the structural characteristics of Caribbean economies
- Analyse the impact of the region's structural characteristics on sustainable economic development

Introduction

Economic growth is defined as the long-term growth in the productive capacity of a country over the long term. Short-term economic growth is achieved through increases in real national income on a yearly basis. **Economic development** is related to factors that represent standard of living and human development derived from sustained long-term per capita economic growth.

Economic growth

Economic growth is measured in two ways:

- Short-term actual growth;
- Long-term potential growth.

Short-term actual growth

- Short-term or actual growth is defined as changes in real GDP on an annual basis.
- If GDP is EC$40bn in 2013 and EC$42bn in 2014, actual growth is equal to 2b/40 x 100 = 5%.
- This growth is possible through the employment of idle land, labour or capital and other spare capacity in the economy.

Sources of short-term actual growth

- **Changes in consumption** Short-term growth may be achieved through changes in consumption as a result of increased consumer confidence, falling interest rates and an even distribution of wealth.
- **Changes in investment** Investment spending increases when business confidence increases. Low interest rates and new technology also serve to increase capacity in the economy.
- **Changes in government spending** Changes in government spending occur through a rise in demand for public and merit goods as shown in Figure 24.1, where short-term growth is represented by Y_0 to Y_1 to Y_2. An increase in exports also plays an important role in short-term growth.

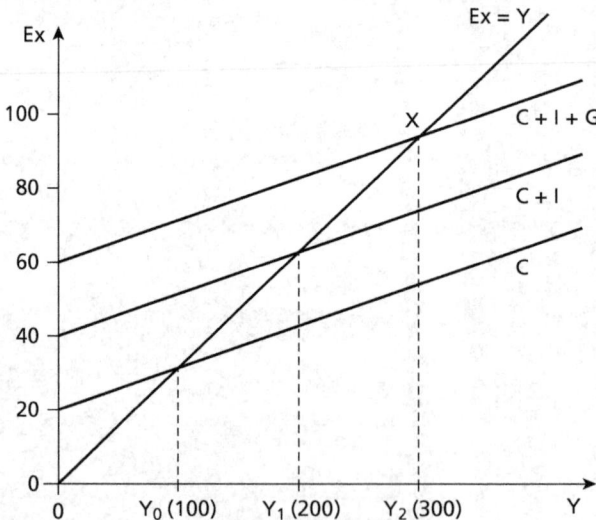

Figure 24.1 Short-term actual growth

ECONOMIC GROWTH AND SUSTAINABLE DEVELOPMENT

Long-term potential growth

Long-term potential growth may result from the following factors:

- Changes in long-run aggregate supply achieved through increasing efficiency in all markets, which creates increases in capacity in the long run;
- Other efficiency measures are incentives to work, to save, to invest, privatization and deregulation;
- The growth in size and quality of the labour force which is achieved through investment in training, health, productivity and safe conditions of work;
- The participation rate (percentage of population in the labour force);
- Investment in capital, which increases the productive capacity of capital investment in conjunction with trained labour equipped with modern tools;
- Modernization of plant and retooling are also major elements of long-term growth;
- The introduction of technology and technical improvements in production, invention and innovation. Invention is the creation of new products and the improvement old ones; innovation is the implementation of new ideas and techniques in commercial use;
- The discovery of new high-value resources and land – e.g. oil and gas;
- Political stability – long-term economic growth is achieved in countries that are not ravaged by civil unrest and war.

> **Exam tip**
>
> Tested at CAPE – Paper 2.

Sustainable growth

- Sustainable economic growth means a rate of growth which can be achieved and maintained without negative economic effects for future generations.
- A fast rate of economic growth may exhaust resources and create environmental problems for future generations – e.g. depletion of non-renewable resources, such as petrochemicals; and global warming.
- The world is united on the issue of preserving the environment and legislation has been enacted to protect the environment.

Exogenous and endogenous growth

- Endogenous growth is achieved through factors within the economy.
- These factors are:
    - Improvements in labour productivity by training and equipping workers with modern technology;
    - The employment of modern techniques in production and management, educating the workforce, targeting labour shortages and growth industries – such as information technology.

Exogenous growth

Exogenous growth is determined by external factors such as tourism, FDI, favourable movements in commodity prices in the world markets, and technical change through the importation of technology.

The economic, social and environmental factors of growth

Government The economic role of government and the private sector contributes to growth.

The government's role is:

- Planning the economic agenda of the country through the budget;
- Implementing monetary and fiscal policy to play a major role in economic activity and economic growth – e.g. infrastructural projects in road building, agriculture, telecommunications and education;
- Overseeing a stable financial system, which is vital for long-term growth.

Private sector initiatives in the primary, secondary and tertiary sectors of the economy also play a significant role in the achievement of economic growth.

Social factors Social factors that impact on growth are related to entertainment, sport, community initiatives such as community self-help, entertainment and cultural activities.

Environmental factors In order to counteract global warming, government legislation, regulation and taxation are implemented to limit greenhouse gases. The private sector's corporate and ethical conduct also address issues such as waste disposal, money laundering, insider trading, and strict compliance with rules of safety.

Indices of human development Real GDP or per capita income are regarded as unrealistic measures of human development. A number of other measures have been developed. These are:

- The **Human Development Index** (HDI), which was developed as a measure of economic welfare by the United Nations and based on measuring four key indicators: literacy levels, school enrolment, life expectancy and real GDP per capita;
- **Measure of Economic Welfare** (MEW), introduced by Nordhaus and Tobin, which adjusts GDP for positive and negative externalities;
- Net migration rates, crude birth and death rates, infant mortality rates, doctors per 1000, and the enjoyment of basic human rights and conditions of work;
- The **Physical Quality of Life Index** (PQLI) incorporates measures such as infant mortality rates, literacy levels and life expectancy, and computes an average value which reflects the basic standard of living.

Structural characteristics of Caribbean economies

- **Small size** Caribbean states are classified as developing small states compared with developed countries such as the USA, Canada, India and China with their huge land masses and populations in excess of three hundred million.
- **Openness** Openness may be measured by the value of imports and exports expressed as a percentage of GDP. This is very high except for Trinidad and Tobago, Barbados and the Bahamas. Another indicator is the trade deficits of these countries, which have a high dependence on imports.
- **Composition of exports** Exports are dominated by primary products – such as agriculture – and tourism, which influences the main type of employment and economic activity in which labour intensive employment is engaged. The effects of negative growth rates of trading partners can be passed on to smaller trade partners.
- **Resource base** Most Caribbean states have a very narrow resource base, which limits the growth of their earnings and GDP. Trinidad and Tobago, and Barbados produce oil and gas; Guyana and Jamaica produce alumina; however, the Windward and Leeward islands have a limited range of products such as bananas, small spices, root crops and tourism.
- **Poverty** The majority of Caribbean citizens live below the poverty line, even in Trinidad and Tobago, and the Bahamas – who both have high per capita incomes in excess of $US10,000. The range of Gini coefficients for Caribbean countries lies between a low 0.42 and a high of 0.55, indicating fairly high poverty levels.
- **Economic dependence** Caribbean countries are very dependent on external factors to manage their economies. Most are reliant on tourism revenues and remittances for foreign earnings; other countries are highly dependent on oil prices, which are determined by the OPEC oil cartel and the winter conditions of temperate countries – e.g. Trinidad and Tobago.

ECONOMIC GROWTH AND SUSTAINABLE DEVELOPMENT

- **High rates of employment** The main reasons for high unemployment rates are a lack of physical capital – such as factories, industrial zones and refineries, a poorly trained labour force, and part-time or seasonal work.
- **Poor infrastructural development** Basic infrastructure – such as the provision of water, roads, power, communications, ports and drainage – is poorly developed and is lacking in most islands .This reduces efficiency and increases costs, limiting the export potential of local output.
- **One-crop dependence** Most Caribbean economies are dependent on a single product for its foreign earning. Agricultural produce and tourism are the main exports but outmoded methods of agriculture, foreign competition and unstable prices result in low foreign earnings.
- **A lack of diversification** A lack of diversification makes Caribbean economies dependent on one main source of earning foreign revenues – such as tourism. There is a need for a long-term diversification plan.
- **Cycle of poverty** A cycle of poverty is caused through obstacles to industrialization – such as the lack of capital due to a low rate of savings. Low incomes in Caribbean states give rise to a low rate of savings. A lack of capital, therefore, reduces productivity, which leads to a repetition of the cycle of low incomes.

Implications for regional economies

- **Dependence on aid** Caribbean states often seek foreign assistance to deal with hurricane damage. Other reasons for dependence on aid are political in nature – aid is given in return for support for strategic initiatives and may be linked to economic objectives related to protecting an export market adversely affected by natural and other shocks.
- **Preferential trade agreements** Although Caribbean states are classified as developing states, most member states have been able to negotiate one-way agreements in their favour with other trading blocs called **non-reciprocating agreements**. These preferential agreements have given rise to complacence and a lack of competitiveness.
- **Foreign direct investment** Foreign direct investment (FDI) may be defined as the purchase, ownership and control of the assets of a country by a foreign multinational company (MNC). Caribbean states use FDI as a mechanism for development. It is estimated that 30% of total investment in Trinidad and Tobago, Grenada and St Vincent has been due to foreign investment.
- **Vulnerability to natural and man-made changes** Internal shocks – such as hurricane damage and the bankruptcy of strategic industries, such as finance institutions – severely affect small Caribbean states. External shocks – such as fluctuations in world commodity prices – have a similar effect.
- **Change in world prices** The dependence on foreign revenue from the exporting of primary products by CARICOM states places them at a serious disadvantage when prices in international markets become depressed. The result is recession, high rates of unemployment, business closures and a depressed economic environment. Such countries then turn to the International Monetary Fund, with unfavourable social outcomes, due to the hardship associated with IMF spending cuts which affect welfare programmes.

The benefits and costs of growth

The benefits of growth are higher living standards; poverty reduction; full employment; an increase in public and merit goods, and other social amenities; increased prospects for wage increases; and income redistribution.

The costs of growth include inflationary pressure, over-consumption, negative externalities, a rise in the consumption of demerit goods, balance-of-payments deficits and the inability to replace non-renewable resources.

Test Your Knowledge

1. Differentiate between economic growth and economic development.
2. List four factors that affect economic growth and how each factor has affected your country.
3. Outline five structural characteristics of Caribbean economies.

MULTIPLE CHOICE QUESTIONS

1. Which of the following is NOT a characteristic of developing countries?
   (a) Economic independence;
   (b) Protectionism;
   (c) Openness;
   (d) Low rates of capital formation.

2. Which of the following defines 'economic growth'?
   (a) The increase in real per capita output over the long term;
   (b) An increase in the standard of living over time;
   (c) The meeting of two production possibility frontiers;
   (d) Replacing existing resources over time.

3. (a) In the table below, showing the human development indices of four countries:
   (b) Which country would have the highest level of development?
   (c) Which country would have the lowest level of human development?

	Country	HDI
(a)	W	0.31
(b)	X	0.66
(c)	Y	0.76
(d)	Z	0.03

4. All of the following are measures of economic development except:
   (a) GNP at current prices;
   (b) The Human Development index;
   (c) The Physical Quality of Life Index;
   (d) Measure of Economic Welfare.

Chapter 25   International Trade

Learning Objectives

By the end of this chapter you should be able to:
- Analyse the role of imports and exports in a small open economy
- Outline the factors that influence exports and imports
- Explain the effects of foreign exchange earnings on a small open economy
- Explain the theory of comparative advantage
- Evaluate the arguments for protection
- Evaluate the arguments for trade liberalization
- Outline methods of trade protection
- Explain the commodity terms of trade
- Interpret changes in the commodity terms of trade
- Calculate the commodity terms of trade

International trade is the buying and selling of goods and services between countries with payment for the goods made in the currency of the seller.

The role of exports and imports creating income for trading partners

Exports as monetary injections have the potential to generate growth in the economy and provide an increase in national income. Export revenue inflows provide a country with sufficient import revenue to purchase goods and services not produced domestically.

The role of imports has a similar effect on the country which supplies the imports in terms of economic growth and employment in that country

Factors that determine exports and imports

The level of exports and imports are determined by:

International prices

The price of a traded good or service in the international market is determined by demand and supply factors.

Demand factors are closely related to the elasticity of demand for the product. Competition is also a key element in international pricing. Other factors are the size of a firm, comparative advantage (see Table 25.2) and production levels.

Most countries that have a comparative advantage also have some degree of price-setting power in the international market.

Domestic production

Domestic production is linked to the supply of factors of production. Land as a resource is immobile, while labour and capital are not easily mobilized across international borders. Countries which have more land than labour and capital tend to focus on agriculture and livestock, while those with more capital and labour concentrate on manufactured goods.

Domestic prices and exchange rates

Domestic prices and exchange rates determine export performance. Domestic prices are determined by cost factors – such as specialization, economies of scale, cost of factors of production, productivity levels and rates of inflation.

High domestic rates of inflation make exports uncompetitive

Exchange rates represent the price of exports. A high exchange rate makes exports uncompetitive in external markets.

The impact of international activity on tourism in the Caribbean Tourism is the economic mainstay of all Caribbean islands, since it is a direct way to earn foreign currency. A wide range of international activity related to sports, cultural and business and eco-tourism activity are determining factors for Caribbean tourism.

Shifts in international demand and the emergence of substitutes

- Shifts in international demand and the emergence of substitutes significantly affect international demand for an exported product.
- Changes in preferences and tastes also cause demand patterns to change – e.g. the shift from tobacco products to health-promoting products.
- The emergence of substitutes has been very evident in the fall in demand for Caribbean sugar in favour of cheaper European beet sugar.

The level of international incomes

The level of international incomes may affect the demand for exports. Tourism is, again, a good example of income elastic demand.

Positive economic growth and rising income levels of trading partners provide a stimulus for export demand. Negative economic growth has the opposite effect.

Foreign exchange earnings from exports and access to capital goods

Export earnings are crucial to economic growth as they enable the importing of capital goods, which can be employed to produce a range of other types of capital and consumer goods.

- **Export multiplier** Exports have the potential to increase national income, economic growth and employment through the multiplier effect, as was successfully achieved in the economies of Singapore and South Korea.
- **Access to consumer goods** A rise in foreign earnings enables the importing of consumer goods and offers increased variety for domestic consumers. Access to foreign goods and services therefore increases the standard of living.
- **Increased domestic production** The investment in capital goods over time leads to increased capacity and to an increase in future domestic production.

The Theory of Absolute Advantage

An absolute advantage in trade exists when a country can produce more of a good than another country where both are using the same quantity and quality of resources. The assumptions of the theory are:

- Two countries, A and B, each produce only two goods – sugar and bananas.
- Each country may have a different quantity of resources.
- Resources can move very easily from sugar to banana production on a 1:1 ratio.
- The level of technology is fixed.
- There are no transport costs.

Exam tip

Tested at CAPE – Paper 2.

Table 25.1 Absolute advantage

	Sugar (tonnes)	Bananas (kg)
A	6	4
B	8	2
Total	14	6

If a worker in Country A can produce 6 tonnes of sugar and 4kg of bananas and a worker in Country B can produce 8 tonnes of sugar and 2kg of bananas, then Country A has an absolute advantage in banana production and Country B in sugar production.

If a country has an absolute advantage in both goods, trade according to absolute advantage is not feasible but can take place in accordance with comparative advantage. Comparative advantage is achieved when a country can produce a good at a lower opportunity cost per unit resource than another country.

Table 25.2 Comparative advantage

	Sugar (tonnes)	Rice (kg)
Barbados	5	10
Guyana	2	6

Exam tip

Tested at CAPE – Papers 1 and 2.

Although Barbados has an absolute advantage in both products, Table 25.2 shows that each country has a lower opportunity cost than the other in a particular product.

Note:

- For Barbados, the opportunity cost of 1 tonne of sugar is 2 kg of rice.
- For Guyana, the opportunity cost of 1 tonne of sugar is 3 kg of rice.
- Barbados has the lower opportunity cost for sugar and should specialize in sugar.
- For Barbados, the opportunity cost of 1 kg of rice is 1/2 tonne of sugar (10/5).
- For Guyana, the opportunity cost of 1 kg of rice is 1/3 tonne of sugar (6/2).
- Guyana has the lower opportunity cost for rice and should specialize in rice production.
- Both countries could then trade according to comparative advantage.

Criticisms of the theories of absolute and comparative advantage

- In practice, countries produce more than two goods.
- Opportunity costs are, in reality, not constant because resources tend to be immobile, or some resources are more suited to certain types of goods.
- Exchange ratios called **terms of trade** usually do not lie between domestic opportunity costs.
  What tend to influence exchange ratios are the demand and supply factors of the trading countries.
- Theory also assumes that domestic ratios (e.g. 1:12) reflect domestic prices; this is not so, if imperfect markets exist.

Protectionism

Arguments for restricting trade

> **Exam tip**
> Tested at CAPE – Paper 2.

Protectionism is the practice of employing barriers to the importing of goods and services into a country. The reasons for doing so are:

- **The 'infant industry' argument** Industries in their 'infancy' should have protection from mature competitors to enable the process of growth that will allow them to compete successfully in international markets.
- **Cheap labour** Imported goods produced with cheap labour are considered unfair competition. However, a country should not be penalized for a low-cost resource that is a comparative advantage.
- **Food security** Protectionist measures are taken to safeguard farmers' incomes. Many countries also aim to ensure food security and a reduced dependence on imported food.
- **The external deficit** When a country's level of imports is persistently greater than its exports, the country may restrict the flow of imported goods in order to reduce the external indebtedness.

Methods of protection

Tariffs

A tariff is a form of indirect taxation on imported goods or services. It is also called **customs duty**. The main effect of a tariff is to cause the price of an import to rise and the demand for it to fall.

> **Exam tip**
> Tested at CAPE – Paper 2.

Figure 25.1 illustrates how a tariff raises the price of imports. WP_1 is the price of the good on the world market. WP_2 is the price when the tariff is added to this price. At price WP_1, 0A is supplied domestically and OB is demanded. At price WP_2, demand falls to OD.

INTERNATIONAL TRADE

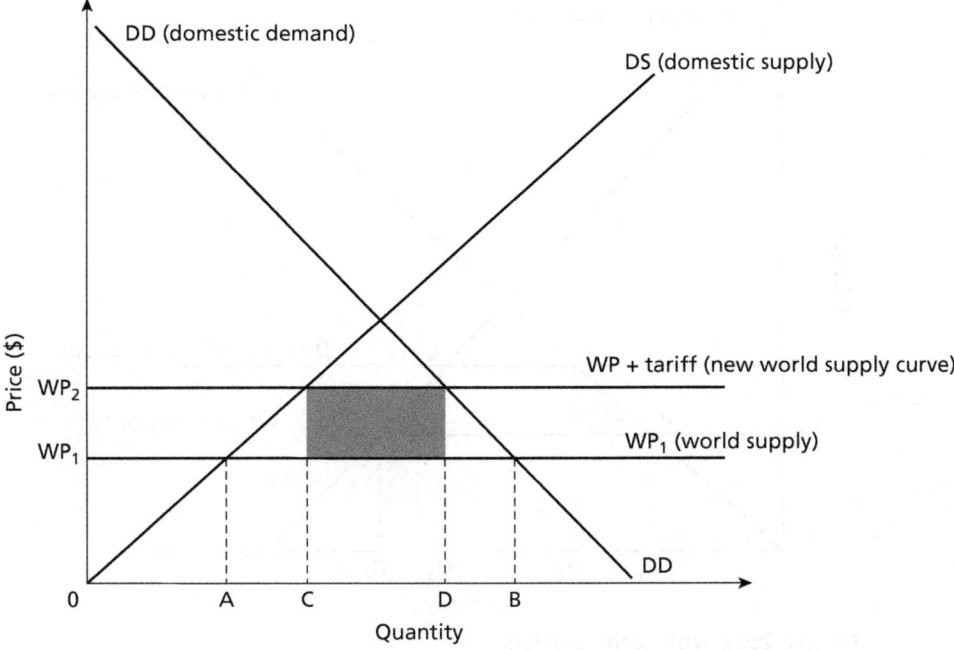

Figure 25.1 The effect of a tariff on producers and consumers

Note:
- Prices are determined where world supply WP_2 equals domestic demand (DD).
- Domestic production increases from OA to OC – an increase of AC, while demand falls from OB to OD by the quantity DB.
- Imports have fallen to the quantity CD whereas, without the tariff, the quantity imported was AB.
- Tariffs not only restrict imports but also raise revenue for the government, denoted by the shaded area.

Quotas

A quota is a specified quantity of a good which the government legally allows to be imported. This raises the price of an imported good and restricts the quantity imported. (See Figure 25.2.)

Note:
- Before the quota, the world price is P_w where domestic demand is OQ_4 and domestic supply OQ_1.
- OQ_1 to OQ_4 is the excess demand which is imported.
- To reduce this quantity imported, a quota of OQ_2 to OQ_3 is imposed on importers, which raises prices locally to Pd.
- Domestic demand is reduced to OQ_3, while domestic supply increases to OQ_2.
- Domestic supply plus quota equals demand at Q_3.
- The government will only raise revenue by this method if import licences are granted.
- In terms of welfare gains and losses, consumer surplus, originally DD DdP_w, is now reduced to DDCP_d – a loss of P_dCDdP_w.
- Producer surplus, originally P_wAO, has increased to P_dBO – a gain of P_dBAP_w.
- The deadweight loss to society – a loss to both consumers and producers – are indicated by triangles ABE and CDdF.
- Licensed importers gain revenue BCFE.

> **Exam tip**
>
> Tested at CAPE – Paper 2.

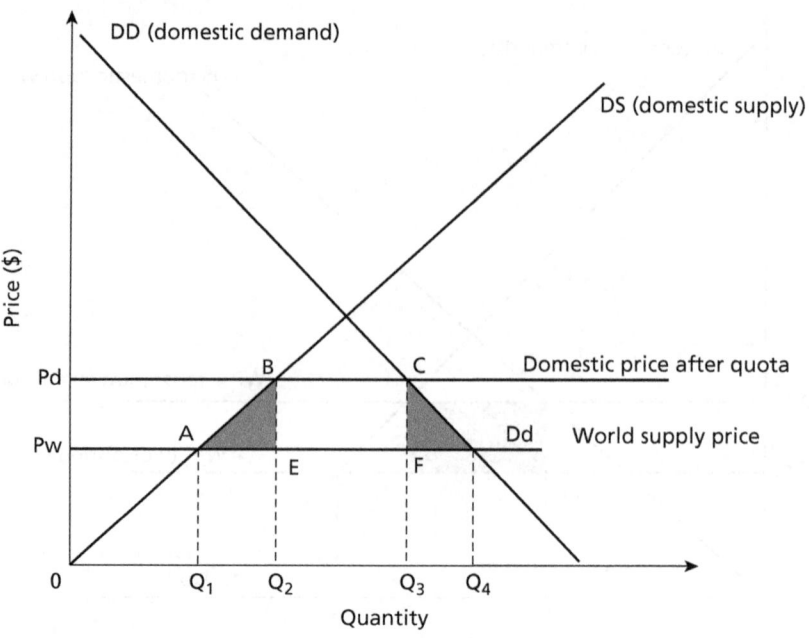

Figure 25.2 Non-tariff barriers

Non-tariff measures

- **Voluntary export restraints (VERS)** VERs are another form of quota that are agreed on (voluntarily) by governments. They operate the same way as do quotas, with the same consequences.
- **Subsidies** State subsidies for exporters make exports cheaper and allow exporters to gain a foothold in foreign markets They are also given to domestic producers to enable lower prices than imports.
- **Government purchasing policies** The government may use its purchasing power to purchase goods from local producers even if the price is above the ruling world price. This is a form of non-tariff barrier.
- **Embargoes** An embargo is an outright ban on imported goods and services.
- **Import deposits** Import deposits require an importer to remit to the government a deposit with the Central Bank before they may be allowed to import goods and services. This reduces the liquidity of the importer and acts as a disincentive to importers.
- **Exchange controls** This method of trade restriction is aimed at an external deficit and the restriction of financing imports as a means of reducing the volume imported. The government could effectively allow only the sale of foreign currency for selected imports and restrict others.

The gains from free trade: the case for trade liberalization

There are four main gains from trade, they are:

- Greater availability and diversity of products now available to trading partners;
- Increased competition between countries;
- Scope for economies of scale where demand comes from very large markets – e.g. NAFTA – 360 million people;
- Comparative advantage.

There are other gains from trade which may be added to the four already identified. These are:

- The spread of technology;
- External trade may enable a country to develop export industries, providing jobs and contributing to economic growth;
- There are welfare gains to be derived from trade when prices are lowered.

INTERNATIONAL TRADE

The terms of trade

The **terms of trade** refers to the rates of commodity exchange between one country's output and another. The terms of trade are expressed in formula as:

$$\frac{\text{Average price of exports}}{\text{Average price of imports}} \times 100 = \text{Terms of trade}$$

When the value of the terms of trade is greater than 100, it is said to be favourable. It could mean that export prices have risen compared with import prices and that fewer exports need to be sold to purchase any given quantity of imports.

Favourable terms of trade may be possible for the following reasons:

- Export prices rising, while import prices are falling;
- Export prices rising, while import prices are constant;
- Export prices rising faster than import prices;
- Import prices falling faster than export prices;
- Export prices constant, while import prices are falling.

Unfavourable terms of trade are indicated by a value of under 100. As long as import prices are relatively higher than export prices, the terms of trade will be less than 100.

Test Your Knowledge

1. To which of the following options may developing economies resort for protectionist measures:
   (a) (i) and (ii) only;
   (b) (i) and (iii) only;
   (c) (i) and (iv) only;
   (d) (ii) and (iii) only.
   - (i) Prevent the collapse of export earnings;
   - (ii) Explain the importance of exports and imports;
   - (iii) Accurately calculate the balance of payments;
   - (iv) Respond to controls imposed by other countries.

MULTIPLE CHOICE QUESTIONS

1. To which of the following options may developing economies resort for protectionist measures?
   (a) i and i only;
   (b) i and iii only;
   (c) i and iv only;
   (d) ii and iii only.
      (i) Resolve a trade deficit;
      (ii) Explain the importance of exports and imports;
      (iii) Accurately calculate the balance of payments;
      (iv) Respond to controls imposed by other countries.

2. What would be the effect on Grenadian imports when Grenada experiences strong economic growth but its major trading partners experience sluggish economic growth?
   (a) Grenadian imports will increase and Grenadian exports will decrease;
   (b) Grenadian exports will be the same as imports;
   (c) A reduction in Grenadian imports and an increase in Grenadian exports;
   (d) There will be no effect on Grenadian imports and exports.

3. Of the options below, what effect will an import quota have on the quantity of wheat imported by St Lucia from the United States?
   (a) (i) and (iii) only;
   (b) (i) and (iv) only;
   (c) (ii) and (iii) only;
   (d) (ii) and (iv) only.
      (i) Increase the volume of wheat that is traded;
      (ii) Reduce the volume of wheat that is traded;
      (iii) Raise the price of wheat in the importing country;
      (iv) Lower the price of wheat in the importing country.

4. Country A and Country B both produce and consume rice and bananas. Both employ the same quantity of inputs for each commodity and produce according to the table below. Which of the following is TRUE?
   (a) Country B is more efficient in the production of both goods;
   (b) Country B has a comparative advantage in Rice production;
   (c) Country A has a comparative advantage in banana production;
   (d) Country A has an absolute advantage in the production of both goods.

Country	Rice (kg)	Banana (kg)
A	45	9
B	30	6

5. Of the following options, which BEST determines the export revenue of a country?
   (a) (i) and (iii) only;
   (b) (i) and (iv) only;
   (c) (ii) and (iii) only;
   (d) (ii) and (iv) only.
      (i) Domestic income;
      (ii) International price;
      (iii) Import restrictions;
      (iv) Domestic production.

Chapter 26

Balance of Payments and Exchange Rates

Learning Objectives

By the end of the chapter you should be able to:

- Explain balance of payments accounts
- Distinguish between the Current Account and the Capital Account
- Explain the calculation of the balance of payments
- Analyse causes and consequences of balance of payments disequilibria
- Identify measures to correct balance of payments disequilibria
- Explain exchange rates
- Explain types of exchange rates
- Explain exchange rate determination
- Explain the effects of exchange rates

Balance of payments

The **balance of payments** is a record of the annual financial flows that take place between a country and the rest of the world.

Financial flows occur for the following reasons:

- The purchase and sale of goods and services;
- Banking and investment;
- Transfers of finance – such as money gifts between residents of different countries.

Any financial inflow is entered as a credit or plus sign, while any outflow is entered as debit or negative sign.

Note:

- If total inflows for the year exceed the outflows, the balance of payments would be in surplus.
- If outflows exceed inflows, the balance of payments would be in deficit.

A simplified balance-of-payments account is made up of four simple sections, the:

Current Account (A);

Capital Account (B);

Financial Account (C); and the

Balancing item (D).

The Current Account

The Current Account is subdivided into four sections:

- The merchandize account balance;
- Services account balance;
- Investment income balance;
- Transfers balance.

The **merchandize** or **visible goods balance** consists of exported goods (e.g. cement) and visible imports (e.g. television sets).

Services account This account records services such as banking, tourism, insurance, transport, accounting, financial services, and so on.

Investment income account Investment income represents interest, profits and dividend income, all of which are also called **property income**.

Current transfers balance A transfer may take the following form:

- Payments or receipts – for example, money gifts – also called **remittances**;
- Government expenditure on embassies abroad called **government transfers**.
- Subscriptions paid to the Caribbean Development Bank;
- Aid received from foreign countries.

When the four sections are added together, the Current Account balance is then determined.

Note:

- The merchandize balance is also called the **balance of trade**.
- The Current Account balance may be positive (surplus) or negative (deficit), depending on whether export receipts are lesser or greater than import payments.

BALANCE OF PAYMENTS AND EXCHANGE RATES

The Capital Account

A simplified Capital Account consists of the following capital flows:

- Fixed or direct capital;
- Portfolio capital;
- Short-term capital.

Fixed or direct capital Fixed capital involves the creation of physical assets – such as factories, firms, mines, or company buyouts between countries.

Portfolio capital Portfolio investment takes place between countries when residents (firms, individuals, public corporations) purchase stocks, shares or foreign government securities.

Short-term capital Short-term capital flows arise through bank transactions involving very liquid assets or hard currencies called '**hot money**' flows.

Financial Account

Official capital flows refers to the following:

- Long-term borrowing by the government – e.g. from a foreign bank – or receipt of a grant;
- The government repayments on external debt, which is an outflow.

The summation of the Current, Capital and Financial Accounts gives the overall balance-of-payments position. This figure may be a surplus or deficit. The balancing item represents errors and omissions which make the accounts balance to zero.

Balance of payments

Current Account deficit

A Current Account deficit is caused when financial outflows exceed financial inflows.

Factors contributing to a Current Account deficit

- Lack of comparative advantage in goods and services;
- High rates of domestic inflation which make exports uncompetitive in the export markets;
- High level of expenditure on imported goods and services – e.g. when an economy enjoys boom conditions, or when interest rates are low;
- Significant outflows of profit from MNCs, along with dividend and interest income associated with FDI;
- Low rates of domestic productivity giving rise to high prices and uncompetitive exports;
- The inability to achieve low cost from scale economies due to limited market size;
- A high exchange rate at which imported goods are purchased and which are inelastic in demand;
- An expansionary monetary and fiscal policy which increases domestic income and supports high import expenditure;
- A lack of resources with which to manufacture exported goods – e.g. arable land, skilled labour.

> **Exam tip**
>
> Tested at CAPE – Paper 2.

Measures to resolve a persistent deficit in the Current Account of the balance of payments

Prescribing measures to resolve a balance of payments deficit on the Current Account may depend on:

- Whether the deficit is large or small;
- The root causes of the deficit;
- The exchange rate mechanism in operation.

Measures to reduce a deficit on the Current Account of the balance of payments will, first, require an expenditure-reducing strategy of a deflationary fiscal and monetary policy designed to reduce demand for imports.

Expenditure switching strategies switch spending away from imports to domestic substitutes – e.g. tariffs quotas, embargos, and other import restrictions may raise the price of imports.

Specific measures to reduce or resolve a persistent deficit may be summarized as:

- An immediate measure to reduce import demand is foreign exchange control. This may be regarded as an expenditure-reducing method with some expenditure-switching effects.
- A short- to medium-term measure is a devaluation of the currency by the monetary authorities – making exports cheaper, which increases export revenue and causes an increase in import prices, causing import demand to fall.

Long-term measures

Long-term measures are employed at the same time as short- to medium-term measures, the difference being that the achievement lag is longer. Briefly summarized, long-term measures include:

- An increased tourism drive;
- The grant of export subsidies, which are designed to reduce the cost of exports and increase their competitiveness;
- The grant of subsidies for products that are intended as substitutes for foreign products – e.g. local orange juice
- 'Buy local' campaigns designed to promote local products and promote awareness of supporting the local economy and jobs;
- Government-sponsored trade missions, to develop external markets;
- Government-promoted trade expositions, which promote a country's products to foreign buyers;
- Development of export processing zones exclusive to exporters – in effect, making infrastructure available at reduced cost;
- Measures designed to improve the productivity of domestic factors of production.

Measures to resolve a Current Account surplus

A Current Account surplus is achieved when financial inflows exceed outflows.

Measures to reduce a Current Account surplus include:

- The removal of import restrictions to increase demand for imports;
- A reflationary fiscal and monetary policy which will cause an expansion in the economy and, hence, stimulate demand for imports;
- Reducing the rate of interest and a decrease in direct taxes to encourage import spending;
- Revaluation of the currency to a higher rate, which will make exports uncompetitive; A revaluation is also likely to cause a surplus to become larger in the short-term.

Exam tip

Tested at CAPE – Paper 2.

Exam tip

Tested at CAPE – Paper 2.

Exam tip

Tested at CAPE – Paper 2.

The positive consequences of a balance of payments surplus

These comprise:

- Export competitiveness;
- Economic strength externally in terms of trade and self-sufficiency;
- Sufficient reserves to finance future imports;
- Reserves to service external debt;
- A fairly strong and stable currency;
- An injection into the economy to promote export-led economic growth.

The negative consequences of a Current Account surplus

These comprise:

- An increase in the money supply can lead to demand inflation;
- A fall in the standard of living, on the basis that a surplus infers reduced access to foreign goods and services;
- A Current Account surplus may mean a deficit with another trading partner who may try to resolve the deficit with protectionist measures;
- A surplus may also lead to a strong currency, which may mean a rise in the cost of trade – also called **Dutch disease**.

Consequences of a balance-of-payments deficit

The consequences of a balance of payments deficit are:

- A Current Account deficit indicates a welfare gain, since the country is consuming more than it is producing;
- The country's reserves will be drawn down, since there will be a need to finance the deficit;
- A deficit can lead to a devaluation of the domestic currency;
- Investor confidence falls due to a possibility of a further devaluation;
- Devaluation leads to higher import prices and contributes to cost inflation;
- Raising interest rates to curb import spending may deter investment;
- A deflationary fiscal policy to reduce consumer spending may lead to unemployment.

Exchange rates

The exchange rate is the price at which one currency is exchanged for another in the international currency markets. Exchange rates are determined by the demand for and supply of a particular currency. Demand factors for a currency such as the Grenadian EC dollar are:

- The demand for Grenadian goods and services;
- Grenadian investors' demand for EC dollars in order to convert foreign returns on investment in foreign securities;
- To purchase Grenadian assets located in Grenada;
- The sending of financial gifts called **remittances** to Grenada from persons residing abroad.

The supply of EC dollars is required for the following reasons:

- To purchase foreign goods and services;
- By foreign firms resident in Grenada to send interest profit and dividends back to their respective countries;
- By citizens who work in Grenada and who wish to send remittances to their respective countries;
- By Grenadian business interests who wish to purchase foreign assets.

Demand for domestic currency

The demand curve for a domestic currency is left to right, downward sloping and negatively sloped, since more domestic currency would be demanded at a lower rate of exchange.

Factors affecting the demand for foreign currencies

A shift of the demand curve to right or left may be caused mainly by the following factors:

- Inflation rates;
- Changes in real income;
- Changes in interest rates.

Other factors which may cause a shift in the demand curve for a currency are:

- External shocks – e.g. the World Trade Centre disaster negatively affected the demand for travel and tourism;
- Political instability may affect foreign investment decisions and, hence, the demand for currency;
- Economic integration – i.e. the formation of trading blocs – can also impact negatively on the demand for goods and services from countries in other trading groups; exchange rates are accordingly affected;
- Aggressive market development and successful market promotion can increase the demand for exports and, hence, create a rise in demand for domestic currency;
- Confidence in a currency may fall, leading to a movement into safe currencies.

The supply of domestic currency (e.g. EC dollars) to the foreign exchange market is left to right and upward sloping – to reflect that more EC dollars will be supplied at a high exchange rate.

The equilibrium rate of exchange

In Figure 26.1, note that DD is the demand curve for EC dollars and SS the supply of EC dollars. The equilibrium rate is TT$3.00 and the equilibrium quantity is equal to $25,000.

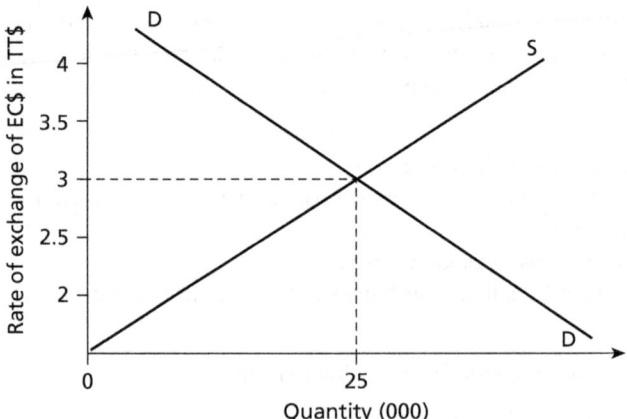

Figure 26.1 Foreign exchange equilibrium

BALANCE OF PAYMENTS AND EXCHANGE RATES

The different types of exchange rates are as follows:
- Flexible or floating exchange rate regime;
- Fixed exchange rate regime;
- Managed exchange rate regime.

A flexible or free-floating exchange rate

A flexible exchange rate is one determined by the free market forces of demand and supply. Demand and supply curves can shift to the right or left, changing the equilibrium rate. The demand curve for EC may shift to the right – e.g. because of an advertisement for a vacation in Grenada. This is called an **appreciation** of the currency. High-priced Grenadian exports will cause the demand curve for its currency to shift to the left and cause a fall in price. This is called a **depreciation** of the currency.

Advantages of a floating or flexible exchange rate

- The balance of payments is kept in equilibrium and facilitates automatic adjustment – i.e. resolves deficits and surplus of the balance of payments;
- There is no need to keep reserves to support the exchange rate or to finance deficits;
- Governments are free to manage the domestic economy, rather than committing economic policy to the external sector.

Disadvantages of a floating or flexible exchange rate

- The uncertainty of exchange rate movements affects the confidence of traders;
- Speculation is encouraged when rates are flexible, leading to unstable rates of exchange;
- Depreciating exchange rates can exert inflationary pressure in the short term;
- Much depends on the price elasticity of demand for flexible rates to be effective.

Note that both appreciation and depreciation could also be caused by a shift of the supply curve.

The fixed exchange rate regime

Refer to Figure 26.2.

A fixed exchange rate regime is in operation when the price of a currency is tied or pegged to another currency – e.g. EC$5 for $US1. This rate is fixed and maintained by the Central Bank of a country on behalf of the government through intervention by means of buying and selling of currency at the fixed rate.

> **Exam tip**
> Tested at CAPE – Paper 2.

> **Exam tip**
> Tested at CAPE – Paper 2.

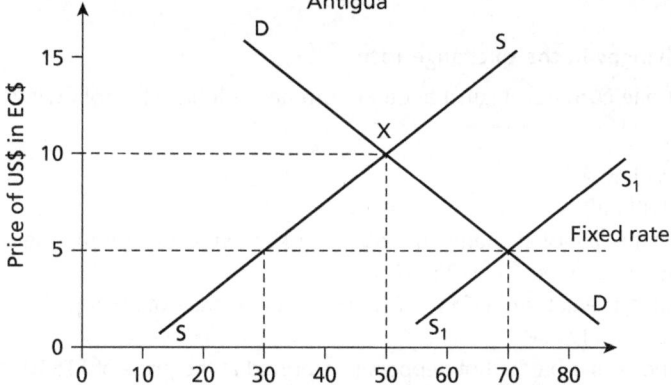

Figure 26.2 A fixed exchange rate

Under a fixed rate of $5, the Central Bank sells from its reserves to meet excess demand of $40m to prevent the price from rising. This is called **intervention to support a fixed exchange rate**.

If there is an excess supply of foreign currency, the price of the currency will depreciate without government intervention. The Central Bank will then enter the market and purchase the excess supply to 'preserve' the fixed rate of $5.

A managed float exchange rate regime

A managed float exchange rate regime is a combination of fixed and flexible rates. The rate of exchange is allowed flexibility within a high and low rate. For example, if the Barbados exchange is managed, then the rate of exchange will be allowed to rise or fall within a range of, say, a low TT$2.50 = Bds$1.00 to TT$3.50 = Bds$1.00, as illustrated in Figure 26.3.

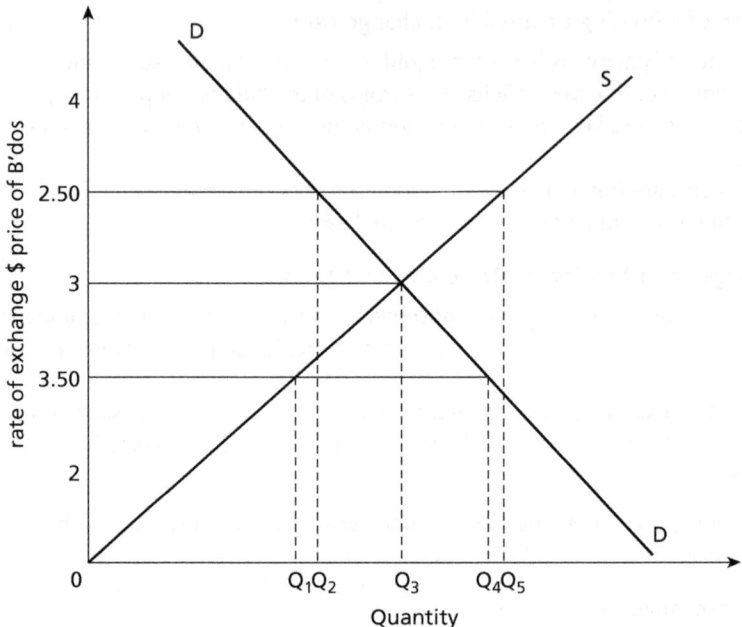

Figure 26.3 Managed exchange rates

Managed exchange rates combine the advantages of flexible and fixed rates of exchange. These advantages are:

- Certainty and stability;
- Automatic adjustment of the balance of payments and protection against inflation.

The effects of changes in the exchange rate

A depreciation of one currency against another currency will have the following effects:

- Import prices will rise;
- Export prices will fall;
- For example, if the rate of exchange is US$1 = TT$5 then a crate of imported apples costing US$20 would cost TT$100;
- If the US dollar depreciates to US$1 = TT$10, the same crate of 20 apple imports would cost TT$200.
- In terms of exports, if a bag of hot peppers is exported at the price of TT$50, at $US 1 to TT$5, a US firm would pay US$10;
- If the TT dollar falls to $US1 = $TT10, the US firm would only have to pay US$5 for the TT$50 bag of peppers;

Exam tip

Tested at CAPE – Papers 1 and 2.

- A greater quantity of exports will be sold but a lesser quantity of imports will be bought, if price elasticity of demand is greater than 1;
- There will be an improvement in the balance of trade and Current Account of the balance of payments;
- For an appreciation of one currency against another, the results will be the opposite to those of a depreciation.

Test Your Knowledge

1. (a) Explain the difference between a Current Account transaction and a Capital Account transaction.
   (b) Explain how foreign direct investment (FDI) is classified in the balance of payments.

2. Which of the following transactions will appear in the Capital Account of Trinidad and Tobago's balance of payments?
   (a) Purchase by a Grenadian investor of an oil refinery in Trinidad and Tobago;
   (b) Purchase of petroleum products from Trinidad and Tobago by foreigners;
   (c) Purchase of cement by a Trinidadian importer from a foreign country;
   (d) The money spent by foreign tourists in Trinidad and Tobago.

3. Explain how the exchange rate is determined in a fixed exchange rate system.

4. Give three advantages and three disadvantages of a fixed exchange rate system.

5. Explain how the exchange rate is determined in a free-floating exchange rate system.

6. Give three advantages and three disadvantages of a free-floating exchange rate system.

7. If a country has a deficit in its balance of payments, then, all else being equal, its money supply is likely to:
   (a) Increase because the foreign currency received from exports will be exchanged for domestic currency;
   (b) Remain unchanged, because its imports were obtained at world prices;
   (c) Fall because the domestic currency will depreciate;
   (d) Remain unchanged, because its exports are bought with domestic currency.

8. Which of the following policies can be used to eliminate a Current Account surplus?
   (a) Devaluation of the currency;
   (b) Introduction of deflationary fiscal policy;
   (c) Imposition of import controls;
   (d) Revaluation of the currency.

MULTIPLE CHOICE QUESTIONS

1. A record of the financial inflows and outflows that arise from economic transactions between one country and the rest of the world is referred to as:
   (a) The merchandize account;
   (b) The balance of trade;
   (c) The balance of payments;
   (d) The Capital Account.

2. The data in the table below refer to the balance of payments of a country. What is the balance of payments for that country?
   (a) $1400 million;
   (b) $1300 million;
   (c) $2500 million;
   (d) $2700 million.

Items	$ (m)
Import of goods	$12 000
Export of goods	$10 000
Invisible balance	$ +600
Investment and other capital flows	$ +100

3. Which of the following is NOT included in a balance of payments account?
   (a) The national domestic debt;
   (b) Financial Account;
   (c) Capital Account;
   (d) Current Account.

4. Which of the following is an expenditure reducing policy to improve the Current Account balance?
   (a) A government subsidy on selected domestic goods and services;
   (b) An increase in income taxes;
   (c) A devaluation of the currency;
   (d) The imposition of an import quota.

5. Which one of the following is an outflow in the invisible section of the Current Account of Grenada's balance of payments?
   (a) Grenada's exports of nutmeg to Europe;
   (b) Grenada's imports of petroleum from Trinidad;
   (c) Foreign tourists spending money in Grenada;
   (d) Payment to American Airlines by Grenadian Travel agents.

6. An advantage of a fixed exchange rate system is that it:
   (a) Forces the government to constantly monitor its value;
   (b) Requires the strong support of government to maintain its value;
   (c) Can provide an automatic solution to balance of payments problems;
   (d) Reduces the uncertainties caused by fluctuating import and export prices.

Chapter 27: Economic Integration

Learning Objectives

By the end of this chapter you should be able to:
- Explain the five main forms of integration
- Evaluate the costs and benefits of economic integration
- Evaluate the objectives of CARICOM and a single market economy
- Explain the significance of the European Union and NAFTA for Caribbean countries

Exam tip

Tested at CAPE – Paper 1.

Regional Integration

There are four basic groupings of regional trade agreements in existence today. These are:

Free trade areas, customs unions, common markets, and economic unions.

All of these agreements are sometimes referred to as **preferential trading** or **multilateral trade**.

Free trade area

A free trade area is a group of countries engaged in trade with one other with no trade barriers among themselves. Each country retains the right to set individual trade restrictions on imports originating outside of the free trade area.

Customs union

A customs union is a free trade area where there is free trading among members of the union. A common external tariff agreed to by all members is imposed on imports coming from outside the union.

A common market

A common market has all the features of a customs union but goes further to include common agreements on:

- Taxation on goods within the union;
- Laws governing employment, trade and marketable products, including safety standards.

Economic union

An economic union is an extension of a common market. Integration extends to a common currency and, hence, a common monetary authority or Central Bank. Further, exchange rates are harmonized, and monetary and macroeconomic policies are decided jointly between members to ensure uniformity.

The economic effect of trade integration: customs union and common market

Trade creation

Trade is 'created' when all tariff and non-tariff barriers are removed when member countries of a region join a customs union or common market, so that the members selling at the lowest cost will gain market share in the union. Specialization and comparative advantage determines market share.

Trade diversion

Trade diversion takes place when a country shifts from trading with a producer with low prices to a producer with high prices when they join a customs union. For example, if CARICOM countries formerly bought low-priced products from China, a common external tariff will raise prices which were previously low.

The costs and benefits of integration

There are various costs and benefits of integration:

Costs

- Firms within the union may try to take advantage of low wages in member countries, leaving short-term unemployment in their own countries.
- Integration may encourage mergers and oligopolistic behaviour in order to retain price control and profits.

Exam tip

Tested at CAPE – Paper 2.

ECONOMIC INTEGRATION

- Beyond a certain size, expanding firms may, in the longer term, experience diseconomies of scale.
- There may be environmental costs from the free movement of large-scale capital projects.
- There may be a net transfer of resources from large to small economies.

Benefits

- Internal economies of scale may be exploited through increased market size.
- Increased competition may lead to increased efficiency.
- Monopolies may be regulated by competition.
- Increased investment may stimulate export-led economic growth.
- Expanding industries would also benefit from improved infrastructure – such as power, communication, banking and insurance.
- Over the longer term, there is likely to be technological transfer between member countries.
- The single market concept enables members, as a collective body, to engage in trade bargaining and better terms of trade.

Regional integration in the Caribbean

Initiatives towards formalizing trade in the region had its earliest beginnings from the West Indian Federation of 1958. Other initiatives aimed at integration are:

- In 1962, a common services conference was convened by Caribbean leaders.
- Also in 1962, Trinidad and Tobago proposed the idea of a Caribbean community, comprising not only 10 members who were in the West Indian Federation, but also other states in close proximity.
- In 1965, Barbados, British Guyana and Antigua entered into discussions concerning the establishment of a Caribbean free trade area called CARIFTA. Shortly after, Trinidad and Tobago, Jamaica and both the Windward and Leeward Islands joined CARIFTA.
- A proposal for the establishment of a common market was introduced. in 1972 at the seventh Heads of Government Conference at Chaguaramas, Trinidad.

CARICOM single market and economy (CSME)

The CSME, which evolved from the 1958 federation initiative, promoted the main objective of the common market agreement in order to present a united front to the other trading blocs of the other regions of the world. Specifically, there is to be free movement of labour, capital in all forms of goods and services within the common market, creating a borderless Caribbean economic village of 7 million people. Over time, fiscal, monetary exchange rate and other macroeconomic policies will become harmonized and, hopefully, evolve into an economic union and, ultimately, a political union.

The benefits of the CSME for the region can be summarized as:

- Free movement of labour and capital among member countries, including joint ventures, mergers and new business development in services such as banking and financing services;
- Increased economic strength as a region when trading with states outside the single market economy;
- Presenting a common position for the Caribbean region in trade matters with other trading blocs;
- Accelerated, coordinated and sustained economic development;
- Improved living standards for all in the region;
- Enhanced competitiveness for regionally manufactured goods and services;
- Net positive impact on the profitability of regional companies;
- Access for producers to the entire CARICOM market and, hence, scope for scale economies.

> **Exam tip**
> Tested at CAPE – Paper 2.

The Free Trade of Americas and Caribbean Economies

The CSME is seen as a negotiating vehicle currently in the negotiations of the Free Trade Area of the Americas (FTAA). While the trade zone starts from Canada and extends to Southern Chile and will be the largest trading bloc of the world with 800 million people, there will be a need for skilful negotiation as a Caribbean region.

The FTAA would consider the following issues:
- Market access;
- Agriculture;
- Services;
- Investment;
- Intellectual property rights;
- Subsidies;
- Anti-dumping and countervailing duties;
- Competition policy;
- Dispute settlement.

The benefits of the FTAA to CARICOM are:

- Access to markets in North America;
- Access to markets in Latin America;
- Trade creation;
- An incentive to increase productivity to compete successfully.

The costs of the FTAA to CARICOM are:
- Increased competition from within the FTAA;
- Higher adjustment costs for CARICOM firms;
- The loss of margins of preference previously gained through other market access – such as CARIBCAN and the Caribbean Basin Initiative;
- Loss of tax revenue from trade as a result of the removal of tariffs.

The North America Free Trade Area (NAFTA)

The NAFTA agreement came into effect in January 1994 when certain trade barriers were removed between the United States, Canada and Mexico. To date, barriers to agricultural goods have been removed between Canada and the United states, while Mexico and Canada are still to agree on dairy, poultry and sugar.

EU and CARICOM

The first LOME convention, signed in 1975, included the United Kingdom and many of the trade privileges enjoyed by the UK also passed on to the former colonies of the UK.

The LOME conventions were premised on trade and development, and involved the movement of resources from the EU to the Caribbean countries via the Economic Development Funds.

Preferential access of Caribbean products to the EU market was a further benefit Caribbean countries inherited from the LOME convention.

There were certain rules which limited the advantages of trade from the LOME convention, however. These included the following:

- Specific types of products that were allowed into the EU market;
- The value added tax based on the stages of product development;
- Quotas on certain primary products;
- Non-tariff barriers on specific food products;
- Specific protocols for selected ranges of products – such as spirits and textiles.

Cariforum

EU assistance to African, Caribbean and Pacific (ACP) nations in 1995 was enabled by the World Trade Organization through a forum for negotiations which eventually led to an Economic Partnership Agreement with CARICOM countries called CARIFORUM. CARIFORUM comprises 15 nations which include Antigua, Barbuda, the Bahamas, Barbados, Belize, Dominica, the Dominican Republic, Grenada, Guyana, Haiti, Jamaica, St Lucia, St Vincent, St Kitts and Nevis, Suriname, and Trinidad and Tobago.

The main concerns identified for consideration are:

- A reduction in fiscal earnings and its negative impact on development;
- The need for a replacement of tariffs with other less onerous fiscal measures;
- Inefficiency in production, which leads to uncompetitive prices of exports;
- The need for improved economic development;
- The need for an increase in capacity in tertiary education, with linkages to global best practices;
- Reduced dependency on mature economies;
- Improved methods of information collection, collation and interpretation;
- The improvement of geographic and occupational mobility within CARIFORUM.

Test Your Knowledge

1. Distinguish between:
    (a) A customs union and an economic union;
    (b) Quota and tariff;
    (c) Free trade area and common market;
    (d) Trade creation and trade diversion.

MULTIPLE CHOICE QUESTIONS

1. Which of the following refers to the creation of a single monetary and fiscal authority having jurisdiction over a number of countries?
   (a) Customs union;
   (b) Free trade area;
   (c) Economic union;
   (d) Common market.

2. What is the difference between a free trade area and a customs union?
   (a) A customs union requires a common currency among member countries while a free trade area does not;
   (b) A free trade area needs to eliminate tariffs between member countries while a customs union does not;
   (c) A free trade area allows the free movement of labour and capital between member countries while a customs union does not;
   (d) A customs union has a common external tariff with the rest of the world while the free trade area does not.

3. When a country joins a customs union and shifts from trading with a producer with low prices to a producer with high prices, this is called:
   (a) A trade deficit;
   (b) Trade diversion;
   (c) Trade creation;
   (d) Trade surplus.

4. When all barriers are removed when member countries of a region join a customs union so that members selling at the lowest cost will gain market share in the union, this is called:
   (a) A unilateral trade agreement;
   (b) Trade creation;
   (c) Regional economies of scale;
   (d) Trade discrimination.

5. All of the following are costs of joining a customs union EXCEPT:
   (a) Firms within the union may try to take advantage of low wages in member countries, leaving short-term unemployment in their own countries;
   (b) Integration may encourage mergers and oligopolistic behaviour in order to retain price control and profits;
   (c) There may be a net transfer of resources from large to small economies;
   (d) A common monetary and fiscal policy may favour larger member states.

6. All of the following are benefits that may arise from a customs union EXCEPT:
   (a) Internal economies of scale may be exploited through increased market size;
   (b) There are more benefits for countries outside of the union than its own members;
   (c) Monopolies may be regulated by competition;
   (d) Increased competition may lead to increased efficiency.

Chapter 28: International Economic Relations

Learning Objectives

By the end of this chapter you should be able to:
- Explain the role and function of the World Trade Organization
- Explain the role of the international financial institutions
- Explain the role of multinational corporations
- Outline the costs and benefits of foreign direct investment
- Explain the term 'globalization'
- Describe the factors which contribute to globalization
- Evaluate the effects of globalization

The World Trade Organization

The World Trade Organization (WTO) succeeded the General Agreement on Tariffs and Trade (GATT) in 1995.

The main purpose of the WTO is to enable free trade among the world's exporting countries.

The main functions of the WTO are:

- Administering trade agreements;
- Providing a forum for trade negotiations;
- Arbitrating in trade disputes between member countries;
- Providing assistance to member countries with respect to the formulation of trade policy;
- Promoting international cooperation.

Rules of the World Trade Organization

Unlike GATT, the WTO has the power of sanction. They deliberate over the following:

- Allowing a country to erect tariff barriers, as in the case of the United States and its steel industry from producers in EU countries;
- The most favoured nation clause is also a concession to one trading partner to extend to other members, except where customs union or free trade areas exist;
- Reciprocity: The mutual lowering of tariff barriers;
- Banning of quotas as a form of protectionism;
- Fair competition: Sanctions are imposed on countries in breach of rules – e.g. illegal dumping;
- Tariff cooperation: Countries cannot raise tariff barriers without first negotiating with their trading partners.

International Monetary Fund

The International Monetary Fund (IMF) came into existence in 1944–45 in Washington, USA, by international agreement, with two main objectives:

- Financial assistance to countries with balance-of-payments difficulties of a short-term nature;
- Access to capital for long-term projects related to infrastructure development – such as ports, drainage, roads, and dams.

Financial assistance required the setting up of the IMF and access to capital required the intervention of the International Bank for Reconstruction and Development (IBRD) also known as the World Bank.

The original objectives of the IMF that were written into its Articles of Association were to:

- Establish a system of exchange rates;
- Monitor and supervise this system in order to promote confidence in international trade, remove exchange rate restrictions and promote exchange rate stability;
- Increase international liquidity by designating financial instruments that are acceptable as payment in international trade;
- Promote international cooperation.

INTERNATIONAL ECONOMIC RELATIONS

In the recent past, the IMF has concentrated on three main areas:

- Financial assistance for countries with balance-of-payments deficits and financial strategies designed to prevent their recurrence;
- Increasing the level of international liquidity;
- Supervising the smooth management of exchange rates among member countries.

IMF financial resources

The financial resources of the IMF come from its members, all of whom must pay a quota or subscription in its own currency. Developed countries pay a larger quota than small developing states.

This pool of resources therefore consists of many of the world's different currencies. The IMF also has a special currency called **special drawing rights** (SDRs).

IMF assistance to member countries

A country in foreign exchange crisis may seek the assistance of the IMF. The IMF provides loans by exchanging a country's quota contribution for foreign currencies – e.g. US dollars. These are called **basic drawing rights** and are loaned in instalments called **tranches**.

Early tranches carry no attached conditionalities; subsequent tranches carry conditionalities which are IMF-designed prescriptions that must be followed and agreed to by the debtor country in a 'letter of intent'. The basic drawing rights mean that funds can be drawn up to 125% of a country's quota for approximately two years.

Additional borrowing

Additional lending by the IMF is granted in special circumstances. This additional funding comes in the form of:

- An extended fund facility, which is to assist countries with longer-term persistent deficits;
- A compensatory financing facility, which is granted if a country's exports have been affected by unforeseen circumstances – e.g. crop damage due to hurricanes;
- A supplementary financing facility – e.g. if a country is affected by rising oil prices;
- A buffer stock facility – to stabilize the prices of primary products;
- An emergency facility – to offer compensation for destabilizing natural disasters.

IMF international liquidity provisions

These provisions are acceptable currencies necessary to finance trade. These are:

- IMF drawing rights;
- Special drawing rights (SDRs);
- Stand-by credit – provided by individual countries.

The IMF also gives approval for countries to borrow from commercial banks, provided they possess the ability to repay.

IMF conditionalities

When debtor countries borrow from the IMF, they are subject to conditionalities – monetary and fiscal targets which must be met before tranches are loaned. In instances of persistent deficit, the IMF may impose austerity measures – e.g. cutting subsidies, removing tariffs.

Devaluation is one of the options available to a country with a persistent deficit on its Current Account. The devaluation is advised with IMF approval.

Other IMF activities

Apart from its three main functions – financial assistance and financial strategies, increasing international liquidity and supervising exchange rates – the IMF also provides:

- Financial advice to member countries;
- Advice on macroeconomic policy – such as monetary and fiscal policy as it relates to the country's fundamentals;
- Advice on weakness in economic management to ensure sustainable growth and positive outcomes for the macroeconomic fundamentals.

World Bank

The World Bank commenced operations on 25 June 1946. The role of this bank is as follows:

- To provide loans or to guarantee loans for productive reconstruction and development;
- To lend finance from its own members and mobilize additional sources of finance from private finance institutions in the world capital markets; the risk of lending is shared by the bank members, according to their economic strength;
- To provide technical advice and training to member countries;
- To promote economic development, mainly through financing infrastructure – such as road building, power and water capacity, schools, hospitals and drainage.

The World Bank includes two specialized lending agencies: The International Development Association (IDA), which was established in 1960, and the International Finance Corporation (IFC), which was established in 1956. These two institutions also make loans, in addition to the World Bank.

International Development Association

The role of the IDA is as follows:

- To provide soft loans for a long-term period, ten year grace periods and interest free. However, a 75% service fee is charged on the paid out portion of each credit in order to cover administration costs.
- IDA credits are designed to assist poorer nations who cannot afford to borrow under the World Bank's strict terms and conditions.
- The IDA finances projects such as agriculture, education, power stations, ports and urban development.
- IDA also provides technical assistance and occasionally makes available foreign exchange to purchase critical imports not related to specific projects.

International Finance Corporation

The IFC is a member of the World Bank group, similar to the IDA. IFC lending is geared towards the growth of productive enterprise in the private sector of developing countries and the IFC operates mainly as a finance provider and facilitator.

In addition, it may itself invest in projects as a partner; establish new businesses; or expand, diversify or modernize existing businesses. Apart from sourcing financial capital for private enterprise, it may also provide technical and managerial support for a project.

INTERNATIONAL ECONOMIC RELATIONS

Investment proposals are considered by IFC in two main ways: as an investment bank and as a development institution. The three basic conditions necessary to IFC involvement are:

- Project earning prospects;
- Benefit for a country;
- Local participation.

The IFC also ensures the following:

- Alternative funding at a reasonable cost, if not otherwise available;
- That financial plans are achievable;
- That there is a potential or existing market for the good or service;
- That there are experienced cadres of business professionals to oversee projects;
- That they have substantial shareholding of the project's stock.

The IFC is also supportive of joint venture partnerships between the state and private enterprise.

Multinational corporations

Multinational corporations (MNCs), also known as **transnational corporations** (TNCs), operate in many countries at the same time and are responsible for the majority of world trade in manufacturing products and service industries.

Common features of MNCs are:

- Significant market power, by virtue of their sheer size;
- The operations and decision-making of such firms are managed from a home country and are therefore centralized;
- Financial strategies are geared towards tax avoidance and low cost;
- In recent times, especially through globalization, the world is regarded as a single market in which the same product is sold – e.g. KFC, Nestlé products, Mac Foods Hamburgers, or oil companies such as BP/Amoco.
- Pricing and output strategies are geared naturally towards profit using a strategy called 'transfer pricing'. This is achieved, for example, by setting prices above or below market prices to avoid paying taxes. If a country has a high corporation tax on profits, MNCs will set a low market price to achieve lower profits, and so a lower taxation cost.

The advantages of producing in a foreign country are:

- A reduction in transport costs of distribution and/or new materials;
- The MNC can deal with the threat of competition to their products better while they are in close contact with the market in a foreign country;
- Wages are low, as are the costs of the inputs required for production (raw materials);
- Avoidance of import restrictions – e.g. when building a plant in a foreign country;
- MNCs qualify for recognized assistance if they set up in a foreign location;
- Employment legislation is less stringent in foreign countries;
- Environmental health and safety standards are lower for MNCs.

Refer to Table 28.1.

Table 28.1 Effects of MNCs on host countries

Benefits for host country	Cost to host country
New technology	Replacement of labour
New managements techniques	Natural resources are depleted at faster rate
Export growth	Their sheer size makes them insulated from government monetary policy
Tax Revenue	They may not strictly adhere to health or safety standards
Corporate sponsorship	They send their profits to their home countries
Good quality, low prices of products	They may shift production around the world, in this way influencing negotiations with unions or government

Globalization

Globalization is defined as an acceleration in the political, social and economic interactions of the economies of the world across borders, acting as a catalyst for development. Globalization is made possible through the following forces:

- Communications technology;
- The removal of trade barriers;
- The formation of trading blocs;
- The operations of MNCs;
- The efforts of the IMF;
- The WTO.

The IMF and the WTO provided a timely boost to the globalization process.

Note:

- The WTO was responsible for promoting international trade between countries.
- The IMF ensured that there was a sound global financial system that would facilitate payments and receipts connected to trade.
- This liberalization of trade provided an accelerated thrust into foreign markets that had been previously protected.

The three most powerful forces which have impacted on globalization were the fall of the Berlin Wall, the movement towards free market economies in the USSR, and the information revolution that coincided with advances in information technology.

The combined effect of all these events served to intensify the connectedness of the economies of the world to the extent that there were spill-over effects that were both positive and negative. These effects influenced the following areas:

- International trade;
- Finance;
- Economic policy;
- Political influence;
- Culture;
- The environment;
- Foreign policy;
- Foreign direct investment;
- The free movement of factors of production and financial capital across borders.

> **Exam tip**
> Tested at CAPE – Paper 2.

> **Exam tip**
> Tested at CAPE – Paper 2.

INTERNATIONAL ECONOMIC RELATIONS

Positive effects of globalization

The positive effects of globalization are:

- The removal of trade barriers between countries, which led to increased competition, increased factor productivity, low prices, increased global output of goods and services, enhanced quality of products, research, and a greater diversity of products for the consumer market;
- Access to a wide range of high-quality and low-priced goods and services, which has contributed to rising living standards across the world;
- Trading activities in foreign markets have created increased opportunities for and benefits from economies of scale and specialization;
- Foreign direct investment is associated with advancements in technology, savings, foreign revenue, modern management, accounting practices, tax revenue and investment;
- Advancements in air and sea transportation arising out of competition for air and sea routes results in reduced costs of international transport;
- The activities of MNCs have created the free movement of labour between international boundaries;
- Globalization has created opportunities for market access through both the removal of barriers and the external networks to which MNCs are connected;
- Globalization has inspired the complementary relationship between communications technology and the movement of financial capital, improving the savings and investment gap;
- The emergence of trading blocs such as the the North American Free Trade Area has a market of 360 million people offering marketing opportunities, and solidarity and cooperation between nations.

> **Exam tip**
> Tested at CAPE – Paper 2.

The negative impact of globalization on Caribbean countries

Since there is a high demand for skilled labour, wages in the skilled sector increase relative to other sectors, which creates a dualistic wage structure. Increased industrial activity and wage inflation pressure are consequences of this development. It also contributes to income inequality.

The activities of MNCs create a phenomenon called **Dutch disease**, which is caused by a high demand for resources that leads to an appreciating exchange rate. Eventually, exports become uncompetitive and the export-oriented sector goes into decline, creating structural unemployment.

Savings related to activities by MNCs have not been available to the domestic capital market and are repatriated to their home countries. Globalization may cause the economic 'shocks' in one country or region to radiate to all countries very quickly.

Other negative consequences of globalization are:

- The spread of international terrorism;
- The undermining of small economies by drug transhipments;
- The spread of fatal diseases – e.g. SARS, AIDS, Avian flu, H1N1 virus;
- Money laundering activities;
- Industrial espionage;
- The subversion of culture – e.g. indigenous music and cultural traditions;
- Environment degradation.

> **Exam tip**
> Tested at CAPE – Paper 2.

Foreign direct investment

Foreign direct investment (FDI) may be defined as the purchase, ownership and control of the assets of a country by a foreign MNC, or the establishment of new enterprise by MNCs that are long-term in nature.

> **Exam tip**
> Tested at CAPE – Paper 2.

There are many arguments for and against FDI with particular reference to small open economies.

Eminent Caribbean economist Sir Arthur Lewis identified growth deficiencies or gaps in the economic growth strategies of small Caribbean states.

These gaps are identified as:

- **The savings and investment gap** The rate of savings in a country is positively related to the rate of investment. Since the level of savings and investment in CARICOM states is low, FDI contributes to improvement in the investment gap.
- **The human capital gap** The transfer of skills from multinationals to the local labour force is seen as a noteworthy objective.
- **The foreign exchange gap** Foreign investment flows and capital equipment are brought into host countries by FDI. This represents a saving in foreign exchange.
- **The enterprise gap** Enterprise by foreign interests is the lifeblood of most small economies. Many small economies in the Caribbean are tourism-based and the level of enterprise is concentrated in micro-enterprises – such as personal services and peasant farming.
- **The management gap** Since multinational corporations have worldwide networks, management of large-scale enterprises is their strength. The transfer of these skills serves to assist a small economy to bridge the management gap.
- **The employment gap** MNCs provide a boost to local employment. In the construction phase of any investment project, many skilled workers are employed. The more sustainable form of employment comes from support services linked to the foreign MNCs – such as power, communication, transport, banking, shipping and packaging.
- **The tax revenue gap** Tax revenue paid to governments by MNCs greatly reduces the debt burden of such governments. When taxes are received through MNCs, the need to raise taxes is reduced.
- **The technology gap** Technological transfer is an important contribution to a small economy. The boost to productivity from modern equipment, tools and processes brings the small economy into contact with modern technology.
- **The networking and external market gap** Since MNCs operate beyond their national boundaries and have secure markets and financial networks in foreign countries, this valuable network is made available to local manufacturers. Increased market size provides welcome opportunities to exploit economies of scale and a competitive edge in export performance.

The disadvantages of foreign direct investment

There are a number of negative arguments that have been advanced against FDI. These are:

- **Property income outflows** Property income outflows includes interest, profit and dividends which are remitted to head offices of the home country, which is viewed in terms of a loss of financial capital.
- **Preferential tax holidays** MNCs hold a negotiating edge with governments of small economies. As a result, tax holidays have, in some instances, been granted for a duration of 8–10 years.
- **High importation of capital and other inputs** Many MNCs import their capital equipment and raw material to manage their operations. The effect of this is that it excludes domestic suppliers.
- **Negative externalities** Environmentalists have expressed serious reservations about the threat to human life, with the siting of plant that poses a long-term threat to local ecology near to rural communities.

- **Political manipulation** MNCs are regarded as very influential with respect to governments' major decisions. In particular, their lobbying powers are considerable when they seek to gain an advantage for themselves.
- **Exploitation of non-renewable resources** MNCs have opted to build plants in foreign countries near to non-renewable raw materials, energy and markets – in part, due to protectionist barriers and high transport costs.

These raw materials are transferred to processing plants in home countries where the full value of the investment is added.

- **Demonstration effect of high wages** Since MNCs tend to offer higher wages than the domestic average, the resulting wage pressures force local industries to pay higher wages.
- **Suppression of domestic entrepreneurship** The vast international networks of MNCs in insurance, banking, communications, mining and hotels vastly outweigh those of the host country, to the detriment of domestic entrepreneurs.

Factors affecting foreign direct investment

Factors affecting FDI are summarized as:

- Favourable demand conditions;
- Exchange rates;
- Tax concessions;
- Low transport costs.

Test Your Knowledge

1. Outline three major features of globalization.

2. Identify three major factors that have driven the process of globalization and evaluate the effectiveness of each factor.

3. Assess the role of FDI in the development of an economy of a Caribbean country.

MULTIPLE CHOICE QUESTIONS

1. If a firm uses its resources to purchase and manage a business operation in a foreign country, then this is referred to as:
   (a) International diversification;
   (b) FDI;
   (c) Cross national investment;
   (d) Domestic investment.

2. Which of the following BEST explains the role of the World Trade Organization?
   (a) Setting the geographic boundaries for the conduct of world trade;
   (b) Executing the taxes and tariffs for world trade;
   (c) Providing protection for less developed countries;
   (d) Setting the rules and regulations for the fair conduct of world trade.

3. An MNC is BEST described as a firm:
   (a) With owners from different countries;
   (b) That conducts operations in several countries;
   (c) Whose product is a household name and is sold across the globe;
   (d) With sale production rights in at least two countries.

4. Which of the following combinations is an example of privatization?
   (a) Deregulation and franchising;
   (b) Franchising and redistribution;
   (c) Contracting out and regulation;
   (d) Deregulation and nationalization.

5. All of the following are negative arguments that have been advanced against FDI EXCEPT:
   (a) Property income outflows are remitted to head offices of the home country and are viewed in terms of a loss of financial capital.
   (b) MNCs hold a negotiating edge with governments of small economies.
   (c) Many MNCs import resources to manage their operations to the exclusion of domestic suppliers.
   (d) Domestic firms benefit from external networks of multinationals.

Answers to multiple choice questions

Chapter 1: The Economic Problem

MCQ1 (c); MCQ2 (b); MCQ3 (a); MCQ4 (b); MCQ5 (b).

Chapter 2: Economic Systems

MCQ1 (a); MCQ2 (a); MCQ3 (c); MCQ4 (d); MCQ5 (d).

Chapter 3: Theory of Demand

MCQ1 (c); MCQ2 (d); MCQ3 (b); MCQ4 (c); MCQ5 (c).

Chapter 4: Theory of Supply I

MCQ1 (c); MCQ2 (c); MCQ3 (b); MCQ4 (c); MCQ5 (d).

Chapter 5: Theory of Supply II

MCQI (c); MCQ2 (c); MCQ3 (b); MCQ4 (a); MCQ5 (d).

Chapter 6: Market Equilibrium

MCQ1 (c); MCQ2 (a); MCQ3 (b); MCQ4 (a); MCQ5 (a).

Chapter 7: The Cost of Production

MCQ1 (c); MCQ2 (b); MCQ3 (b); MCQ4 (a); MCQ5 (b).

Chapter 8: Price, Revenue and Profit Concepts

MCQ1 (c); MCQ2 (b); MCQ3 (b); MCQ4 (b); MCQ5 (d); MCQ6 (b).

Chapter 9: Imperfect Competition: Monopoly and Monopolistic Competition

MCQ1 (b); MCQ2 (b); MCQ3 (b); MCQ4 (c); MCQ5 (a); MCQ6 (a).

Chapter 10: Oligopoly and Contestable Markets

MCQ1 (c); MCQ2 (a); MCQ3 (d); MCQ4 (d); MCQ5 (c); MCQ6 (c).

Chapter 11: Market Failure

MCQ1 (b); MCQ2 (a); MCQ3 (b); MCQ4 (b); MCQ5 (c); MCQ6 c.

Chapter 12: Role of Government and Market Failures

MCQ1 (c); MCQ2 (a); MCQ3 (b); MCQ4 (a); MCQ5 (d).

Chapter 13: Theory of Income Distribution

MCQ1 (a); MCQ2 (b); MCQ3 (a); MCQ4 (b); MCQ5 (c); MCQ6 (b).

Chapter 14: Wage Differentials

MCQ1 (d); MCQ2 (c); MCQ3 (b); MCQ4 (a); MCQ5 (c).

Chapter 15: Income Inequality, Poverty and Poverty Alleviation

MCQ1 (b); MCQ2 (d); MCQ3 (c); MCQ4 (d); MCQ5 (c).

Chapter 16: National Income Accounting

MCQ1 (c); MCQ2 (b); MCQ3 (a); MCQ4 (a); MCQ5 (a).

Chapter 17: Classical Models of the Macro-Economy

MCQ1 (b); MCQ2 (a); MCQ3 (c); MCQ4 (d); MCQ5 (b).

Chapter 18: The Keynesian Model of the Macro-Economy

MCQ1 (b); MCQ2 (b); MCQ3 (c); MCQ4 (c); MCQ5 (a); MCQ6 (c).

Chapter 19: Investment

MCQ1 (d); MCQ2 (b); MCQ3 (d); MCQ4 (d); MCQ5 (a).

Chapter 20: Unemployment and Inflation

MCQ1 (a); MCQ2 (d); MCQ3 (b); MCQ4 (a); MCQ5 (b); MCQ6 (a).

Chapter 21: Monetary Theory and Policy

MCQ1 (a); MCQ2 (b); MCQ3 (d); MCQ4 (d); MCQ5 (a).

Chapter 22: Fiscal Policy

MCQ1 (c); MCQ2 (d); MCQ3 (c); MCQ4 (a); MCQ5 (a).

Chapter 23: The Public Debt

MCQ1 (c); MCQ2 (a); MCQ3 (b); MCQ4 (c); MCQ5 (a).

Chapter 24: Economic Growth and Sustainable Development

MCQ1 (a); MCQ2 (a); MCQ3 (c), (d); MCQ4 (a).

Chapter 25: International Trade

MCQ1 (a); MCQ2 (d); MCQ3 (c); MCQ4 (d); MCQ5 (d).

Chapter 26: Balance of Payments and Exchange Rates

MCQ1 (c); MCQ2 (b); MCQ3 (a); MCQ4 (b); MCQ5 (d); MCQ6 (d).

Chapter 27: Economic Integration

MCQ1 (d); MCQ2 (b); MCQ3 (b); MCQ4 (b); MCQ5 (b); MCQ6 (b).

Chapter 28: International Economic Relations

MCQ1 (b); MCQ2 (d); MCQ3 (b); MCQ4 (a); MCQ5 (d).

Index

A
Absolute advantage, 191–192
Absolute poverty, 118
Accelerator principle of investment, 150–151
Adverse selection, 89, 93
Aggregate demand (AD), 129–130
    discretionary fiscal policy and, 174
Aggregate supply (AS), 129–130
    long-run curve, 131–132
    short-run curve, 130–131
Allocative efficiency, 85
Appreciation, currency, 203
Asymmetric information, and market failure, 89
Automatic fiscal policy, 174
Autonomous investment, 148
Average physical product (APP), 31, 32
Average propensity to consume (APC), 137–138
Average propensity to save (APS), 139
Average revenue (AR), 58
Average total cost (ATC), 50–51

B
Balance of payments, 198
    Capital Account, 199
    Current Account, 198
    deficit, 201
    Financial Account, 199
    surplus, 201
Balance of trade, 198
Banking, adverse selection in, 89
Barometric price leader, 79
Basic drawing rights, 215
Basic needs measurement, poverty, 118
Beneficial externality, 119–120
Break-even point, 61
Budget, 176–177
Budget line, 16–18

C
Capital Account, 199
Cardinalist theory of demand, 13
CARICOM single market and economy (CSME), 209
CARIFORUM, 211
Cash reserve ratio (CRR), 169
Change in quantity demanded, 21
Classic economics, 129–134
    AS/AD model, 129–130
Collectivist economy. see Planned economy
Collusive oligopoly, 79
Command economy. see Planned economy
Commodity money, 164
Common market, 208
Company voluntary agreement (CVA), 94
Compensating, wage differentials, 112
Conditions of demand, 13
Conditions of supply, 36
Constant returns to scale, 33
Consumer equilibrium, 14, 18
Consumer surplus, 15
Consumption
    defined, 137
    determinants of, 139
    factors influencing, 138
    fixed/autonomous, 137
    induced, 137
    and savings, 139–140
Contestable markets, 79
Contractionary fiscal policy, 174
Contractionary monetary policy, 168
Convertible bank notes, 164
Corporate code conduct, 94
Corporate ethics, 94
Cost efficiency, 85
Cost push inflation, 157–158
    measures to curb, 160
Costs, of poverty, 119
Costs, of production, 50–55
    average total cost, 50–51
    long-run average cost, 53–54
    marginal cost, 51–52
Credit creation, 169
Cross price elasticity of demand (CED), 26–27
Current Account, 198
    deficit, 199–200
    surplus, 200
Customs duty, 192
Customs union, 208

D
Deadweight loss, 88, 89
Debt for equity swap, 182
Debt ratio, 182
Debt refinancing, 181
Debt rescheduling, 181
Debt restructuring, 182
Debt trap, 182
Debt write off, 182
Decreasing returns to scale, 33
Deflationary fiscal policy, 159
Deflationary gap, 144–145, 154
Demand/demand theory
    cardinalist theory of, 13
    change in, 21–22, 44–45
    conditions of, 13
    defined, 13
    derived demand, 97
    indifference curve, 15–16
    non-price factors and, 13, 22
    price factors and, 13
Demand pull inflation, 156, 157
Demerit good, 87
Depreciation, 123, 148
Depreciation, currency, 203
Deregulation, 94
Derived demand, 97
Discount rate, 168
Discretionary fiscal policy, 174
    and aggregate demand, 174
    and balance of payments, 175
    and unemployment, 175

Discrimination, and poverty, 118
Diseconomies of scale (DOS), 54
Domestic currency, demand for, 202
Domestic debt, 180
Dominant price leader, 79

E

Economic benefits of poverty alleviating measures, 119–120
Economic costs, unemployment, 154
Economic development, 184
Economic efficiency
    allocative efficiency, 85
    and Pareto optimality, 85–86
    productive efficiency, 85
Economic growth
    benefits of, 187
    defined, 184
    factors of, 185–186
    long-term potential growth, 185
    short-term actual growth, 184
Economic integration, 208–211
    costs/benefits, 208–209
Economic rent, 103
Economic system
    defined, 8
    free market system, 8–9
    mixed economy, 10
    planned economy, 9–10
    subsistence economy, 8
Economic union, 208
Elasticity of demand, 22–24
Embargoes, 194
Employer's associations, 112
Employment
    classical theories, 132–133
    defined, 154
Employment gap, 220
Endogenous growth, 185
Enterprise gap, 220
Equalizing, wage differentials, 112
Equilibrium output, 60
Equilibrium rate, 134
Excess liquidity, 134
Exchange rates, 201
    effects of changes in, 204–205
    equilibrium, 202
    national debt and, 181
    types of, 203–204
Exogenous growth, 185
Expansionary fiscal policy, 174
Expansionary monetary policy, 168
Expenditure method, national income accounting, 124–125
Explicit costs, 50
Exports, 190
    factors determine, 190–191
External debt, 180
External economies of scale, 55
Externalities, and market failure, 87–88
External marginal benefit (EMB), 88
External market equilibrium, 134

F

Fiat money, 164
Financial Account, 199
First law of demand, 14
Fiscal indiscipline, 180
Fiscal policy, 173–178
    aims of, 174
    automatic, 174
    discretionary, 174
    objectives, 173
    potency of, 177–178
Fixed/autonomous consumption, 137
Fixed capital, 199
Fixed costs, 50
Fixed factor, 30
Flexible exchange rate, 203
Foreign currency
    demand for, 202
    investment in, 169
Foreign direct investment (FDI), 219–221
Foreign exchange gap, 220
Formal collusion, 78
Fractional reserve banking, 169
Free market system, 8–9
Free trade area, 208
Free Trade Area of the Americas (FTAA), 210
Frictional unemployment, 155

G

General Agreement on Tariffs and Trade (GATT), 214
Geographical mobility, 101
Geographic immobility, 107
Giffen good, 20–21
Gini coefficient, 116
Globalization, 218–219
Government, and market failures, 92–94
Government expenditure
    economic reasons, 176
    social reasons, 175
Government transfers, 198
Gross domestic product (GDP), 123
    nominal, 126
    real, 126
Gross investment, 148
Gross national product (GNP), 123

H

Head count index, 118
Herfindahl-Hirschman Index (HHI), 82
Hot money, 199
Human capital gap, 220
Human Development Index (HDI), 118, 125, 186

I

Imports, 190
    factors determine, 190–191
Incidence of tax, 46–47
Income
    circular flow of, 123
    functional distribution of, 115
    size distribution of, 115
    uneven distribution of, 93
Income effect, of price change, 18–19

Income elasticity of demand (YED), 27
Income inequality, 115
  factors causing, 117
  Gini coefficient and, 116
  Lorenz curve and, 115–116
  measures designed to reduce, 117
Income method, national income accounting, 124
Increasing returns to scale, 33
Indifference curve, demand theory, 15–16
Indirect tax, 46
Individual demand curve, 22
Induced consumption, 137
Induced investment, 148
Inferior goods, 19–20
Inflation
  causes of, 156
  consequences of, 158
  cost push, 157–158
  defined, 156
  demand pull, 156, 157
  measurement, 160–161
  measures to control, 159
  Monetarist theories of, 158
  national debt and, 181
  unanticipated, 158–159
Inflationary gap, 145
Informal collusion, 78
Internal diseconomies of scale, 54
Internal economies of scale, 51
International Bank for Reconstruction and Development (IBRD). see World Bank
International Development Association (IDA), 216
International economic relations
  World Trade Organization, 214
International Finance Corporation (IFC), 216–217
International Monetary Fund (IMF), 214–216
  conditionalities, 215
  financial resources, 215
International trade, 190–195
  absolute advantage and, 191–192
  protectionism, 192–194
International unemployment, 155
Investment, 148–151
  accelerator principle of, 150–151
  categories of, 148
  defined, 148
  in foreign currency, 169
  portfolio, 199
  rate of interest and, 150

K
Keynesian fiscal policy, 174
Keynesian model, 140–145

L
Labour force, 154
Labour immobility, and market failure, 92
Law of constant opportunity costs, 4
Law of decreasing opportunity cost, 4
Law of diminishing marginal utility, 14
Law of diminishing returns, 3
Law of equi-marginal returns, 14–15
Law of increasing costs, 3
Law of increasing returns, 4
Law of variable proportions, 31
Leakage, income, 140
Legal tender, 164
Liquidity preference theory, 165–167
Loanable funds, 101
Long-run average cost (LRAC), 53–54
Long-run average total cost (LRATC), 65
Long-run law of returns to scale, 33
Long-run period, production, 30–31
Long-term economic growth, 4
Long-term potential growth, 185
Lorenz curve, 115–116
Loss minimization output, 63
Lump sum tax, 71–72

M
Macroeconomics, 145
Managed float exchange rate regime, 204
Management gap, 220
Marginal cost (MC), 51–52
Marginal efficiency of capital (MEC), 148–149
  criticisms of, 150
Marginal efficiency of investment (MEI), 149
  curve, factors shifting, 149
Marginal physical product (MPP), 31, 32
Marginal physical product of labour (MPPL), 97–98
Marginal propensity to consume (MPC), 137, 138
Marginal propensity to save (MPS), 139
Marginal Rate of Substitution (MRS), 16
Marginal revenue (MR), 58
  in perfect market, 59
Marginal revenue productivity (MRP) theory, 97–104
  limitations of, 102
  and rate of interest, 101
Marginal utility, 14
Market concentration, 81–82
Market demand curve, 22
Market equilibrium, 43–47
  effects of taxes/subsidies on, 46–47
Market failure, 86–89
Measure of Economic Welfare (MEW), 126, 186
Merit goods, and market failure, 87, 92
Mixed economy, 10
Momentary period, 30, 39
Monetarist fiscal policy, 174
Monetary policy, 167
  contractionary, 168
  expansionary, 168
  instruments of, 167–168
  limitations of, 170
  and national income, 170
  targets of, 168
  working of, 168–169
Monetary validation, 158
Money, 164
  characteristics of, 164
  demand for, 164–165
  functions of, 164
  speculative motive for, 165–166
  types of, 164

Monopolist, 68
  in long-run equilibrium, 69–70
  in short-run equilibrium, 68–69
Monopoly, 58–60
  lump sum tax and, 71–72
  and market failure, 86
  perfect competition vs., 72–73
  subsidies and, 72
Monopsonist, 109
Moral hazard, 89, 93
Moral suasion, 167
Multinational corporations (MNCs), 217–218
  advantages of producing in, 80–81
  features of, 80–81
Multiplier (K), 142–143

N
National debt, 180–182
  burden of, 181
  causes of, 180
  effects of, 180
  and exchange rates, 181
  and inflation, 181
  managing, 181–182
  output and investment decision, 181
National income
  expenditure method, 124–125
  income method, 124
  Keynesian model of, 140–145
  monetary policy and, 170
  output method, 125
  statistics, 125
National income equilibrium, 140–145
  algebraic model, 144
Natural monopoly, 71
Negative externality, 88–89
Net investment, 148
Net national product (NNP), 123
Non-price factors, and demand, 13, 22
North America Free Trade Area (NAFTA), 210

O
Occupational mobility, 101, 107
Oligopoly, 78
  collusive, 79
  Sweezy model of oligopolistic behaviour, 78–79
Open market operations (OMO), 168
Opportunity cost, 2–3
Optimal purchase rule, 14–15
Output method, national income accounting, 125

P
Pareto optimality/efficiency, 5, 85–86
Perfect competition, 62–63
  vs. monopoly, 72–73
Perfectly elastic demand, 26
Perfectly inelastic demand, 25
Perfect market, 58
  marginal revenue in, 59
Phillips curve, 161
Physical capital, 148
Physical Quality of Life Index (PQLI), 186
Planned economy, 9–10

Planned investment, 148
Policy conflict, 177
Portfolio investment, 199
Poverty
  absolute, 118
  costs of, 119
  factors contribute to, 118
  measurement of, 118
  persons susceptible to, 118
  relative, 118
Poverty line, 118
PPF/PPC. see Production possibilities frontier/curve (PPF/PPC)
Precautionary demand for money, 165
Price ceiling, 45
Price control, 45, 93
Price discrimination, 70
Price elasticity of demand
  perfectly elastic demand, 26
  perfectly inelastic demand, 25
  total expenditure method, 24–25
Price elasticity of supply, 38–39, 104
  determinants of, 39–40
Price factors, and demand, 13
Price floor, 45–46
Private goods, 87
Private marginal benefit (PMB), 88
Privatization, 93
Producer surplus, 44
Production, 30
  cost of, 50–55
  function, 30
  long run, 33
  periods of, 30–31 (see also specifc periods)
  stages of, 32–33
Production possibilities frontier/curve (PPF/PPC), 2–5
Productivity, defined, 31
Profit, 61–62, 102
Profit maximization, 60–61
Property income, 198
Protectionism, 192–194
Public debt, 180–182
Public goods, and market failure, 86–87, 92
Public Sector Debt Repayment (PSDR), 180
Public Sector Net Cash Requirement (PSNCR), 180

Q
Quotas, 193

R
Rate of interest, 101
Rate of interest, and investment, 150
Regional economies, 187
Regional trade agreements, 208–211
  common market, 208
  customs union, 208
  economic union, 208
  free trade area, 208
Relative poverty, 118
Relative poverty line, 118
Remittances, 198, 201
Rent, 102
Repo rate policy, 168

Index

Reserve ratio, 168
Reserve requirement ratio, 169
Retail Price Index (RPI), 160–161
Revenue
    in perfect market, 58–59
    types of, 58 (see also specific types)

S

Savings
    consumption and, 139–140
    defined, 139
    determinant of, 140
Savings and investment gap, 220
Scarcity, 2
Search unemployment, 155
Seasonal/casual unemployment, 155
Short-run period, production, 30–31
Short-run supply curve, 65
Short-term actual growth, 184
Short-term capital, 199
Social costs, 50
Social costs, unemployment, 154
Social marginal benefit (SMB), 88
Social responsibility, 94
Social welfare, 119
Special drawing rights (SDRs), 215
Spillover, 88
Stagflation, 161
Standard of living, 125–126
Structural unemployment, 155
Subsidies, 194
    effects on market equilibrium, 46–47
Subsistence economy, 8
Substitution effect
    of price change, 18–19
    of wages, 99
Supply
    change in, 37, 44–45
    conditions of, 36
    defined, 36
    factors affecting, 36
    price elasticity, 38–39
Sustainable economic growth, 185
Sweezy model of oligopolistic behaviour, 78–79

T

Tariffs, 192–193
Tax and Price Index, 161
Taxes/taxation, 92
    effects on market equilibrium, 46–47
    indirect, 46
    lump sum tax, 71–72
Tax revenue gap, 220
Technological unemployment, 155
Terms of trade, 195
Third party effects, 88
Time period, 39
Token money, 164
Total expenditure method, 24–25
Total physical product (TPP), 30, 31
Total revenue (TR), 58
    in monopoly market structure, 59–60
Total utility, 13–14
Tradable permits, 94
Trade liberalization, 194–195
Tranches, 215
Transaction demand for money, 165
Transfer earnings, 103
Transfer pricing, 81
Transnational corporations (TNCs), 217

U

Unanticipated inflation, 158–159
Underemployment, 154
Unemployment
    causes of, 154
    costs of, 154
    defined, 154
    discretionary fiscal policy and, 175
    types of, 155 (see also specific types)
Unions, 110–111
Unplanned disinvestment, 148
Unplanned investment, 148

V

Variable costs, 50
Variable factor, 30
Voluntary export restraints (VERS), 194

W

Wage differentials, 107–112
    compensating/equalizing, 112
    demand factors, 107
    employer's associations, 112
    supply factors, 107
    unions and, 110–111
Wage price spiral, 158
Wages
    in imperfect labour market, 109
    in perfectly competitive industry, 108–109
    substitution effect, 99
Wage/wage spiral, 158
Welfare equity, 119
Withdrawal, income, 140
World Bank, 216
World Trade Organization (WTO), 214